WONDERFUL WEEDS AND VARIOUS VARMINTS

D1446760

The world is too much with us; late and soon,
Getting and spending, we lay waste our powers:
Little we see in Nature that is ours

WILLIAM WORDSWORTH

Familiarity with the natural world provides
a valuable anchor in reality.

ROLAND C. CLEMENT

Vice President, National Audubon Society, from the Foreword
of the 1977 edition of Lawrence Newcomb's *Wildflower Guide*

WONDERFUL WEEDS AND VARIOUS VARMINTS

The Natural World in our Backyards and Beyond

BOB COLLIER

Illustrations by Gale Hinton

THE UNIVERSITY OF TENNESSEE PRESS

Knoxville

Copyright © 2018 by The University of Tennessee Press / Knoxville.
All Rights Reserved. Manufactured in the United States of America.
First Edition.

Library of Congress Cataloging-in-Publication Data

Names: Collier, Bob (General surgeon), author.
Title: Wonderful weeds and various varmints: the natural world in our
backyards and beyond / Bob Collier; illustrations by Gale Hinton.
Description: First edition. | Knoxville: The University of Tennessee Press,
[2018] | Includes bibliographical references and index. |
Identifiers: LCCN 2018006246 (print) | LCCN 2018008042 (ebook) |
ISBN 9781621904502 (pdf) | ISBN 9781621904496 (paperback)
Subjects: LCSH: Nature—United States—Anecdotes. |
Seasons—United States—Anecdotes.
Classification: LCC QH81 (ebook) | LCC QH81 .C64 2018 (print) |
DDC 508—dc23
LC record available at https://lccn.loc.gov/2018006246

To Louise, dear Spouse of these many decades,
who has made life so well worth the living

CONTENTS

Spring

Summer

Fall

Winter

FOREWORD

The shelves of bookstores are filled with the latest data on the destruction of Earth's ecosystems: the demise of the monarch butterfly, honeybee die-off, the bats' white-nose syndrome, climate change affecting bird populations, and on and on. These are all very important studies for our times. But rare is the book that digs into all these subjects and others, not just as a serious intellectual study, but as a very personal day-by-day, season-by-season journey in which the reader experiences the fragile beauty of Mother Nature just outside the door.

This is Dr. Bob Collier's way of writing. His communication style makes you feel as if you are walking on a trail talking with someone who is totally engrossed by the sights and sounds of nature, which just happen to be to the left or right, above or below, at that particular season of the year. Bob's enthusiasm is contagious. It makes you want to get *out the door* and experience all of it for yourself.

If you don't think you will ever want to go outside and let the fragile beauty of the natural world touch your heart and soul, then it's best that you not read Bob's book, for in reading it, you probably won't be able to resist going out the door.

Bill Nickle
Narrow Ridge Earth Literacy Center
Washburn, Tennessee

INTRODUCTION

Ecotourism is a burgeoning business, and a growing number of people are finding themselves with the available free time and sufficient means to avail themselves of the manifold wonders of nature by way of such luxurious travels. Kenya? Antarctica? New Guinea? Pick your exotic location, anywhere on Earth.

Then there are the vigorous, fit, and young trekking types, who can choose from a world of challenging trails, high mountains, and hidden valleys to answer their call from the outdoors—total immersion for days at a time.

All well and good; all to be encouraged. But nature is not just for those of us fortunate enough to be affluent or young: it's for us all. People respond to nature in a myriad of ways, probably in as many ways as there are people. A trip outdoors can amount to as simple an exercise as a turn around the yard in the afternoon to check the flowers for bugs, or a look at the night sky before bed to see if Venus and Jupiter made it up that evening. Just a small dose of the outdoors does the body and the spirit a world of good.

And yet, there are some who don't find being out in nature such an enriching experience. Whether due to matters of health or mobility; phobias toward bats, snakes, bugs, or spiders; or a just a feeling of discomfort with being outside, the outdoor world is not for everyone. Nevertheless, even indoor armchair adventures into the great kingdom of the natural world can be remarkably absorbing, and a source of considerable diversion and pleasure.

Nature is there for you, whether you're reading about it at home in your favorite chair or watching it outside your kitchen window, whether gazing out on row upon row of hazy blue ridges from the top of the Great Smoky Mountains or intently observing the microcosm of creatures eating and being eaten on the flowers in your backyard garden.

Our innate responses to our natural surroundings have a certain deep-seated commonality, perhaps because human beings are actually an integral part of their surroundings. We all are just as much a part of nature as the penguins and the giraffes, the maple trees and the moss. Nature, it turns out, isn't something "out there" that one has to make extensive plans to go away and visit somewhere. It's right outside your door, and it's everywhere! We breathe it, we drink it, and we eat it. We are totally dependent on it, whether we live in a remote forest cabin or in downtown New York City.

But as for the living, growing, dynamically interrelated parts of it, yes, some purposeful effort must be made to be aware, to look and see, to smell and feel all the wonders conjured up by the word "nature."

Down through the ages, many words—often times eloquent or poetic—have been written extolling the virtues of nature. A great number of them have inferred that humans' true place is at the top, to manage, exploit, even control all the natural goings-on here on our tiny blue sphere. But gradually, more people are coming around to a more realistic view of our place in the system: We're actually all in this thing together, each of us interconnected parts of the same world—and often troublesome and destructive parts at that.

The challenge is huge, to get all the world's inhabitants on board with the idea that we're living together on a single planet, all of whose life forms we have the potential to destroy. But I feel that we must all hold on to the possibility of making the world into a place of peace and abundance; maybe not a Garden of Eden, but hopefully something considerably closer to it than we've managed to achieve so far.

It should be apparent to everyone that you can't know your place in the system unless, of course, you know your place. That would be the place where you find yourself to be, where you spend your life going through all the tasks and experiences involved with being "in your place." So many ideas—nuanced, slanted, incorrect, or patently false—are being proclaimed about the status of our world and our place in it, veiled in political, religious, and/or economic jargon, that there is a monumental disconnect between words and reality.

Perhaps the most logical place to begin trying to get several billion human beings to start paying attention to all this is with the group that probably offers us the most hope: the youngsters. Children's sense of wonder, their minds' propensity to absorb everything they encounter, and their innate ability to discern what's actually real make them perfect ambassadors for the ultimate preservation of this planet that we call "our place."

We live in a country where many of the rural folks have moved to the cities, and we are discovering that many of those urban people grow up having never walked on grass, having never been out of sight of buildings, or having never grown a flower. Our children spend hours—cumulatively *years*—staring at small square monitors and screens. Many are never told to go outside and play; they may seldom use their imaginations or ever experience even a small, real, outdoor adventure. Experts routinely express their concerns about the measurable effects on our youngsters' mental and emotional health and their worldview, resulting from this striking lack of contact with the natural world. One author has famously coined the term "Nature-Deficit Disorder" to describe this state of affairs.

On the other hand, we learn that even city kids (and grownups as well) can reconnect with their place in the world with small forays out the door. There is a tree out there to be climbed, or have an appreciative hand laid on its trunk. There is a bird or flower waiting to be observed, a patch of grass to be felt underfoot, a spot of open sky to be gazed into.

But someone has to take youngsters outside and help them realize they can explore and discover those wonders for themselves. And, hopefully, they will find that the world outside is exciting and full of as much beauty and complexity as anyone could wish to see or learn about. Sky, weather, trees, creatures, flowers . . . things to stimulate the mind and soothe the weary soul.

I feel fortunate to find myself living in a part of the world where I can experience four distinct and different seasons year after year. Day by day, each season enriches our lives, unfolding its own unique gifts, changes, and happenings, big and small. A great many of us enjoy the seasons, and all of us could if we just slowed down enough to pay attention. The seasons give us marvelous experiences that we can all have in common—to see, share, learn more about, and discuss with one another.

Your author, from birth an outdoor person, incongruously enjoyed a 45-year practice of general surgery in the Knoxville, Tennessee area, confined daily to small rooms with no windows. My very patient wife of nearly six decades, Louise, has been a constant and enthusiastic companion in the majority of our outdoor experiences. She is referred to as "Spouse" in the stories compiled here, an appellation that seems peculiar to some but perfectly logical to me.

We both gratefully acknowledge our indebtedness to our late friends, Dr. Bob and Lavada Harris, who introduced us to the wonders of birding in April of 1985 in the Snowbird Mountains of North Carolina. From that momentous beginning grew our ever-widening interest in the behavior of the flora and fauna coexisting with us here in our part of the world and beyond. All this eventually led to an invitation by another significant person in the journey, Sandra Clark, editor of our local weekly newspaper, the *Halls Shopper/News*. Way back in 2003, Sandra suggested that I might do a weekly nature column for her. It began as a bird column; the series was 20 columns along before a non-bird column appeared, "Nature Strikes Back," found in the Fall section of this book.

The weekly bird columns gradually evolved into a monthly nature column, with free-range privilege to cover most anything outdoors, local and farther away. They were mostly inspired by simple daily experiences and observations enjoyed through the different seasons, generally in the outdoor environs of the ridge-and-valley region here in East Tennessee. Backyards and gardens, farm hayfields and woods, nearby roadsides, meadows and mountains hold many things that people often look at but seldom really *see*. With my columns, I hoped to remind those who had seen them to look at them again. Many of my friends and neighbors, who had looked but hadn't seen, have often responded with "Interesting! I didn't know that it/that/those were even there."

Some of the essays go farther afield with trips to the Florida Keys, Montana mountains, and Vermont forests. I hope you find yourself momentarily surrounded by the nature of those places as well; fascinating, different, but certainly related in many ways to the sights and sounds found in the hills and valleys and mountains of East Tennessee.

I would like to also acknowledge our gifted and indefatigable illustrator, artist Gale Hinton, whose enthusiasm about this project to benefit Narrow Ridge, and about life in general, was both infectious and encouraging. Thank you, Gale.

The stories in this book are loosely arranged by season, beginning with spring—a logical place to begin a year, I suppose. Mostly observations and few explicit conclusions, they are generally quiet celebrations of discovering what's out there in the great outdoors with a few aggravations and irritations thrown in for seasoning, as life generally has a way of happening. I hope these stories serve as reminders and enticements to each reader heading out the door.

So, what is the above-referenced "Narrow Ridge"? It is a remarkable community of people living on 700 beautiful hill-country acres in Grainger County, Tennessee, a place called The Narrow Ridge Earth Literacy Center. They are off the grid—no connections to public electric lines or public water systems. They teach in schools and colleges, grow gardens, keep bees, love the outdoors, and have a wonderful sense of community. Their primary goal is to show how it is possible, and ultimately essential, for us all to learn the principles of living sustainably. Their attractive lifestyle there at Narrow Ridge demonstrates sustainability. The Earth Literacy Center is accredited to teach all that wisdom to college students and faculty from across the country, a timely enterprise now as more and more colleges are offering studies in sustainability. Their founder and my good friend, Bill Nickle, is hereby acknowledged as having suggested compiling my *Halls Shopper/News* columns into this book. All proceeds from the sale of the book will go to support the visionary programs of Narrow Ridge. Enjoy!

WONDERFUL WEEDS AND VARIOUS VARMINTS

SPRING

SOME REFLECTIONS UPON SPRING

Why would anyone want to live in the Southeast? Well, for May and October, of course! At least, that's what we say when we're enjoying one or the other of those two glorious "mini-seasons." And we certainly long for them when it's August or February.

The real message though is that we have four distinct seasons in these parts, every year. Those of us who grew up accustomed to each year unfolding in such a dependable fashion are actually discomforted when transplanted to a place without changing seasons. I remember being surprised by a friend's comment years ago; he had been given the perfect assignment: 3 years in paradise . . . Hawaii! He related how he eventually reached the point of grumbling each morning, "Oh, man, not another perfect day." It seems that when you're accustomed to seeing it from time to time, you begin to actually miss some less-than-ideal weather.

Seasons and weather set us up to expect and tolerate the inclement and to rejoice in the better days. And along the way, we come to actually appreciate the variations. Springtime has to be Exhibit A for this idea. For one thing, the joy of spring is amplified by its juxtaposition to winter, a damp, chilly, gloomy 3 months that by late February feels like it will never end.

For another, there's something new and exciting going on in the spring for just about anyone with even a small interest in nature. Early wildflowers, some even coming up through the snow . . . waves of migrating spring birds, back in again from South America, familiar friends here again for an extended visit . . . gardens to be planned and planted . . . hungry trout to be

3

coaxed from your favorite local waterway with cleverly-tied flies, designed to imitate the latest hatching bugs . . . greenways and trails to be conquered without piling on layers of clothes.

My earliest memories of being excited about spring revolve around one of my most favorite people ever—my Granny Collier. After the passing of my Grandfather Collier back in 1934, Granny moved back to the family farm in the Powell community and lived there, independent and alone, for over 30 years . . . well, sort of alone. She had two faithful dogs, a collie named Jerry and a Scottie named Inky. She had a couple of jersey milk cows and two retired working farm mules, Red and Jack, a bunch of chickens, and . . . a huge garden.

I still remember the first time Granny let me plant the beans. I was about age 7. Kentucky wonders, they were. Amazingly, they came up. And even more wondrous, they produced beans! I was as proud of them as if I had invented beans myself. That experience triggered some sort of latent gardening gene in my DNA that has remained active for the ensuing seven decades. It seems to be at its most intense each year in the early spring. And its influence seems to have spread from just growing my own garden to a fascination with whatever Mother Nature is growing in *her* spring garden, from the tiny bluets to the tallest budding trees.

Days at Granny's farm were spent seamlessly blending family and people with the natural world we found all around us. There were possums and snakes, birds and flowers. The garden was coming up with summer's vegetables, and the sorghum field was sprouting with what would become next fall's sorghum molasses for our morning biscuits.

On Sundays we feasted on the world's most delicious chicken and dumplings, whose main ingredient, the chicken, had been chasing grasshoppers in the yard the day before. We finished with deep-dish apple pie made from apples off Granny's favorite tree that we could all see from where we sat at her dining room table. Observations, connections. . . . It just all fit together in a marvelous, comfortable way!

Spring seemed to get it all started every year, taking the world outside from gloom to joy, almost overnight. So then let's proceed and see what we find as we emerge from hibernation and take a look or two outside.

SO, WHAT'S "BIRDING"?

You have to start somewhere. Many an avocation begins with a small "aha!" of discovery. A sentence in a book, a DIY program on TV, a visit to a friend's flower garden or the county fair, and an "I really like that" or "I could do that" moment becomes a lifelong passion.

For the last thirty years or so, birding has been the main focus of my outdoor activities, but it hasn't been that way forever. Growing up, it was fishing. At first it was mostly fishing on the creek bank with a cane pole, using grasshoppers for bait; then gradually moving up to the more refined sport of tying and fishing with flies. Some years farther along, the US Air Force took me to Utah, where I discovered the world of rock hounding, combing acres of ground for geological treasures and digging a lot of big dusty holes. And finally, to the delight of Spouse, who responded to rock hounding with a folding chair and a good mystery book, we discovered birding. No holes to dig; no tons of gathered material to lug home. All we needed was binoculars, and we had a whole new reason to be outside, a world full of colorful flying wonders to become acquainted with.

In general, when we speak of a "birder," we are referring to an average citizen with a pair of binoculars, a bird field guide or two, and possibly a spotting scope or long-lens camera. This person would have a good and growing knowledge of at least their local bird life and where to find it, and a constant, nagging need to be out somewhere seeing birds.

Numerous activities are connected with the sport of birding, such as club meetings, field trips, reading great magazines, and travel. There are local, state, and national birding organizations, all with endless opportunities for learning experiences both out in the field and in evening gathering spots, together with like-minded individuals. Birding goes on all year, but there's a definite peak in interest and activity during spring and fall migration each year, as less familiar birds travel through the area.

With extensive travel and lots of time in the field, it's possible to eventually see 600 or 700 or more different species of birds just in the area of North America beyond Mexico's border. Individual states, especially those that find themselves with a good variety of habitats such as mountains and seacoasts, likely boast lists of several hundred birds. Individual counties may have a couple hundred; the Great Smoky Mountains National Park has a list of over 200 species. Birders usually learn their local birds and become familiar with them and enjoy knowing from day to day which ones are around. They then are more likely to recognize the occasional unusual avian visitor to their area.

Which brings us to the phenomenon of finding rare birds. "Rare" means birds not common to your area, maybe seen once in a while or once in a decade, or even once in a lifetime. Birders familiar with as many common local species as possible can then recognize a rarity as something worth serious attention—a very exciting event, and one that seems to be happening ever more frequently in these days of multiple means of instant digital communication.

When birders get together, talk invariably focuses on the birds they've seen lately and where, the last time they saw them and with whom, and what the weather and other circumstances were at the time. Birders are nice people—curious and interested—and nearly always eager to share their knowledge and experience, especially with beginners.

We were outdoor people already, but our discovery of birding served to refocus our interests in the whole world of nature, and the study and enjoyment of the greater world of natural history gradually unfolded from there—trees, flowers, butterflies, dragonflies—all of it. Interest in the natural world can begin with rocks, bugs, trees, or birds. It's a most intriguing journey, wherever you start and regardless of what becomes your primary interest. Most people find that it enlarges their whole world. Spouse and I welcome you to ours.

A TRIP TO THE LOW COUNTRY

When you grow up within sight of the Great Smoky Mountains and you're an outdoor person, I suppose it's only natural that "being outside" calls up images of cool high elevations, rushing clear streams with clean gravelly bottoms, tall, straight poplars and thick, full evergreens growing up from dense rhododendron thickets, and hiking trails that go either uphill or downhill most of the time.

It turns out that there are other outdoors out there, some of them a lot different from the environs in our neck of the woods. In fact, there are places where "high" means 1 or 2 feet above sea level, where the rivers and streams have water the color of tea, and the currents flow slowly back and forth, rising and falling twice a day. The groves of stately pine trees grow on land as flat as a tabletop, a dense undergrowth of palmettos at their feet, between miles of grass-filled salt marsh. The other trees—the massive, gnarled old live oaks—stand on the higher ground, embellished with ferns and Spanish moss.

This is the "foreign" land you encounter all along the coasts of South Carolina and Georgia, from the beaches inland for 30 miles or so; it's the Low Country. Armadillos and alligators, snakes and mosquitoes—what more could an outdoor person want?

This particular year, the weatherman was calling for snow the first day of spring. Spouse and I decided we needed to be somewhere farther south, hopefully some place with a lot of birds already there and not just expected in a month or so. We had already been wanting to add some more birds to our Georgia list. The middle of March, the state of Georgia, lots of birds,

an easy day's drive away. And so it was decided . . . we headed for the Low Country, and Jekyll Island seemed to be the right destination. The barrier islands along the coast of Georgia—Tybee, Ossabow, St. Simons, Jekyll, Cumberland, and others—are different from the long, narrow ribbons of sand we're used to visiting along North Carolina's Outer Banks. On the Georgia coast, because of the shape of the coastline and the work of the wind and tides, the barrier islands are plump, wider, higher affairs with well-established maritime forests of live oak, pine, and palmettos.

The Low Country is a land of water. The gentle 2-foot tides of the Outer Banks are replaced here by big 6-to-8-foot tides. The boat docks you see with many steps up and down to their landings attest to the significant twice-daily water-level changes. Eight major rivers flow into the ocean in the 100 miles between Savannah, Georgia, and the Florida state line, not to mention sounds, creeks, and marshlands without number. The early colonists depended on the waterways for their transportation, at least as far inland as they could navigate.

After the Native Americans, the Spanish, and the British came and went, those hardy early settlers established homes in the Low Country and built large rice plantations there, in a land that I would consider uninhabitable before the days of air conditioning and window screens. And I recall that the folks in Boston and Philadelphia chose to harvest the oak trees for sailing vessels from those islands in the winter because, as many historic records attest, not even the toughest crew of timbermen could tolerate the snakes, bugs, alligators, and deadly fevers of the Low Country summers.

But early spring is really nice. There's not a lot going on, tourist-wise. Just about the only people around are the locals, some indoors-type snowbirds, and the fishermen and birders . . . which brings us to the birds. The ocean, beaches, woods, ponds, and marshes give you a wide variety of places to look for our winged friends. And there are some great manmade places as well. Several wildlife refuges have been developed using the ponds and dikes from the old rice plantations; on one of those ponds we saw hundreds of nesting wood storks and scores of yellow-crowned and black-crowned night herons. And we saw lots of alligators . . . big alligators.

All that added up to a marvelous 3 days of dawn-to-dark birding, and a list of 111 species sighted on the trip. Some were exciting single sightings: one glossy ibis flying over; a yellow-throated warbler in the Spanish moss, possibly a month before it would be singing for us up in the pines of Cades Cove in the Smokies. We spotted a little chickenlike sora rail skulking through the marsh grass and a plump little long-distance-migrating shorebird called a red knot, hunkered down among a flock of other species, as if trying to keep a low profile and avoid any publicity.

There were some "oh, wow!" moments, like when Spouse and I saw 20 white pelicans soaring high over the marsh in the morning sun, just as a bald eagle flew across the sky in front of them. And then there were what I like to call "the way nature was intended to be" moments, where the abundance of life is just too much to count. We stood and watched a thousand little sandpipers and plovers feeding on a mud flat at low tide; suddenly they would all swirl into the sky and sweep around like a single huge organism, and then calmly settle back down to begin feeding again as if nothing had happened, only to repeat the whole drama once more minutes later.

Out on the beach, this scene repeated itself, only bigger and noisier. There, the larger birds—gulls and terns, black skimmers and oystercatchers—were hanging out, and they did the resting and swirling thing, too, but with a lot more squawking and calling. You just won't see birds like that in the Smokies; it was like being at Disney World for birdwatchers!

Given a little space, nature produces beautiful things in numbers and varieties beyond our imaginations. A few days at the right times and in the right places could convince even the most committed indoor person of the truth and wonder of that.

When it stops snowing, we'll be on the road again.

MIRACULOUS SPRING

Mother Nature seems to tease us with the promise of spring. At first, little tantalizing bits for a day or so, and then weeks of fits and starts. In addition to the deliciously warm sunshine we begin to feel on our backs, there are more and more sights and sounds of spring to enjoy. And there are seemingly miraculous things going on behind every sight and sound.

Take spring peepers, for example. These tiny frogs, the size of your thumb, spend the winter hibernating under logs and leaf litter, showing no signs of life and sometimes frozen solid. And then at the first hint of spring, there they are in *every* puddle and ditch, peeping by the thousands, sometimes with snow and ice still around the edges of their wetland.

And just like the peepers, everything else out there seems to be chomping at the bit, eagerly waiting to burst forth into song or blossom. Cardinals and tufted titmice have been singing for weeks. Their spring hormones kick in when the days begin to reach some mystical length, snow or not. And this all seems to work pretty well, as it has for thousands of years now.

Over the course of many, many years, I have come to regard the many happenings of spring as nothing short of miraculous. When you stop and think about it, just the fact that birds can fly is miraculous, and a lot of them do it spectacularly well. For example, that little shorebird called the red knot, the one that we were so delighted to see during our trip to the Low Country, is a world champion of flyers. It comes some 7,000 miles each spring from its wintering grounds in southern South America to nest and raise its young in the tundra of far northern Canada.

Our ruby-throated hummingbirds, very tiny creatures compared to the red knot or even a robin, fly nonstop across the Gulf of Mexico each spring to show up at our hummingbird feeders and raise their young in our neighborhoods. Miraculous? Consider this: These countless miles of travel are guided by amazing skills built into their little bird brains. They can navigate by the position of the sun, compensating automatically for the time of day. They fly by night, guided by the stars. Clouds and fog? They have a wired-in navigation system that uses the Earth's magnetic field. All these are feats we humans can do only with an airplane and a sophisticated guidance system.

And then, a fall miracle to follow the spring ones: The young birds that hatched this year head south, on their own, guidance systems in operation, to a place they've never been, the wintering areas their parents headed north from earlier in the year.

Of course, bats can fly, too. They're the only mammals that can fly, and they're really good at it. And so can thousands of bugs and butterflies. So, birds don't have exclusive rights to flying, but they *can* claim exclusive bragging rights to a couple of other miraculous things: feathers and singing. Those amazingly complex structures, the feathers—apparently originally worn by the dinosaurs—give birds all those bright crisp spring colors, keep them warm, and enable them to fly. And what about the singing thing? Well, frogs and katydids sing, but not melodious songs like a robin or a wood thrush, or the entertaining melodies and mockeries of our Tennessee state bird, the mockingbird.

In spring, robins, cardinals, titmice, and mockingbirds go at it for hours every day, soon joined in the chorus by very vocal bunches of migrants. Now, I'm sure that most of you know that they aren't singing just to entertain us human beings! They're actually singing to establish their own individual nesting territories and to attract a mate. Presumably, the best singer gets the best territory and the best mate. It happens that, years ago, I got a very good mate, but I'm really thankful that the process didn't depend upon my singing! We humans have worked out a somewhat different system for courtship, but fortunately for us all, the birds' remarkable system is one that fills our springtime with music.

One thing that not everyone realizes is that each species of birds has its own specific song or set of songs, recognizable in the field, from bird to bird. Most good birders have learned to "bird by ear"; they know which of their feathered friends are in the vicinity just by listening to the songs around them. It's also very helpful to know who's singing when the bird in question is very high in a leafy tree or tucked into some dense underbrush.

Some folks are a lot better than others in their ability to remember and recognize bird songs and calls. Some gifted few can remember thousands of them. But everyone can learn the familiar ones—robin, cardinal, bluebird, mockingbird—and then progress on from there, a few at a time. Birding by ear opens up a whole new dimension for enjoying the outdoors.

There are lots of other springtime miracles happening now. Consider how the wildflowers suddenly transform the seemingly lifeless forest floor into a garden of the first order. Bloodroots come up through the snow and bloom for us along the Norris River Bluff Trail even when it's really too chilly for us to want to go out. They are being joined by a dozen other species of beautiful early spring flowers, including a few thousand trout lilies carpeting the floor of the woods.

And how about those butterflies? People have regarded caterpillars from last fall, emerging from their strange transformation into spectacular spring butterflies, as miraculous for centuries. We still don't understand the details, and it is truly a wonder of nature. Those tiny Eastern tailed blues and little white moths are already flitting about on any warm sunny afternoon, and the heavy hitters such as silver-spotted skippers and tiger swallowtails will be along soon.

Speaking of insects, thousands of tiny gnats and flies, caterpillars and inchworms come out, just in time to feed the waves of warblers and vireos, swifts, and swallows that are even now on their way up from South and Central America to Sharp's Ridge, Norris Songbird Trail, and your backyard. The birds will eat literally *tons* of them. It all seems to work out in miraculous fashion, and we all need to remember that our awareness and care are part of what will enable these miracles to continue on into the future.

THE EARLIEST BIRDS

Polar vortexes, snow and ice, used-up snow days, rain and gloom. By the first week of March, I imagine there aren't many of us who wouldn't love to see spring burst forth. We're all really ready for some warm sunshine, blue skies, green grass, and lots of trees and flowers in bloom.

For the hardy birdwatchers among us, there is one more spring thing we eagerly anticipate: the arrival of the spring migrants. It's our biggest happening of the whole year! Early spring brings hints of changes coming. Our year-round birds—the chickadees, titmice, song sparrows, robins, cardinals, and Carolina wrens—perk up and begin singing as soon as we have a few mild sunny days, and of course we're glad to have them here to announce spring.

But those migrants! Dressed in their resplendent new spring plumage, they arrive in East Tennessee from their tropical winter homes in the Caribbean and Central and South America with their hormones raging. In the bird world, that means being hungry, good-looking, and conspicuous, courting the ladies and challenging your rivals, and singing for hours on end.

They go away in September, a long 6 months, so we content ourselves with our faithful resident birds plus a few winter visitors from farther north, like the white-throated sparrows and the yellow-bellied sapsuckers, and a few gulls, ducks, loons, and grebes on the lakes. We might even see a couple of rufous hummingbirds, a western species, wintering at feeders here, and last month we enjoyed the amazing appearance of a beautiful male painted bunting, a bird of the Southeast coast and Texas, coming regularly to a feeder in Maryville, in the shadow of the Smoky Mountains.

But as the time approaches for the real migrants, our bird populations more than double, as will the number of species, as the birds of spring begin to return. First comes a trickle in February, more in March, and a huge flood of them in April. Records can tell interesting stories, and birders have always kept lots of records. They show a notable change in the dates of the spring arrivals over the past several decades. As the climate warms, some birds arrive at their usual nesting grounds up to 3 weeks earlier now than they did even as recently as the 1950s, and many species are nesting much farther north now than a few decades ago.

But overall, the change is slow, and in spite of being subject to problems of local daily weather as they travel, our migrants generally return on a fairly predictable schedule. And thankfully, Mother Nature doesn't blast us with everything all at once. The spectacular scarlet tanagers, Baltimore orioles, rose-breasted grosbeaks, 25 species of warblers, the vireos, and the hummingbirds would be overwhelming if they all showed up at the same time!

But it turns out that, instead of some of those more spectacular species, our earliest birds are a bunch of hard-working, perpetual-motion, blue-collar, somewhat less flashy guys and gals, the swallows. Here in the East, we have six species of swallows to look for. The two "mud swallows"—the barn swallows and the cliff swallows—build cup- or jug-shaped nests of mud clinging to barn walls and the underside of bridges. Two species tend to nest in burrows in banks and cliffs: the bank and northern rough-winged swallows. And then there are two that prefer to live in houses and hollows in trees: the purple martins and the tree swallows.

Of all those, the ones that get the most attention are, of course, the purple martins. They have an army of dedicated landlords and landladies waiting for them. Purple martin people are experts at the game of watching for the earliest spring bird and claiming bragging rights over their neighbors for having the first one arrive at their housing.

And early they are: The average earliest purple martin sighting here in East Tennessee is right around March 8th to March 12th, and sometimes they're much earlier. But overall, the earliest swallows around here, and thus the earliest spring migrants, are the beautiful tree swallows. They can show up any time around the first of February. Our earliest ones are usually seen at a wonderful birding locality called the Eagle Bend Fish Hatchery. Located in the big U-shaped bend of the Clinch River at Clinton, some 20 miles north of Knoxville, it is one of 10 state fish hatcheries run for us by the Tennessee Wildlife Resources Agency (TWRA).

Spouse and I were looking around the hatchery on the morning of February 18th when, zounds, there they were! Two tree swallows, with shiny blue-green backs and snow-white bellies, zipping over the fields, catching early spring flying insects. Those first spring migrants are always cause for rejoicing! The following Monday, master birder Ron Hoff observed a flock of 150 tree swallows at the fish hatchery, a big flock either arriving to spread out and nest in these parts, or maybe just working their way north. They depend on halfway decent weather for their food supply, and they nest as far north as northern Canada and Alaska, places that are at this time of year still in full-blown deep winter.

Tree swallows like to nest in old abandoned woodpecker cavities near water. One of their favorite places around Knoxville, and a great place to observe them, is Cove Lake State Park, another 15 or so miles north, where they naturally live in hollowed-out dead willow snags standing in the edge of the lake. When a suitable willow tree isn't available, though, they will also take readily to a bluebird house. Often, if a string of bluebird houses is too close together to suit the bluebirds (they like to be a respectable distance from other bluebird neighbors), the tree swallows will move into a house between the bluebird-occupied ones.

Like all the swallows, tree swallows feed on the wing. Masters of speed and agility, they course over fields, ponds, and lakes throughout the day, nabbing untold tons of flying insects. They're beautiful to watch for themselves, and even more so when you know they're the vanguard of all those feathered friends heading this way. Time to dust off the binoculars. Good birding!

IT'S SPRING FOR SURE,
BUT WHAT'S THAT GREEN?

By early April we've already enjoyed two weeks of official springtime. And it has started getting nice, with warm days, cool nights, and occasional rain showers. The redbuds are bursting into their usual luscious spring glory, and the cedars and elms are making pollen. (Your sinuses will likely be taking notice.)

Most of the trees, though, are still a little skeptical of it all; the buckeyes and wild cherries are barely starting to peek out with some leaves. The wily walnut trees know better. They're waiting, as the seed packets say, until all danger of frost has passed. Nevertheless, as we drive around in our overall area, we see a lot of bright, spring-fresh new green leaves. But notice, though: They seem to be growing on only a couple of kinds of plants—tall bright green trees and shorter bright green undergrowth bushes.

Could we have something strange going on here? Look at the edges of the woods along Interstate 75 or State Highway 33. Those early green trees? They're out way ahead of the usual earliest trees such as the poplars and the maples, producing some serious competition for sunlight and nutrients. Alas, they aren't from around here, as we say in East Tennessee. They are from across the water, brought to us from China by none other than the US Department of Agriculture back around 1965: the now widespread Bradford pear.

To make matters worse, all that exuberant understory shrubbery that has been up and growing for weeks now, completely filling some areas under the trees and lining our highways, is another foreign invader, native to China, Japan, and Korea and brought to us compliments of the New York Botanical Garden in 1898. The dreaded Amur bush honeysuckle.

Now, we know that there are at least two sides to every story. Staunch differences of opinion are normal human behavior. Just look at politics and religion! It's that way with Bradford pears. Lady Bird Johnson called them "the perfect tree." The Tennessee Department of Environment and Conservation, in their publication *The Tennessee Conservationist*, calls them "evil dressed in white."

Perfect tree? Well, yes, in a number of ways. The people who love them point out that they grow very fast, which is a great feature for contractors, making them useful for quickly transforming a brand-new subdivision into a tree-lined neighborhood. The trees are a uniform, lollipop shape, and they bloom profusely early in the spring and have lovely red-to-maroon foliage in the fall. And they are disease and insect resistant; not even Japanese beetles will eat them.

But the "perfect tree" has a dark side. The Bradford pear's rapid growth also makes it typically have a short lifespan, an average 20 years or less. It is famously vulnerable to wind damage, with broken limbs and split trunks. Furthermore, the monotonous, uniform, stamped-from-a-pattern lollipop appearance of the trees is disagreeable to a lot of folks who prefer to see the expected natural variety in the shapes of their trees. The flowers of the Bradford pear are notoriously malodorous, a smell described by some as resembling that of rotting flesh. The fruits, eaten mostly by starlings, drop in yards and onto cars as they deteriorate and smell unpleasant as well.

And yet, the worst part is this: Our cultivated Bradford pears are clones produced from a mutant form of a tree called the Callery pear. When those seeds are eaten by birds and dispersed far and wide, and germinate and grow, they revert back to their ancestral Callery pear. Then they grow in dense thickets, and many of them bear fierce, strong thorns that can penetrate a tractor tire or workboot. They aggressively crowd out our native trees and shrubs, the classic behavior of all invasive species!

Those widespread bush honeysuckles? Well, they don't sprout thorns, which is probably the nicest thing you could say about them. But like many other invasives, they come out earlier in the spring; go dormant later in the fall; are disease and insect resistant; and outcompete native shrubs, ground covers, and wildflowers, spreading and growing fast and aggressively.

The bush honeysuckle's bright red berries, a selling point for them as an ornamental planting early on, are attractive to many bird species, and so get dispersed, likewise far and wide, often miles from the mother plant. The plants are versatile enough to grow in full sun and deep shade, in wet or dry locations, and they line the roadsides all over the eastern United States except for arctic Maine and tropical Florida. They have been banned in Connecticut and Massachusetts—believed to attract deer and bring an increase in Lyme disease—and they have been labeled a "noxious weed" in Vermont and are on Tennessee's invasive species list.

These two bad actors are the ones that stand out at this time of the year, but there are many others. Think Japanese honeysuckle, Chinese privet, mimosas, kudzu, and the tree-strangling Oriental bittersweet. Garden escapees such as winterberry, English ivy, burning bush, and nandina become serious invasives, too. So, what to do, besides wringing our hands and grumbling? Mostly, I would say, read up, be informed, remove exotics from your corner of the Earth, and above all shop wisely for whatever you plant and grow. The websites for the Tennessee Native Plant Society (http://www.tnps.org) and the Tennessee Exotic Pest Plant Council (http://www.invasive.org) provide lots of useful information for those who wish to put some native plants into their landscape.

In checking the internet, I found nurseries still offer both Bradford pears and bush honeysuckles for sale! Find a good, reputable plant nursery to do business with, and let them know that you're aware of the problems with invasives and don't want them on your property. Try landscaping with natives you haven't used before. Hooray for redbuds, dogwoods, wild plums, serviceberries, sugar maples, black cherries, silverbells, witch hazels, and sourwoods!

MIGRATION

On a recent Tuesday I took a stroll around the grounds between rain showers, just to get a little outdoor air before the rest of what was shaping up to be an indoor-type day. My Granny Collier's double jonquils, lovingly salvaged from her old house site, were blooming, the old cool-weather bluegrass was bright green, and the birds were singing.

Really singing, as if they thought it was already spring, which was still officially 3 weeks away. The cardinals and the tufted titmice led the chorus, with support from the field and song sparrows, the eastern towhees, and the Carolina wrens. All those guys had hung in there with us through the whole dreary winter, along with the mockingbird, the brown thrasher, the blue jays, and the robins.

In early spring, with all that morning chorus, it's hard to believe that in just 6 weeks, the birdsong will more than double! With the arrival of the spring migrants, the songs multiply so that some mornings it is hard to sort them all out. Swifts and swallows, vireos and gnatcatchers, catbirds and wood thrushes, cuckoos and nighthawks, and hummingbirds and wood warblers all come back. Species that through the eons have developed a lifestyle that many of us would envy—they live in a world where it is always summer.

Actually, they live here with us less than half the year. We are loathe to admit it, but they are really South American birds that have found great success in raising their young by coming north for a few months each year. Here, they are able to raise their babies on the high-protein diet of insects that explodes around us every spring—gnats, worms, bugs, and caterpillars.

Animal migrations have fascinated and mystified people through the ages. Birds aren't the only animals that do it. Great herds of animals migrate across the plains of Africa, and herds of caribou migrate in the vast far north of our continent. Monarch butterflies migrate from as far as Canada to a site in Mexico, to a place where not a single one of them has ever been before. But for sheer huge numbers—think billions—and sheer unimaginable distances—often thousands of miles a year—nothing in the natural world matches the spectacle of the spring and fall flight of the birds.

These comings and goings are part of the local people's lives. Consider the storks returning over the centuries to the chimneys of Europe. The cliff swallows of San Juan Capistrano, having wintered 6,000 miles to the south in Argentina, have traditionally returned to the mission outside Los Angeles each spring on St. Joseph's day, March 19th. And then there are the turkey vultures of Hinckley, Ohio, faithfully returning each March 15th, just in time for the town's big Buzzard Day Festival.

The seasonal disappearance of the birds mystified the ancients (and not-so-ancient folks) who were observant and curious about such things. All those flocks of blackbirds and swallows, even the small songbirds—where did they go? There were theories that the swallows buried themselves in the mud of ponds to sleep the winter away. People surmised that hummingbirds flew south riding on the backs of the geese; they were obviously too small to get very far on their own!

Even in more recent times, with worldwide travel and many scientists and naturalists out there searching and observing, many of the details of migration remain unknown. Research has revealed that birds find their way using a combination of amazing inborn skills, among them the ability to navigate by the Earth's magnetic field and to tell the time of day by the sun, and then apparently remembering the previous year's local geographic landmarks as they go along. Birds are able to travel thousands of miles every spring, and end up for nesting in the same field or yard each spring . . . amazing!

But discovering where some species go to spend winter has always been a challenge. Some species seem to just disappear into a trackless jungle to the south or to go out across the ocean to Goodness Knows Where. Bird banding has been used extensively to examine this question, and has occasionally provided some critical answers. Hundreds or thousands of individuals of a species were fitted with tiny ID leg bands, and then by sheer luck, one or two would be recovered from birds on the wintering grounds. That is how a dedicated birder from Memphis surprised the ornithological world by discovering that chimney swifts spend their winters in the jungles of Peru.

Bird banding is a very labor intensive and low-yield enterprise. But we've put men on the moon and landed a vehicle on Mars, and we now have high-tech help in solving some of the mysteries of bird migration. An April issue of *Birdwatching* magazine contains an article about that very thing. It seems that a gentleman with the interesting name of Vsevolod Afanasyev, working with the British Antarctic Survey, developed a device called a geolocator and used it to track the legendary wandering albatross on their decades-long travels across the endless southern oceans.

One of his colleagues, engineer James Fox, then adapted the device into a tiny 0.018 ounce gizmo that can be attached to the back of a small bird. A sparrow weighs in at about 0.7 ounce; a catbird, around an ounce. The geolocator contains a clock, battery, light sensor, and microprocessor, squeezed into a miniature device that causes these small birds no distress or problems with their flight. There are some downsides, however; each geo-locator costs $200, and they only recover about 20% of them for analysis. Cloudy weather and even prolonged shade can make evaluations difficult.

But with the geolocators, scientists have already made many remarkable discoveries into the details of when, where, how far, and how fast various bird species travel. They've found that our purple martins use a broad area along the Amazon River for their wintering grounds; flocks of one of our eastern shorebirds, the willet, fly 2,800 miles each fall, before hurricane season, to gather for the winter in a small area on the northern coast of Brazil.

Probably the most spectacular example of this is the story of two birds called northern wheatears. Northern wheatears are small, black, white, and gray sparrow-sized birds that nest in the far north of North America. The two wheatears at the center of our story were fitted with geolocators. After their migrations, they were recaptured and the devices analyzed. The two little birds had left Fairbanks, Alaska, flown over the Bering Sea, through Russia, across the Arabian desert, and wintered in central Africa—an average round-trip distance of 18,640 miles, the longest-known migration of any songbird!

Research using geolocators is just beginning. We're learning that whales can dive more than a mile deep in the ocean, and birds can fly nearly 20,000 miles in a year's migration. And, yep, there are still an awful lot of things we don't know. But we surely do know that the arrival of all those singing spring birds each year is an event little short of miraculous, and they'll be here soon. Be watching!

STALKING THE WILY WILDFLOWER

Around these parts, the appearance of the spring wildflowers is a really big deal. Testimony to that statement is the huge annual Spring Wildflower Pilgrimage headquartered in the City of Gatlinburg and enjoyed throughout the Great Smoky Mountains National Park. Since its inception in 1951, the three-day event has drawn thousands of visitors from across the nation. They enjoy indoor exhibits of native wildflowers, attend informative evening programs, and participate in many of the guided wildflower, birding, and general nature-oriented field trips.

In March, the trees are bare, the shrubs are bare, and even the forest floor is bare. Then, within days the first spring ephemerals pop up from underneath the remains of last autumn's decaying leaves. The bloodroots are generally first, with their pristine white blossoms appearing seemingly overnight, sometimes through a lingering patch of late-spring snow. They are quickly followed by all manner of shapes and sizes of stems, leaves, and blossoms, many of them white, but here and there a yellow, a pink, and even a maroon or two.

Not to be forgotten are the trees in the spring. Across the mountainsides, way before the leaves, we see splashes of white and pink here and there. These early birds are the silverbells, the serviceberries, and the dogwoods, along with their pink cousins, the redbuds and fire cherries. All signs of life return and morph rapidly into an overwhelming abundance. All are eagerly awaited and then enjoyed by a lot of winter-weary people here and across the country.

Interest in wildflowers has been around ever since human beings came trudging along and discovered them. Back in hunting-and-gathering days, the flowers often served as little flags to indicate a plant that could be used for food or medicine. A lot of trial-and-error practical wisdom was gained and handed down through the centuries. Later, cultivated flower gardens grew in popularity, some reaching spectacular proportions and becoming symbols of great wealth and status.

Widespread interest in wildflowers as a pastime for the average citizen has been around mostly in the last two or three centuries and has evolved in a fashion similar to bird watching. Each of those fields of interest first began as a subject of study by the scientific community, and then was discovered by myriad avid amateurs who not only enjoyed them as a diversion, but who added another dimension of practical knowledge and experience to the discipline.

In our part of the world, popular interest in birding can be traced back in good measure to the likes of Roger Tory Peterson, whose wonderful field guides redefined the pastime of birding from that of collecting birds with a shotgun to one of using binoculars to identify and observe birds, something we all could learn and enjoy.

Similarly, the mysterious botanical world has been revealed to us by a series of people who had the gift of sharing their knowledge of wildflowers with a bunch of very interested amateur botanists. One such person was Mrs. William Starr Dana, who authored *How to Know the Wildflowers*, a landmark wildflower guide, published in New York back in 1893. It is full of flowery nineteenth-century prose and bits of poetry by some of her contemporaries—Thoreau, Bryant, Emerson, Whittier, and others—plus lots of botanical history and folklore. It was originally illustrated only with blackand-white line drawings, but color plates were added to the 1921 edition.

And as proof of the popularity of wildflowers back then, the first printing sold out in 5 days. Revised and enlarged several times, Mrs. Dana's book was last produced in a cloth edition in 1940. But it was a piece of pioneering work, remains a classic, and is still an interesting read to this day.

Another major addition to the present-day body of wildflower field guides was published in 1977. *Newcomb's Wildflower Guide* had the ambitious subtitle of "An Ingenious Key System for Quick, Positive Field Identification of the Wildflowers, Flowering Shrubs and Vines of Northeastern and North Central North America." In the introduction the author, Lawrence Newcomb, explains that his key system will allow the flower enthusiast to quickly identify any of the 1,375 wildflowers, shrubs, and vines of the northeastern United States and neighboring Canada. Well, maybe not all of them and maybe not so quickly, but the book was a big step forward and does have excellent illustrations, done in an orderly manner. Newcomb's classic book is indeed a helpful reference and still a go-to book for a tough wildflower identification problem.

And now in the twenty-first century, we have an abundance of beautifully illustrated flower guides covering just about every part of the country. Many of them are specific to individual states, national parks, or certain mountain ranges and river valleys. A voice of experience here will advise you that, sometimes, it pays to have more than one book on the same area; you may not find the flower you're trying to identify in one book, but it may be clearly and fully illustrated in another.

Guide books can also help with common names. Every nook and cranny of civilization calls their wildflowers by a different common name. The Latin scientific name for a plant is the same everywhere, but the common names? All over the place. Many guide books will give more than one common name for a given plant, and some even provide a concordance of sorts, with a list of known names for the plants.

All those spring flowers are out there for everyone to enjoy. You can find them in your backyard, along your nearby roadsides, and in your neighboring fields and parks. And they're good for you! Newcomb's book states it very well: "Familiarity with the natural world provides a valuable anchor in reality." And the author expressed hope that his new wildflower guide would facilitate people's search for a meaningful grasp of the world around us. And who among us wouldn't welcome some help with that?

SPRING AND THE SIGNS

Springtime just has a special feeling to it. The feeling came to me last week, as I stood and admired my first jonquil, a neat double blossom whose ancestors graced my grandmother's yard well over 75 years ago.

The last of February can have a lot of March days: sun, clouds, gusty winds, and showers. And then the buds come out on the elms, the maples, and the willows. And the cardinals, tufted titmice, field sparrows, and Carolina wrens sing every morning.

I suppose, through the years, the single event that always meant spring had really arrived was when we started planting our garden. It was a magical day, when the ground was just right to work and the sun was shining, and in went the onions, the spinach, and lettuce. What a great feeling!

Folks around here know gardening. Our forebears had done it since before they left their home countries and came over the mountains. And it wasn't done just as a cheery outdoor experience, the reason many of us plant gardens today. There were many hungry mouths to feed, and besides, nobody had eaten anything fresh since the last greens of fall. Our local gardening traditions go back a long way. Take seed companies and their catalogs, for example. Think how scanning those pages of showy, weedless flowerbeds and luscious, ripe, always bug-free vegetables get the old juices flowing during those last dreary days of winter!

The Landreth Seed House in Philadelphia, started up in 1784, is apparently the oldest seed company in the country and the fifth oldest corporation in North America. They introduced the zinnia in 1798 and later the white potato and Bloomsdale spinach. Can you imagine a garden without a crop of all three of those? They also apparently started the tradition of all those tempting, beautifully-illustrated seed catalogs. The Park Seed Company was started up in 1868 by an enterprising 15-year-old, and 8 years later, Burpee Seeds was started by an equally enterprising 18-year-old.

The Shakers also had a lot to do with how we do seeds today. They had put out a catalog of garden seeds in 1831. Using the official name of The United Society of Believers in Christ's Second Coming, they lived in several areas across the United States, from Maine to Kentucky, in communal settlements of strictly celibate men and women (no offspring). They survived as a group by taking in an occasional new member and by adopting orphans, but they have finally all but died out. They left behind many remarkable accomplishments, including their tradition of simplicity in their lives, and their beautiful furniture.

But in 1916 they developed the concept of packaging garden seeds for sale in small paper envelopes, the way we see them in stores today. (They're getting so expensive, it wouldn't surprise me if they didn't start selling them by the seed. But, oops! That sounds like something my grandmother probably might have said 60 years ago!) To continue with the story, the enterprising Shakers also made small wooden boxes for packing and distributing the seed packets to the country stores, where the customers picked their selections straight out of the boxes. Decorated with pictures of flowers and vegetables, those boxes are big-ticket collectors' items today; even modern facsimiles are expensive.

Well, after you have gleaned your ideas from the seed catalogs, and gone down to the store for your packets of seeds, there's still the preparation and planting. Do you just go out there and toss your seeds into the ground? Certainly not, if you believe in planting by the signs! My favorite planting-by-the-signs person was the late Mr. Earl Conner, of the large Powell Conner clan. A master farmer and gardener, Earl used to plow our garden every spring, without telling us when he'd come beforehand and without any thought of our paying him for the work.

Earl was a believer and practitioner of planting by the signs. For you city folk who might not be familiar with the practice, it involves timing all your farming activities— removing brush, digging postholes, plowing and planting—according to the signs of the zodiac.

Foolishness, you say? Not if you had seen Earl Conner's garden! It always looked like a page from a seed catalog. The Conner farm was next door to the Collier place, and you could see his garden from mine. Well, there was no contest: Earl's corn would be 8 feet tall while mine was just peeking out and trying to decide whether to go on and grow.

Other than years of experience like Earl's, how does one come to know about all this zodiac stuff? Why, from the *Old Farmer's Almanac*, of course! The almanac was first published in 1792, and is the oldest continuously published periodical in North America. It contains weather forecasts, tide tables, planting charts, and all the zodiac-related times to do various farming chores, or even more importantly, when not to do them. For example, if you dig postholes when the signs are wrong, your fenceposts are going to loosen up; if the signs are right, the posts will tighten up in their holes "like they growed there."

And you don't just throw all your seeds in the ground under the same sign—heavens no! Some signs are right for the aboveground crops, and some are right for the root crops. Plant your 'taters when the signs are in the feet, and they'll all have little toes growing on them. The list of possible gardening misadventures is long; consult your almanac. The almanac is also famous for its weather predictions, although its accuracy varies a lot according to who you ask. At any rate, it is a legendary part of life in rural America.

Every garden is as different as its gardener: scientific or by the signs; organic or full of dust, spray, and fertilizer; weed-free or laid-back. But they all have the common thread of that hard-to-describe feeling that every gardener shares in some way, when those little seeds come up, by golly, living and producing for yet another season. It will make you want to hum a little tune as you pull those pesky weeds!

RIGHT PLACE, RIGHT TIME

Most folks who know about our Great Smoky Mountains National Park are familiar with the tremendous role the Civilian Conservation Corps (CCC) played in its development. Some 4,000 young men showed up just as the park was authorized for development. Living in 17 US Army-supervised camps, they built the area's infrastructure including roads, bridges, buildings, and trails. They were in the right place at the right time, both for them, and now some 80 years later, for us, as we use the park in the present day.

On an April birding trip to Illinois and Kentucky, Spouse and I came to realize that the CCC had a far wider impact than we had ever appreciated. We encountered two state parks, one in Illinois and one in Kentucky, where the impressive results of the CCC's work added much to our travels. But first, a bit of history.

The stock market had crashed in October 1929, and by 1933 millions of people were unemployed, tens of thousands of farms were foreclosed, and people were starving. Our nation was in a state of extreme distress, nowhere worse than here in the Southeast. Abject poverty and hopelessness stalked the land. In April 1933, President Roosevelt signed the CCC into being. Called a "miracle of cooperation," it succeeded because of a remarkable degree of coordination among four federal departments: War, Interior, Agriculture, and Labor. It ultimately involved more than 3 million young men, aged 18 to 25, with about 500,000 serving at any one time.

These enrollees, as they were called, were organized into more than 2,500 camps of around 200 men each, spread across the country in 48 states and territories. Their camps were supervised by army officers and their work organized by an array of surveyors, engineers, and landscape architects. The men were paid $30 a month—the "Dollar-a-Day Army," as they were called. They got $5 a month to spend, and the remaining $25 each month went directly home to their families. With the average income of a western North Carolina farm family running at $86 per *year*, the CCC money their young man earned meant food on the table, shoes for the younger siblings, and an easing of the misery at home.

Many of the enrollees learned skills such as heavy machinery, carpentry, stonemasonry, surveying, and landscaping. One hundred thousand were illiterate when they signed up; they were taught to read and write. Those 3 million men were indeed in the right place at the right time.

The purpose of our spring road trip, in addition to general enjoyment, was to see how many species of birds we could find in Illinois and Kentucky. We've found through the years that the best places to start exploring a new state for birds are its state parks. They are generally great natural areas, with woods, fields, and a lake or stream, and lots of local birds. And so, in southern Illinois, we came upon a place called Giant City State Park. While birding in the park amid its woods and geological wonders, we were given a valuable tip by a friendly local lady school bus driver, waiting with her big bus for a load of high school science students to return from a hike. "Be sure to eat at the lodge," she advised.

Being that it was around noon and we were far from anyplace else, we took her advice and sought out the lodge. It was a cavernous, stately place, two stories of stone and logs, with a massive fireplace sporting an elk head with huge antlers and a full-sized stuffed bison standing in the lobby. And wouldn't you know, it was "all the award-winning fried chicken you can eat" day. With all the trimmings! Mercy. But about the lodge: It had been built by their local CCC camp in 1935 and 1936. Still solid and beautiful, it provided regular daily service. It was one of those places that you just want to stand and stare at. I purchased an excellent book at their gift shop by Ren and Helen Davis entitled *Our Mark on this Land*, a detailed history of the whole CCC program.

The high point of our trip was a 2-day visit to the John James Audubon State Park in Henderson, Kentucky. Audubon lived and worked in Henderson for a while, less than a mile from the banks of the Ohio River. The park has woods, trails, wildflowers, and, of course, lots of birds. The centerpiece of the park is a mansionlike building, complete with a medieval-style, three-story tower, and built by the CCC and finished in 1940.

That stately stone structure is now a museum, and it houses the largest collection of Audubon material found anywhere. It has a diorama of

Audubon in his study, working on a painting and surrounded by all sorts of collected critters. There are lots of various nonbird pieces of artwork, as well as photos, maps, and letters. But most especially, there are all four volumes of the original huge, elephant-folio-sized *Birds of America*, each one displayed in a large museum case. Each volume has one page carefully turned by a white-gloved attendant each day. Some of the few remaining original copper engraving plates from which the monumental prints were made are on display as well. Even a nonbirder might be impressed with the estimated value of the big books—around $12 million each. As if they would ever sell them. . . . It is a remarkable small museum, all the more interesting because of the origin of the structure itself and its history.

For us here in East Tennessee? The Davis' CCC book categorizes the Great Smokies as a "destination park," and its photographs include one of the beautiful stone, four-arch Elkmont bridge while it was under construction, as well as one of the then newly-completed Mount Cammerer fire tower. We don't have to go far to see some of the best examples of CCC work anywhere.

The CCC came to an abrupt end in 1942, with the start of World War II. Most of the young men entered military service. But in its 9 years, the CCC worked across the nation in 71 national parks, 405 state parks, and hundreds of other developing areas. They reclaimed lost land and planted 3 billion trees. They built hundreds of miles of roads, hundreds of bridges and buildings, and hundreds of miles of trails. No wonder we keep running into signs commemorating the CCC in so many places! Sturdy reminders of tough times being overcome by hard work. They were certainly there at the right time, in a lot of great places, for those young men, and for us still today.

TROUT LILIES SPRING UP

This news just in: trout lilies found blooming in woods near Portsmouth, New Hampshire, on April 25th! Not much of a news item for us, but for our friends 1,000 miles north of here who thought winter would never end, they were an awesome sight. In one recent year, our trout lilies were late due to the Easter Week snows and generally chilly weather. Nevertheless, we found them in full bloom along the Norris River Bluff Trail on March 29th, a full month earlier than the ones in New Hampshire.

We were on an early spring birding trip through Pennsylvania and New York, and we had hardly seen any flowers. When we came upon the trout lilies in New Hampshire, we were reminded of how fortunate we are to live in the Southeast. We can enjoy the early flowers near home, then follow spring up the slopes of the hills and mountains and find them still blooming in the high places like Mount LeConte, Clingman's Dome, and the Cherohala Skyway into May and even June, around the same time residents of New Hampshire and Vermont are enjoying theirs.

Do you have a favorite spring wildflower? Mine is usually the one I'm looking at in any given moment. But overall I think the trout lilies are near the top of my list. They aren't generally the first ones to bloom, but when they do, a couple acres of thousands of little nodding golden bells do a great job of announcing that spring is finally here. It was a sprinkly 45 degree day when we found them in big patches along the Norris River Bluff Trail with most of their usual early spring friends, many looking as if they had come up only the day before.

The bloodroots, often among the first flowers to bloom, were there, many of them blooming out even before their leaves had unrolled. The hepaticas were in full bloom up on the rocky cliff faces, and the little white-and-pink-striped spring beauties were coming out along the path. About the only usual early flowers not yet in bloom were the trilliums—the yellow sessile ones and the purple wake robins. They were up, but with only leaves and buds thus far, blossoms coming soon.

There were blue wild phlox and white twinleaf. The deep yellow of celandine poppies was just beginning to show. We had wondered if we were too early for the Dutchmen's breeches, another dependable favorite along the trail. But then there they were, hundreds of them, toward the end of the lower part of the trail. First one, then several, then oh my goodness! The whole forest floor was covered with them, little stalks of white and yellow upside-down pantaloons, like tiny clotheslines full of freshly washed laundry. It's always fun to suddenly come upon a thousand of something that you've been searching carefully for, hoping to find maybe just one.

Ah, but the trout lilies! There they were, covering the lower slopes, on up to the foot of the bluffs, uncounted numbers of yellow bells and speckled leaves. A trout lily by any of its other names—fawn lily, adder's-tongue, dog-toothed violet—is still a trout lily, one of nature's loveliest ways of announcing spring. Named "trout lily" because its speckled leaves reminded folks of the speckled sides of the brown trout, it so happens that their emergence usually coincides with the beginning of trout season. And sure enough, standing just a few yards away in the cold waters of the Clinch River, there they were—the ever-hopeful trout fishermen.

Like most of its lily cousins, trout lilies come up each year from bulbs (properly called corms). Beginning as a seed dropped from a dried seed pod, little runners go out and sprout into new lily plants. Each seed can develop as many as ten runners and corms over the course of several years. This is what leads to the extensive carpetlike colonies of trout lilies that cover the bare, leafless early spring forest floor. The yellow bell-shaped flowers open up more and more each day but tend to close up at night, or even on cloudy days. I can tell you from personal experience that this tendency of the trout lily is very frustrating at times for the wildflower photographer!

Unfortunately, most of the wildflowers that grow from bulbs—trout lilies included—fall prey to a number of predators that find the bulbs delicious. Though the bulbs are usually tiny, a sufficient number of them add up to a tasty night's meal. The most destructive are wild hogs; they can root up half an acre of bulbs in an evening and destroy whole colonies of lilies in a few hours.

As is often the case with wild plants, people have found reasons to value trout lilies in addition than their beauty. From ancient times, Roman soldiers used a poultice of trout lilies to ease the miseries of foot blisters and corns. (With as much walking as they did, I would imagine they were experts in such matters.) Native Americans used tea made from the lily leaves to treat stomach cramps and other disorders. And studies have proven that water extracts of lily leaves do indeed have antibacterial properties.

East Tennessee is a great place for wildflowers, and we have lots of places to see them. Already mentioned is the annual Spring Wildflower Pilgrimage held in Gatlinburg and the adjacent Smokies. There are numerous other springtime wildflower-centered activities and events all around the region to be discovered and enjoyed; find one handy to your location.

All the delicate early flowers are called "spring ephemerals." My favorite definition for "ephemeral" is "here and gone in a day." They really don't last very long. All traces of many of them are gone by the time the trees standing above them have fully leafed out. But don't give up on them; you can still seek them out in the higher elevations of the Smoky Mountains, at the same time our neighbors in New Hampshire are finding theirs. At low elevations or high, now is one of the best times of the year to go out and see the springtime wonders unfold. They won't last long. Try to take the time to see some of it; you will be enriched.

WOOD WARBLERS—WOW!

Every birdwatcher has his or her favorite birds. Mine happen to be wood warblers. They're the birds that really enticed me into the world of birding, and they have had that effect on a lot of other people, too. These little birds are found only in the New World: North and South America, Central America, and associated islands. There are 115 species of wood warblers, and some 57 of those species nest in North America north of the United States–Mexican border.

Generally, there are more species of birds out west than here in the eastern part of the country. Take woodpeckers, for example, where the West outnumbers the East 16 to 8. Or hummingbirds, where they beat us by 17 to 1! But, happily, with the warblers, the reverse is true. The majority of species of wood warblers is concentrated in the eastern United States and Canada, highest along the Appalachian Mountains, the Maritime Provinces, and eastern Canada.

What are they? Roger Tory Peterson, in his remarkable way of succinctly describing things the way they are, called the wood warblers "the butterflies of the bird world." They are small, active, insect-eating, mostly brightly colored birds with a wide variety of plumage patterns and songs. They arrive every spring, migrating from winter in northern South America, Central America, Mexico, and the Caribbean by the millions. They land along the Gulf Coast and make their way north day by day, 10–30 miles or so a day. They eat and sing their way along until they reach their ancestral nesting grounds, wherever those may be. They end up everywhere from the swamps of southern Georgia to the Great North Woods and tundra of Canada.

The wood warblers come in a variety of patterns and colors, but they are all small, about the size of small sparrows. They all have thin pointy beaks, and all are in constant motion, searching the ground, the bushes, and the trees for insects and caterpillars.

Colors? You name it. Just look at any one of the many birding field guides and scan the wood warbler pages. One of the earliest to appear is the black-and-white warbler. He sings a high squeaky song like a wheel needing oil and is dressed out in sharp black and white stripes. The blackpoll is another spiffy warbler in black and white.

Lots of warblers have yellow somewhere on their bodies. The numerous yellow-rumped warblers have some pale yellow on their sides and a bright butter-yellow rump, which helps to identify them on the spot. Prothonotary warblers, which like to live near water—you can find them at Cove Lake State Park—have a blue-green back and a deep yellow breast that has earned them the alternate name of "golden swamp warbler." And the widespread yellow warbler is a bright yellow all over, with some red speckles on the male's breast.

Some warblers do spectacular things with yellow and black. The prairie warbler has a yellow breast with black streaks on its sides. The magnolia warbler has a different back and head, but a yellow breast with even bolder black streaking. And the Canada warbler, which can be found along the higher trails of the Smokies, has a striking black "necklace" over its bright yellow chest area. Redstarts have orange spots on a background of black, and the Blackburnian warbler displays a fiery, brilliant orange throat that, when seen in the spring sunshine against a background of blue sky, is unbelievably beautiful.

As you may have surmised by now, we're talking about a bunch of really colorful little birds, but out there in the field the warblers are notoriously hard to see because of their small size and active nature. They are not at all interested in posing on a nice open branch; they are busy looking for edibles. The challenge to adequately see them adds to their fascination. One sure way of increasing your enjoyment of the warblers, and significantly increasing your chances of finding them, is to learn their songs.

The warblers are, more often than not, heard before they are seen. Each species has a fairly basic song, and some are very distinctive and easy to learn. Get those first, and then work on the harder ones. If you know a certain bird is near you by hearing its song, your chances of finding it are significantly better.

The best way to get started is to bird with someone who knows bird song. A number of good CDs and cell phone apps are available that feature bird songs, pictures, and helpful explanations that help you know what to listen for.

As with most birds, it is best to look for warblers when they are most active, from daylight till late morning. The best areas to look have a lot of woods. In Knoxville, the road along the top of Sharp's Ridge Memorial Park looking down on north Knoxville provides excellent viewing. The Great Smoky Mountains National Park also comes to mind. Thirty-six species of warblers have been seen in the Smokies park; twenty-two of them nest up there, which means they will be there all spring and summer to find and marvel at!

For other great warbler-viewing areas, try the Cherohala Skyway, which runs from Tellico Plains, Tennessee, to Robbinsville, North Carolina, reaching elevations over 5,000 feet; it's like the Smokies with no traffic! Then there's Cross Mountain, up in Campbell County above Caryville, which is home to the scarce cerulean warbler and many others. And excellent warbler viewing can be had at Frozen Head State Park near Wartburg in Morgan County. (That park is great for wildflowers, too.)

With some patience and experience, you can see 20 or more species of those "butterflies of the bird world" every spring. So go out and give them a try. You will be amazed at the array of warblers. But do so carefully; wood warblers can be very habit forming!

LOOPERS FOR LUNCH

We had an uninvited guest at dinner just the other night. Well, just uninvited to me but definitely unwelcome to Spouse. Upon aiming for my first bite of salad, I spied something walking down the right sleeve of my shirt. Not walking, exactly, either, but getting along by a mode of travel the caterpillar people call "looping": front feet out and down, bring the back ones up, repeat.

Yep, a nice, vigorous inchworm was heading down my sleeve, trying to get to the salad bowl ahead of me. They must be fond of salad. Spouse and I recalled with a chuckle an episode wherein I found an inchworm in my salad at a now-long-gone Italian restaurant in Knoxville. I just sat him over on a nearby potted fig tree and continued to eat my salad, so as not to cause a fuss.

Anyhow, caterpillars make butterflies, so after dinner I got out my trusty *Field Guide to the Caterpillars of Eastern North America*, an excellent guide by David L. Wagner that is full of illustrations that you just don't find in other butterfly books. I was hoping to find out what sort of butterflies inchworms morphed into after their worm stage.

As is the usual case with things I decide to check into, what I knew paled into insignificance compared with the expertise the field guide had to offer. Firstly, there wasn't just one inchworm; there were photos of 84 different *species* of them, with a reference to a US Forest Service bulletin showing 187 species of them. And then, to add to my feelings of inadequate savvy, the book said that inchworms don't even turn into butterflies. . . . They all become moths!

Now, all the butterflies and moths are in the order of insects called *Lepidoptera*. There are approximately 11,230 species of lepidopterans in North America. By far, the most familiar lepidopterans are the spectacular, colorful butterflies. But there are only 760 species of butterflies, and the remaining 10,470 species are moths.

All those inchworms? They turn into part of that horde of more than 10,000 species of North American moths as adults. So do a bunch of other familiar "worms": the troublesome tobacco hornworm, the dreaded tomato hornworm, and all those tent caterpillars munching on your cherry trees right now.

If moths outnumber butterflies by nearly 14 to 1, how come we see so few of them? One main reason is that moths are mostly nocturnal, going about their lives on the 11 p.m.–7 a.m. shift, so that even the big spectacular ones are rarely seen. And then, over half the moths are in a group called the microlepidopterans; they are very small and inconspicuous, with lifestyles that keep them hidden and out of sight—think clothes moths, eating your favorite wool sweater. But back to the inchworms.

As a group, they are masters of camouflage and disguise. Their colors are mottled or striped browns and grays, and they sport various bumps and knobs to make them look remarkably like sticks and twigs. One, the camouflaged looper, actually attaches little bits of leaves or blossoms to its body as a disguise; they should be the envy of any turkey hunter, trying his best to look like a tree.

At spring migration time, this quote from the field guide really catches my eye: "In terms of abundance and biomass, loopers are among the most important forest lepidopterans in eastern North America. They are an especially important component of the spring caterpillar fauna of deciduous forests, where they are the staple in the diets of many forest-nesting birds."

Well, there you have it! Inchworms are warbler food and a staple in their diet, no less. All those little worms that are riddling the new tree leaves with holes, and dangling in front of your eyes on threads attached to some twig higher above, plus all those scores of species of inchworms, are timed to hatch out just as the fresh green leaves appear. This, in turn, at least in an average year, happens to be just when all those hungry migratory birds are arriving here to nest for the season or to fuel up and continue on to nesting places farther north.

Biologists tell us that if migratory birds didn't show up for some reason, many or most of the trees would actually be defoliated by the millions of worms per acre munching away at them. It is interesting to see how the migration process unfolds every year, with the leaves and worms sometimes coming out 2 or 3 weeks ahead of the main waves of migrant birds, and sometimes the birds mostly ahead of the worms.

Tradition has it that finding an inchworm walking along on your shirt means you're being measured and are about to get a new shirt. If that's not reason enough to be nice to inchworms, remember that they're also a certified high-quality spring warbler food!

REDBUD TREES, BUGS, AND BEES

We've been having a redbud season that must rank up there among the best. The past couple of weeks had given us abundant sunshine, steady warmish temperatures, and frequent rain showers, and our wonderfully native and widespread redbud trees have responded with a huge flower show.

Walking around the grounds enjoying all those exuberant blossom-filled trees with their pea-type flowers—they are in the legume family; take notice of those peapod fruits later in the year—I stopped at one big redbud in particular. There amongst the blossoms was a little yellow-rumped warbler, not 10 feet away, briskly checking out every twig nook and bark cranny for whatever tiny insects it could ambush. And it was indeed finding a steady supply of minute, mobile bits of protein, so small that I couldn't even see what it was catching. Just what a hyperactive, carnivorous little bird needs to build up for spring— courting, nest-building, brood-raising activities!

But as I watched the bird feeding on all those "invisible" critters, something else struck me about that tree full of blossoms: It was alive with bigger things, too—a cloud of flitting, buzzing, flying things, all working over the tree's flowers and, luckily for them, apparently not on the bird's menu. Bugs! Entomologists divide the enormous world of insects up into various orders and families, and in the precise way that they do it, bugs or as they like to say "the true bugs," are one specific group of insects, with leathery wing covers and piercing and sucking mouth parts (yuck!). They include the likes of bedbugs, stink bugs, squash bugs, and those flashy orange-and-black milkweed bugs.

But to us mere mortals, "bugs" is a wonderfully useful word for any small crawly thing we might encounter and, probably, look upon with suspicion, distrust, or fear. These might include bees, beetles, spiders, ticks and mosquitoes, even crawfish (also called mudbugs), and viruses (the flu "bug").

And as my redbud tree demonstrated, springtime brings bugs out in droves. I'm sure you've heard someone say, "What we need is a good cold winter to get rid of all those bugs." That won't happen, friends, unless we have another Ice Age. This past December, I watched a hatch of swarming little mosquito-sized gnats outside our front window on a nice mild day being nipped out of the air by our busy little year-round flycatcher, a hungry phoebe. Those gnats, and most other bugs, are pretty much undeterred by a stretch of even severely cold East Tennessee weather.

But back to the redbud tree! All that buzzing and flitting got me looking around to see what else was going on in my redbud tree. And sure enough, there was a lot more—not just in the air, but on the ground and under it. I noticed scattered here and there a bunch of newly constructed ant colonies. Not just a hill, but a spread-out operation with piles of excavated earth over maybe a couple of feet of real estate. And there they were— dozens of quarter-inch black ants going about in businesslike fashion, some carrying loads of stuff three times their size.

A March/April issue of *The Tennessee Conservationist* contains an article by Lizzie Wright entitled "The Ants of Tennessee." She relates that, of the 13,000 species of ants on Earth, some 127 species live in Tennessee. And that doesn't include those dreaded invaders from South America, the fire ants, spreading ever northward and now making a home in Tennessee . . . a wider variety of ants than you could ever imagine! Except for occasional visits to our kitchens or picnics, we almost never notice all those millions of ants there beneath our feet. The northern flickers surely do, though. The part of the woodpecker family most likely to be seen on the ground, flickers like nothing better than to sit beside an ant colony and pick them off one by one.

But what about all those things humming and buzzing in the air? As far as big hard-working families go, bees are the flying counterparts to our subterranean friends the ants. And like the ants, there are a lot more of them than you might think. Of course, there are our familiar honey bees. Interestingly enough, honey bees aren't native to North America; they are immigrants to North America, like most of our ancestors. In fact, many of our ancestors brought colonies of honey bees with them from their homelands in Europe.

It turns out, though, that there were a lot of other bees already here in North America when those newcomers arrived—a lot more. These would be our perhaps less-famous, but decidedly very important, native bees. There are 20,000 species of bees in the world, and 4,000 are native to the United States. They range in size from a one-twelfth-inch-long speck to a more-than-one-inch-long behemoth. Over 90% of the species are solitary; their families consist of one mama bee and her few offspring. The rest live in the various-sized, multiple-bee colonies that we're more familiar with.

And what good are those bees? Well, they pollinate over 75% of all our food crops. Without bees, we'd have no fruits, berries, vegetables, nuts, chocolate, or coffee. And our honey bees have been declining at an alarming rate due to disease, insecticides, and herbicides. In a major apple-growing area of China, people on ladders hand-pollinate each apple blossom, one by tedious one, to produce apples. They've sprayed all their local bees into extinction! In our country, native bees are shouldering more of the load on crop pollination. Farmers are learning more about how important the native bees are becoming to crop production (and actually, always have been) and are taking measures to protect and encourage them. Studies are showing that it's working.

Then how about all those bugs as major bird food? Of course, the birds eat tons of caterpillars and grasshoppers. As previously noted, we wouldn't have many leaves left on anything if it weren't for the birds. But in the air? Those swifts, swallows, nighthawks, kingbirds, and phoebes aren't swooping around up there just for the exercise. Some curious scientists have rigged up a variety of airborne devices fitted with bug traps and have come up with the astonishing figure that 1 square mile of air, just over our heads, can contain as many as 32 million flying insects! Good for the birds, and very good for us earthlings here below, that the birds are up there consuming zillions of bugs daily.

There are a lot of other bugs we haven't mentioned, many that make our world look, feel, and sound more like home to us. There are bugs that eat the bugs that would be eating our stuff. Some bugs, for example, make a profession of eating aphids. And others spend their waking hours eating mosquitoes. Butterflies, dragonflies, crickets, and katydids. . . . They'll all be here come summer, adding a splash of color and some lovely evening music. All part of that big web of Life unfolding out there in April. It's really worth a closer look!

CACOPHONY ON THE RIDGE

Spouse and I get top-notch periodicals from each of our favorite nature- and conservation-related organizations, and I look forward every month to looking through them for the newest developments and the latest findings. One article that really caught my eye recently offered an explanation for what to me has become a worrisome situation here in East Tennessee. Part of the National Wildlife Federation's publication, the article's clever title was "Coping with Chronic Clamor."

Now, we've all heard about light pollution, the brightening of our night skies by all the lights of urban sprawl. Those of us near town can hardly see the stars any more; the Milky Way, almost never. But, noise pollution? It's a pretty unrecognized problem, but we are actually afflicted more by noise pollution than by light pollution because noise is with us 24 hours a day.

We've become accustomed to the background hum of traffic, machinery, air-conditioning and heating units, and entertainment devices. Known for a long time now to have negative effects on birds and other wildlife, it certainly affects us humans, too. We were originally designed to function in a quiet world of natural sounds, aware of what is happening around us. Sadly, we are losing those skills as we become immersed in constant noise.

The article on chronic clamor related a series of studies on the effects of modern-day noise pollution on the lives of our birds. The first one examined saw-whet owls, little bitty guys that make their living catching mice in the dark by ear. The researchers found that natural gas compression stations near where they lived in Idaho could make so much noise that the owls couldn't hear their surroundings well enough to catch mice. I can picture the maintenance guys out there scratching their heads, wondering why they're having all those mice messing up their equipment!

Another study, from San Francisco, examined the various songs white-crowned sparrows had historically sung and found that their songs had all devolved into one, single, loud note, to enable the birds to hear each other over the noise of the traffic. In other words, the sparrows are evolving a way of surviving by degrading their eons-long communication systems into a single homogeneous noise. One wonders where that could lead in the coming centuries.

But the study that really caught my attention, because it had direct applications to us here in Knoxville, was about the effects of traffic noise along a usually remote, quiet wooded ridge in southern Idaho. Normally, migrating birds stop on the ridge to rest and fuel up on energy-rich caterpillars, to allow them to continue flying on. The scientists had rigged up a "phantom road" by placing several sets of loudspeakers along the ridge that played traffic noise that mimicked the usual sounds of traffic in a national park. They found that the noise caused a full third of the migrating birds, unable to safely communicate with one another, to avoid pausing there in their travel, presumably moving on to a quieter place elsewhere.

And how does all this apply to us here in Knoxville . . . especially the birders? Well, we have a nice wooded ridge—Sharp's Ridge—that has served as a premier spring migrant refueling stop over the years. *Bird Finding in Tennessee*, a book published by Nashvillian Michael Lee Bierly nearly 40 years ago, introduces Tennessee birding site #85 this way: "Where in 1.3 miles can you see 28 species of warblers and 80 species of birds in a morning's walk in May?"

The answer, as every local birder would know, is Sharp's Ridge, known more properly now as Sharp's Ridge Memorial Park. The ridge has always been a destination for birders, beginners to advanced. The Knoxville Bird Club has four weekly spring bird walks there, the last part of April and first part of May. My 1992 edition of *Birds of Sharp's Ridge*, put out by City of Knoxville Department of Parks and Recreation with the guidance of the Knoxville Bird Club, lists 153 species of birds that had been sighted there as of that time. That included an astounding 36 species of warblers, essentially all the warblers found in eastern North America.

But as the years have gone by, the older birding veterans have seen those wonderful, warbler-filled April mornings become increasingly few and far between. We already know that our songbirds have decreased in number by 50, 70, and 90% in some cases, over the past 60 years or so. These sad numbers are mainly attributed to loss of wintering grounds due to deforestation and loss of food sources and nesting habitat from insecticides, herbicides, development and urban sprawl.

These facts certainly account for most of Sharp's Ridge's fading glory, but the article about the quiet ridge in Idaho made me wonder if the absence of the birds up there on the ridge might not also be related to noise. After all, Sharp's Ridge has experienced an exponential increase in noise since the 1960s, from Interstate 275 on the west, Interstate 640 on the north, and Broadway on the east. And then on the south, we have the cacophony of Knoxville: trucks and cars, machines, trains, sirens, and horns. Then there are the housing developments, condos, and businesses, all marching along the sides and up the slopes, working their way toward all the communication installations strung out along the top of the ridge. It's truly noisy up there.

Of course, *all* of our quiet places are under pressure from things that make noise. A perfect example is the Great Smoky Mountains National Park. You would think it's a place of peaceful, natural quiet. But until the Park Service put a stop to it, there were entrepreneurs up there flying helicopters into the park to dump happy tourists off for a mountaintop picnic experience. The noise of a helicopter is very disruptive at best, and very unwelcome overhead to someone who believes that his or her 12-mile hike into the wilderness has earned them a special level of peace and quiet. This is said of course with due deference to those brave helicopter pilots whose rescue missions into the Smokies are legendary. But just the present-day clamor of normal daily life overrides a great many of the natural sounds we once enjoyed, and which the youngsters growing up now may never have heard. *Somewhere* in East Tennessee there must be a remote, quiet, wooded ridge where, every spring, waves of wood warblers appear, along with scarlet tanagers, Baltimore orioles, and rose-breasted grosbeaks, resting, feeding, and singing. Quiet? It would be hard to find such a spot in these parts. I hope you'll let me know if you do.

REALLY BLUE

With the middle of April upon us, the spring migrants are beginning to show up, one species at a time. My blue-gray gnatcatchers have been busy all week, working over all the yard trees for insects. They'll be nesting soon. And as I was winding down my yardwork one Saturday evening, I heard, and then saw, my first two chimney swifts of the year. They zoomed over the yard several times, as if to be sure the place hadn't changed too much while they'd been spending the winter in Peru. And on the day before that, a black-and-white warbler appeared in the yard around seven o'clock in the evening.

Lots more spring arrivals will show up over the next 2 or 3 weeks. One of our smaller-sized, but more conspicuous and colorful visitors is the indigo bunting. They go from a zero population in the winter to very numerous in the summer, joining right in there with the other two of our Big Three blue birds, the blue jays and the eastern bluebirds.

Indigo buntings bring a whole new level of blueness to the business of being blue! The males in summer are a rich deep blue that's so dark that they look black unless they're viewed in good sunlight. Then they light up with the great, bold color that gives them their name. Indigo buntings have a bright, loud, persistent song, sung in phrases that are suggested by "here, here, where, where, see it, see it," over and over through the day. One especially nice thing about them is that, in contrast to a lot of our more shy birds, indigo buntings love to sing from the tip of the highest tree around, as if to show the world what handsome birds they are. Nice for us birdwatchers, because if you hear one singing, you can usually just look around at the treetops till you spot the small dark source of all that song, grab your binoculars, and feast your eyes on all that beautiful blue.

Female indigo buntings are a drab brown and buff color, providing camouflage on the nest. They make a well-woven nest of grass and plant fibers and prefer a brushy site, located from near ground level to as high as 15 feet up in a tree. They lay from three to five eggs, and tend to raise two broods a summer.

Indigo buntings usually arrive in our area around the third week of April. They will nest, raise a family, and stay around Knoxville with us until October, when they finally head back south for the winter in Mexico or the Caribbean. Like all the bunting family, they are seed and berry eaters, though they will munch a tasty bug if one is handy.

An interesting bunting family note: A very close first cousin to our indigo bunting, the painted bunting, is a really spectacular little bird. They don't live in East Tennessee, though we had one as an aberrant winter visitor once out in Maryville. They live mostly along the warmer coastal plain areas of the Southeast and on out into Texas, are not nearly so numerous as their cousins the indigos, and are declining in numbers. One could not imagine a better-decorated bird. The same size and shape as the indigos, the painted buntings are bright red on their underside and rump, bright blue on the head, and green on their back. Native American legend has it that when the Great Spirit came to paint the birds their colors, he was nearly out of paint when he reached the painted bunting, so he just used dabs of the different colors he had left. A truly striking little bird, especially for North America!

If you'll be traveling somewhere they might be, painted buntings are certainly worth the time it takes to look for them. We once saw a group of four of them at the same time on a feeder in a county park near Homestead, Florida. . . . WOW! Grab the camera!

But for the stay-at-home types among us, we can be well satisfied by getting an eyeful of our resident super-blue birds all spring and summer, and enjoying their lively song.

HIS NAME IS MUDD

Sometimes a birding experience can be combined with another experience—music, museums, sports, history. Imagine a nineteenth-century fort, complete with moat and drawbridge, with dark, damp prison cells, stories of conspiracies and murder, pestilence, and disease. Picture nesting colonies of thousands, even tens of thousands, of tropical birds found nowhere else in the United States, and hundreds of northbound migrant birds, coming and going in a steady stream, stopping in for a brief rest before heading on.

Put it all together on a couple of tiny dots of islands in the Gulf of Mexico, surrounded by 100 square miles of protected reefs and ocean, 68 miles due west of Key West, Florida, and you have the Dry Tortugas National Park. Spouse and I visited the Dry Tortugas on a birding trip, but the heavy mists of history were hanging over our destination as surely as the excitement of seeing thousands of new-to-be-seen seabirds.

Our South Florida/Keys birding trip had taken us through the congested, sprawling mess of Miami, where we saw tropical rarities such as red-crowned parrots, red-whiskered bulbuls, and spot-breasted orioles. We escaped to the lonely pinelands of central Florida, where the scarce red-cockaded woodpeckers can be seen only when they emerge from their tree holes at dawn and the endangered Florida scrub jays eat peanuts out of your hand.

In the Keys, the Overseas Highway runs along the chain of islands from just below Miami and west for 150 miles until it ends at Key West. From there, it takes either a boat or a floatplane to cover the 68 miles of open ocean to remote Fort Jefferson and the Dry Tortugas, sitting alone out in the Gulf of Mexico. We got to do it in a boat, a speedy big catamaran, up in the bow, sort of like old Shep on a road trip with his head hanging out the window, ears flapping in the wind. Our destination islands were discovered by explorer Ponce de León in 1513 and named for the turtles—las tortugas in Spanish—he found there. The little sandy dots on the nautical charts were soon labeled "Dry Tortugas" to let sailors know there was no fresh water to be had on the islands.

The Tortugas have long been known to be home to lots of birds. John James Audubon studied the colonies of seabirds there in 1832. The US military soon recognized the strategic value of the Dry Tortugas to guard the shipping lanes of the entire Gulf coast, and construction of Fort Jefferson was begun by the US Army Corps of Engineers in 1846. Work continued for nearly 30 years, utilized slave labor until the beginning of the Civil War, and involved the use of nearly 16 million bricks. The fort was one of the largest ever built in the Western Hemisphere and one of the last of the medieval-style forts, soon to be rendered obsolete by the new, powerful rifled cannons. For its time, Fort Jefferson had some of the most advanced weapons available, including 15-inch Rodman smoothbore cannons that could fire a 432-pound projectile a distance of 3 miles.

Although as many as 2,000 people occupied the fort at its height in the 1860s, it was never finished or fully armed. During the Civil War, it was also used as a prison, mostly for Union deserters, but also for a more infamous one, Dr. Samuel Mudd. The expression "Your name is Mudd!" had been used earlier, apparently first noted in a Vaudeville act, but it certainly applies to Dr. Mudd, if only by coincidence.

The story on Dr. Mudd goes like this: Actor John Wilkes Booth shot President Lincoln at Ford's Theatre in Washington, DC, on April 14, 1865. He then jumped from the presidential box onto the stage, where he himself had acted on occasion, breaking his leg in the process. He limped away to a waiting horse and escaped across the Potomac River into Maryland. There, on April 15th, he had his leg splinted and spent the night at Dr. Mudd's home. He was cornered in a barn in northern Virginia on April 26th and fatally wounded by a Union cavalryman. Investigation and prompt trial by a military tribunal ensued, and eight conspirators were convicted. Four, including a woman, were hanged. (Mary Surratt was the first woman executed by the US government.) Dr. Mudd escaped that fate by only one vote of the tribunal trying the case. He and three others were sent to Fort Jefferson in the Dry Tortugas.

Three of them, including Mudd, were sentenced to a life of hard labor. They arrived in July 1865 and settled in to await whatever would become of them. Then, in 1867, an epidemic of yellow fever broke out at the fort, eventually afflicting most of its inhabitants. It quickly killed the prison doctor and his child. Dr. Mudd and another physician from Key West rose to the occasion, doctoring many back to health and saving many lives. The grateful troops petitioned Tennessean President Andrew Johnson on Dr. Mudd's behalf, and he was eventually pardoned in 1869.

He returned to his farm in Maryland, had five more children, and spent the rest of his life farming, doctoring, and denying that he had anything to do with a conspiracy. Word went around that Dr. Mudd was really just an innocent victim of circumstances and didn't know John Wilkes Booth, so much so that Presidents Jimmy Carter and Ronald Reagan both wrote to Mudd's descendants, expressing their belief in his innocence.

However, recent historical research has revealed that Dr. Mudd had made John Wilkes Booth's acquaintance 5 months before the Lincoln assassination and talked with him on more than one occasion. Booth spent a couple of nights at Dr. Mudd's Maryland home, and Mudd arranged for Booth to buy a horse from Mudd's next-door neighbor. At trial, Dr. Mudd's main defense was that when Booth showed up at his door, had his leg set, and stayed the night, he was disguised, and therefore Mudd never recognized Booth. Although Booth was a noted actor, one has to wonder if he was really *that* good. The debate continues on to this day.

So, curious history buffs and nature lovers come together for the 2.5-hour boat ride to Fort Jefferson. The low-lying structure rises up out of the ocean ahead of you, and the boat docks at the pier. The boat is your only source for food, water, and bathroom facilities. There is a small, 10-site campground on the island but absolutely no food, water, or phone service. You bring everything you can anticipate needing, and come and go by arrangement with the boat company.

Once there, you can go on a 45-minute history tour. Sure enough, Spouse and I saw Dr. Mudd's cell, a dark stone chamber with two little windows looking out on the bright Gulf sky and water. And wow. . . . There are the birds! There are huge colonies of two species of terns—brown noddies (4,500 of them) and sooty terns (80,000 of them). There are masked boobies, brown boobies, and magnificent frigatebirds. All five of these species have their only significant nesting areas in the United States right there in the Dry Tortugas, and eager birders from all across North America go there to add those more tropical, ocean-going birds to their lists. Bird watching heaven! And there's a steady parade of spring migrants, dropping in to rest and refresh from their nonstop flights across the Gulf of Mexico: cuckoos, thrushes, warblers, short-eared owls, and scarlet tanagers.

On the Dry Tortugas tour, you get to stay about 4 hours, and then it's back aboard your catamaran. You glide back eastward toward Key West, the sun at your back, the sea breeze in your face, sipping a refreshing beverage, and napping in the tropical air. Certainly not a bad way to have a history lesson.

WHAT'S FLYING AROUND AT YOUR PLACE?

Spring azure, mourning cloak, Eastern comma, clouded sulphur. There are some really neat things out there announcing the arrival of spring besides flowers and birds. Butterflies, for example. The above-named four critters are some of the earliest butterflies seen in East Tennessee. In fact, some of them fly so early in the year that they show up while it is still winter!

We often think of butterflies as the big flashy swallowtails and monarchs of summer fields and meadows, rather than one of our first hopeful signs of spring. But here they are, often flying before even the first wildflower peeks out from under the leaves, and long before the first migrant bird finds its way back to East Tennessee.

I've seen all four butterflies—spring azure, mourning cloak, Eastern comma, and clouded sulphur—flitting around my yard at various times over 3 or 4 weeks in early spring. It is always a pleasant surprise to be grumping my way to the mailbox bundled up in my old warm coat and see a bright blue or yellow butterfly flapping merrily along as if to say "What's your problem, buddy?"

Butterflies are fun, and a lot of birders gradually learn to be butterfly enthusiasts, too. Butterflies are a nice addition to any birding outing. For one thing, they are often out and about in the middle of the day, when birding gets slow, and you're out there with your binoculars in your hand anyway! Binoculars are a real help, bringing the butterflies up close while you remain far enough away to avoid spooking them (at least sometimes). There are about the same number of North American butterfly species as there are species of birds, and butterflies can prove to be even more of a challenge to see well and to learn.

The little spring azures, a little over a half-inch long, may be one of our earliest signs of spring. Widespread and common across the United States, they begin to fly as early as February in Knoxville. They are a nice pale blue above and light blue-gray with little spots below. Their close relative the Eastern tailed blue, another little early blue butterfly, is similar to the azure but has little tails and orange spots on its hindwings.

The mourning cloaks are beautiful and interesting. They are easy to recognize—larger and slower, sporting a rich brown color with a clear yellow border along their trailing edge. These guys are among the longest-lived of all our butterflies, living as long as 10 months; many species live only a few weeks. The mourning cloaks hatch out in the summer and become adults by fall. Unusual for butterflies, they hibernate over winter as adults and so are ready to fly again as soon as the temperatures approach the 60-degree mark, even if it is still winter.

Eastern commas are a little harder to spot: They are strong, fast fliers that often land on tree trunks. Above they are orange with a bunch of brown spots, but when alighted with their wings folded to show only their undersides, their brown-patterned, irregularly shaped wings look exactly like a dead leaf. You've probably mistaken one for a leaf on more than one occasion. The comma and its nearly identical first cousin, the question mark, get their names from a tiny silver comma (or question mark) on the underside of their back wings.

One of our most widespread groups of butterflies, the sulphurs, have lots of species in their family, but the most likely ones to see around these parts beginning in March are the clouded sulphur and the cloudless sulphur. They are both yellow medium-sized butterflies of field and meadow, differing slightly with regard to the amounts of color in their forewings. Their caterpillars like to eat clover and alfalfa, so as farming increases in a given area, so do the numbers of sulphurs. Male sulphurs are all yellow, but females of these two species can be either yellow or white. So, if you see a yellow butterfly out in your field flying around courting a white butterfly, be reassured: They know what they're doing, and everything's OK.

Watching butterflies is like watching birds or stalking wildflowers; it can be an addictive pastime. For pure visual enjoyment, there are the different species of swallowtails and fritillaries. For making friends, there are the confiding and easy-to-observe buckeyes and hackberries. And if you want challenge and intense study, there are species such as the dreaded skippers—dozens of species of skittish, fast-moving lookalikes that can send you to your field guide scratching your head.

There are numerous excellent guides to help you learn about the butterflies in your area. Two that I have found to be very useful, out of many, are the *Stokes Butterfly Book* by Donald and Lillian Stokes and Jim P. Brock and Kenn Kaufman's *Field Guide to the Butterflies of Eastern North America.* Spring is here! It's time to begin enjoying the flowers and the birds, but also check out the butterflies. Early spring is a good time to begin looking for them, when there aren't so many different ones out and about. Then, as the season unfolds, you will already be familiar with some of them and ready to proceed on to greater levels of butterfly knowledge. Photographing them, which requires considerable patience and persistence, takes the adventure up another notch and adds to the challenge. Don't let yourself be outsmarted by an insect!

BIRD'S NEST TIME

A gardening friend of mine showed me a new and active bird's nest last week. It was situated in a small flame azalea bush, no leaves on it yet, but the birds apparently had confidence that the leaves would be there in time to hide and shelter the soon-to-be-born baby birds. The nest was a thing of beauty, precisely constructed and containing four little blue eggs. It got me to thinking about bird's nests, both in general and on a personal level.

Lots of us have memories of bird's nests past, of watching eggs become baby birds, being fed constantly for days by attentive parents and quickly growing into feathered, then flying, creatures. We watched a transformation nearly as amazing as the drama of a caterpillar becoming a butterfly.

As I mulled all that over, a bird nest memory from almost 40 years ago came to mind. My dad was finishing a hospital stay from a serious spell of what would eventually prove to be a terminal illness. We took him to our house for a few weeks to help him get back on his feet, a trying and worrisome time for him, us, and the grandkids.

Robins to the rescue! Like a small miracle, a pair of robins decided to build a nest on the windowsill of his room, at eye level, seemingly in the room with Dad. They finished it up, laid four eggs, and proceeded to raise the babies, worm after worm. Grandpa and the grandkids kept close watch on the proceedings, until after about 2 weeks, amid much chirping and cheeping, and several anxious spectators, the fledglings did their first-day attempt at flying . . . and were gone. And by then it was time for Grandpa, much improved, to go back to his house, and the two nests back there were empty. Those two robins with their nest of youngsters turned a sad and

stressful situation into a time of excitement and fun, a long-remembered piece of family history.

But, let me tell you about that latest nest, the one in the azalea bush. It turned out to be a chipping sparrow nest. Chipping sparrows are one of our common local sparrows, and one of our smallest, with a light gray, unstreaked breast and a spiffy rufous-brown cap on their head. They make a neat little nest, about 4 inches around, of fine strands of dead grass and rootlets. They make the inner lining of the nest out of soft stuff, and their favorite material is hair, preferably horse hair or dog hair, sometimes plucked from its owner. The most interesting thing about the chipping sparrows' nest was that they had woven into it some thin strips of plastic material my friend had used to protect her garden plants from the frost—a neat piece of handiwork! The four eggs were robin's-egg blue, but only about half the size of a robin's egg. If things went well, they would hatch in 11–14 days, and fly away in another 14.

Note I said *if* things go well, and there is a great big "if" in the situation. It's the same "if" that all the birds face in raising their young each season. Many songbird species are known to produce a successful nest of young only 50% or less of the time—not a very good average. Just imagine some of the problems that face a pair of birds as they set out to raise a family: Their offspring begin as eggs, with breakable shells, that have to be kept intact, safe, and warm. Then the eggs become noisy, ravenously hungry, featherless little creatures—mostly mouths—that have to be corralled somehow so they can be fed constantly, every daylight hour, till they can fly away on their own.

Birds don't have hands, and they do all this activity, as one author has put it, as if their hands were tied behind their backs. But, through the millennia, birds have worked out the solution by building a nest. And nests, like birds, come in all shapes and sizes. The very simplest ones are called scrapes: just a flat place that they dust off and declare it to be a nest. Our best example around here is our inland shorebird, the killdeer. Loud and vocal, (their Latin name is, appropriately, *Charadrius vociferous*), we see them around playgrounds and ballparks. They make their nests on flat roofs, in gravel driveways, and in baseball and softball outfields, sometimes causing considerable, if only temporary, inconvenience to the sympathetic humans trying to avoid any harm to nest or young.

Then there are platform nests. Take mourning doves, for example. They toss a few sticks together in a tree in a couple of days and lay their eggs. Their nests are so flimsy that you can often see the eggs as you look up through the bottom of the nest. By contrast, bald eagles take their platform nests very seriously. Made from big sticks and branches, their nests are built to last. Used year after year and often for decades—and added to every year—the nests sometimes reach the size of several hundred pounds.

The ducklike grebes build nests that float among the reeds of their marshy homes. Kingfishers nest underground, digging a horizontal tunnel 6 feet or more into a streambank. Baltimore orioles weave amazing long hanging baskets, suspended from the fork of a branch. And think of the contrast between the massive pile of sticks in the eagle's nest and the tiny but highly effective, 1-inch jewel of cobwebs and lichens put together by a mama hummingbird!

An expert in such matters can tell at a glance which species of bird made any given nest. Each member of a given species makes their nest in pretty much the same way. Nobody teaches the birds how to make a nest. It's all in there, programmed in their tiny bird brains, along with how to migrate to our yards from South America every spring and home again in the fall, as well as what's good to eat and how to find it. It's a complicated, exacting, amazing process. It happens millions of times every spring. It's one of the true wonders of nature!

MR. BUSHYTAIL

Mr. Bushytail, tree squirrel, eastern gray squirrel. . . . He goes by a number of different names. People may love him and think he's terribly cute, or enjoy hunting him and even eating him, or curse him for eating their garden or robbing their birdfeeders. But whatever your point of view, our commonest squirrel in these parts, the Eastern gray squirrel, is familiar to just about everybody who's ever been out in the yard, park, or woods.

Squirrel stories abound. I've had a friend who fed her favorite neighborhood squirrel so many cashew nuts that the little beast became too fat to climb a tree. And another friend who grew tired of having his birdfeeders robbed clean every day and began trapping squirrels and hauling them off to an undisclosed location. He gave up at squirrel number 95. I've always been unsure whether it was the same squirrel returning day after day, or maybe he had tapped into a completely unlimited source of them. I suspect the latter.

There are a couple of other species of tree squirrels in the eastern United States. Widespread, but concentrated more in specific areas, are the larger, reddish-brown fox squirrels. They have habits and lifestyles similar to gray squirrels, but they tend to come down out of the trees more and do better in places with smaller, scattered woodlots and more widely spaced trees.

Then there's the "boomer," our smaller Great Smoky Mountain red squirrel. Also known as pine squirrel and spruce squirrel, they live at all elevations in the park, but they really prefer the higher spruce-fir forests. And they tend to be very loud and vocal, as those of you who spend time in the higher Smokies are well aware.

Back to our run-of-the-mill cute gray squirrels. Most of them actually are gray, but they can range in color from white to black. Often, the more unusually colored ones live in large colonies with individuals of similar colors in a fairly specific location. Everyone is familiar with the typical pose of a squirrel, sitting on its haunches, holding food in its front paws. Well, there's more to that pose than meets the eye. Squirrels examine their food carefully, by feel, sight, and smell. It is critical to their survival through the winter that they distinguish between foods that will keep well over the winter and not spoil versus foods that won't keep well and tend to spoil or are infested by weevils and the like.

With the mighty chestnut trees out of the picture, squirrels have to depend heavily on acorns as a staple in their diet, along with beech nuts, walnuts, hickory nuts, and pinecone seeds. Although squirrels slow down in the winter, they don't hibernate. When the weather is mild they are out and about and so must depend on the food they stored up in the summer and fall. It turns out that acorns begin to lose food value as soon as they sprout. The white oak family of trees has acorns that tend to sprout quickly in the fall. So, when the squirrels check them out, they usually eat white oak acorns rather than storing them. Red oak acorns, on the other hand, sprout the next spring. They also have more chemicals, called tannins, in them, which makes them store better. So, they get put away for later—usually. Squirrels are very picky about their food, though. If they find a red oak acorn infested with an acorn weevil or some other pest, they instinctively know it won't keep and they don't hide it away; they will usually just eat it, worm and all.

Speaking of hiding things away, gray squirrels are what biologists call "scatter hoarders." They hide their food supplies one at a time, in a lot of different places scattered over a wide area. The boomers, in contrast, are called "cache hoarders." They put all their winter food stores in one place in the middle of their territory and then defend it fiercely from all comers.

Gray squirrels are clever hiders, too. They will often take a nut and pretend to bury it in up to half a dozen spots before they really put it in the ground and cover it up. They have remarkable memories and can later recover up to as many as an amazing 95% of the food items that they have hidden months earlier. But even so they miss a few, and in so doing, they become the Johnny Appleseeds of the oak trees. Many of those forgotten nuts sprout, often at some distance from their mother tree, gradually spreading the oak forest a few hundred yards at a time.

Squirrels have a social life, but it's pretty strange. Female squirrels are receptive to male squirrels for just 6 to 8 hours once or twice a year. The rest of the time, the sexes stay mostly separate; there's certainly no family life.

About the only time they associate with one another is at sundown, when groups of several females, or several males, bunch together in a nest for the night. These nesting groups are usually blood relatives, and they are exclusive clubs. They generally don't let anybody else in, even if they really try.

Then every morning they go their completely separate ways. They hunt and find their own food items, and eat them or hide them entirely on their own, with no cooperation and no sharing.

Mama squirrels usually have one or two babies, once or twice a year, but they are programmed to be more or less productive, depending on conditions of plenty or of want. Around 75% of young squirrels fail to live through their first year, but those who do can live up to 10 years or more.

Squirrels are notorious for their creativity in robbing birdfeeders. Whole books have been written on how to outwit squirrels; whole businesses thrive on making allegedly squirrelproof birdfeeders. After a long and unpleasant history of long ropes, metal poles, axle grease, and barbed wire, do I have any advice for all you bird feeding enthusiasts out there? Nope, sorry! it's just like all those squirrels we talked about—you're on your own for that problem.

CADES COVE

Through the years, Spouse and I have found that just a single day in Cades Cove will serve to properly reset our relationship to the world around us. That being the case, naturally one spring day we decided to go up and get a much-needed Cades Cove fix. The weather was sunny, temperatures were in the upper 70's, and the wildflowers were coming on strong. We hadn't tried out the newly paved Loop Road and given it our stamp of approval. And, in rummaging through some stuff, I had come upon a Cades Cove Auto Tour Guide booklet that was published in 1965, which I'm sure we acquired around 1970. So, we packed a lunch and headed for the hills to see if we could get a newer version of the tour book to compare with our nearly 50-year-old one.

A brochure put out by the Great Smoky Mountains Association makes this striking statement: "Even if Cades Cove were to secede from the rest of the Great Smoky Mountains National Park, it would still be on the list of the ten most-visited national parks!" With no waterslides, bumper cars, bungee jumps, or fast-food restaurants, no motels or casinos, and still with 2 million visitors a year, you'd think there must be something pretty good going on up there. Indeed, there is!

Taken together with its rim of massive mountains, millennia of natural history, and centuries of people history, Cades Cove is a spell-binding place. The Smoky Mountain coves—with names like Cades, Wear, Tuckaleechee, and Cataloochee—are geologically unique places. Their flat, level floors are made of younger limestone rocks surrounded by overlying, older, acidic shales and sandstones making up the mountains. This situation gives the cove floors sweeter, less acidic soil than the rocky hillsides, excellent for growing corn, wheat, vegetables, and grass for grazing and for hay—potentially a great place to settle.

There is no evidence that the Cherokee had ever set up actual residence in the Cove. The first permanent white settlers were John and Lucretia Oliver, who arrived in 1818. The area was very remote. The nearest town was Maryville, a 3-day road trip. Many of the early folks lived their entire lives without ever leaving the Cove. Never very crowded, the Cove population rose and fell through the years, peaking at around 685 in 1850 and at 708 in 1900. There were still about 100 families living in the Cove when the state of Tennessee began buying up the land for the national park in 1928.

Which brings us up to the present. Sort of. One of the most fascinating parts of the history of the park, to me at least, is the difficulty the founders and early leaders had in deciding what to do with the park once they had it. Some people wanted to make it another great wilderness park like the ones out west, complete with dude ranches and lots of horses. They imported rainbow trout and stocked the streams with that nonnative fish so that anglers could experience some "real " trout fishing, like out west.

Others wanted a network of paved roads throughout the park, so everyone could experience every part of the park from their car windows. They wanted big, multistory, rustic hotels like those in Yellowstone, Yosemite, and Glacier national parks, with plenty of restaurants and amenities. And the one that really gets me—and it was seriously considered and debated, and favored by the first park superintendent, J. R. Eakin—dam up Abrams Creek, flood Cades Cove to form a lake just over 3 miles long and 1 mile wide, and have a huge lodge on the lakeshore with a carillon bell tower and paddleboats for the visitors. How's that for preserving nature for future generations?

Thank goodness much more farsighted and wiser heads prevailed. They decided to preserve the Cove so natural features like the forest-covered mountains and the clear, free-running streams could be protected and still show us twenty-first-century people how life was lived in those mountains nearly 200 years ago.

So now, as Spouse and I meander through the Cove, the forested mountains look down on a new and nicely improved Loop Road with paved turnoffs and smooth stream crossings. We can visit half a dozen beautiful old log homes, a couple of magnificent cantilevered barns, a working grist mill, and four "modern" frame buildings dating from the early 1900s—the three churches and the Becky Cable house at the Cable Mill area.

The main difference between the 1965 Auto Tour and the present one? In 1965, the Cove's fields were leased out by the Park Service to fortunate individuals to cut hay and graze cattle, supposedly to maintain the farmlike atmosphere of the place. Three residences for those people were listed on the Auto Tour, and along the road, fenced fields full of fat cattle were seen grazing on imported fescue grass. They are gone now—people, residences, and cows. And now the fescue is going away, too.

Happily, the fields are being carefully restored, one at a time, to the way they would have looked in the 1800s. The park staff are planting the fields with native warm-season grasses, from seed found to remain in a few areas of the Cove. These grasses make excellent food and cover for the creatures that have lived in the Cove for centuries, although various critics complain that the native grasses make the landscape look "weedy."

River otters, wiped out in the Smokies early on for their fur, once again swim in Abrams Creek. Peregrine falcons, once extinct east of the Rockies because of DDT, again fly over the Cove, and raise a couple of young up on Duckhawk Ridge every year. A Day Hikes Guide we got along with our new Auto Tour Guide lists 28 species of birds you can expect to see in the Cove. Deer and turkeys abound. And flowers! We saw some 25 species that day: showy orchis, crested dwarf iris, and bouquets of yellow trilliums with red fire pinks. An amazing natural flower garden!

As we destroy our ridgetops, muddy our streams, and fill the landscape with abandoned big-box stores, it's a comfort to know that there are yet a few sanctuaries where the natural world can go on as it was intended. The 800 square miles of mountains, streams, and forests preserved within the Great Smoky Mountains National Park serve to show us what nature can create if given a few thousand years here and there. And a little time spent in Cades Cove can serve to show that independent and determined people can adapt to life in the rugged natural world, and live in it successfully for their whole lives. You should try to spend a day in the Cove!

REGAL MONARCHS AND TOXIC MILKWEEDS

Large, striking orange-and-black butterflies, gliding along with a stately, measured flight, are making their way to East Tennessee from some mysterious place south of here, but from exactly *where* is a recent discovery. For years people had suspected that eastern monarch butterflies migrated somewhere to the south every autumn. The western population of monarchs was not a big mystery; they migrated to several small California towns each fall, arriving as regularly as the swallows returning to San Juan Capistrano. One such town is Pacific Grove, some 60 miles south of San Francisco. Known as Butterfly Town USA, Pacific Grove has an annual parade and festival to celebrate the butterflies' arrival.

But the millions of eastern ones—where did they go? Thousands of volunteers tagged hundreds of thousands of monarchs, and people to the south recovered a few of them. Their trail seemed to head west into Texas, but then the trail seemed to go cold. It remained a scientific mystery until it was finally solved back in 1975.

A Canadian zoologist named Dr. Fred Urquhart had been working on the monarch question for many years, since 1937. In 1972 he put notices in various Mexican newspapers, requesting volunteers for tagging and observers to look for butterfly wintering grounds. A Mexico City man named Ken Brugger saw one of the notices and responded. He then crisscrossed the Mexican countryside for 3 years, looking for the butterflies' winter destination. Finally, with the help of some Mexican tree cutters, the site was found. On January 9, 1975, Ken Brugger called Dr. Urquhart from Mexico

saying, "We have located the colony! We have found them—millions of monarchs—in evergreens beside a mountain clearing."

Sure enough, all those millions of monarchs from across eastern North America were there, blanketing the trees and the ground, in a 20-acre grove of trees located at 9,000 feet in the mountains of central Mexico. One of the guides estimated that there were 1,000 trees, each one enveloped in a solid, moving sheet of butterflies. Dr. Urquhart described the scene: The butterflies "filled the air with their sun-shot wings, shimmering against the blue mountain sky and drifting across our vision in blizzard flakes of orange and black." What a sight it must have been!

And those monarchs that head back north in the spring? They mate, lay their eggs, and die. Their children hatch, grow, fly farther north, and repeat the cycle, to at last reach their summering destinations. Finally, in the fall, several cycles later, a larger, stronger fall generation appears, equipped to once more make the journey south to the ancestral wintering grounds, a place they have never seen. Guided only by instinct, they drift away south at 10 miles an hour to the mountains of central Mexico.

The whole story is an excellent example of the remarkable complexity of nature. The more we learn, the more there seems to be to the story. And it's true of this one as well. . . . There's more! Because now we encounter the next actor in the monarch drama, the milkweed plant.

There are numerous species of milkweeds, but here we concern ourselves with common milkweed, a tall robust plant with stout stems and large leaves. Its trademark blooms are unusual 2-to-3-inch balls of around 50 tightly arranged, five-petalled, pinkish-white flowers that tend to blend in with their surroundings. They like to grow in unmown fields, along roadsides, and in median strips. They can be easily overlooked if you aren't actually looking for them.

The milky white sap that gives the milkweed family its name has some unusual properties, too. For instance, when a plant gets injured, say, a leaf broken off or chomped on by something, the sap immediately oozes out and hardens into a rubbery seal for the area. It is so rubbery, in fact, that our military studied it as a possible source for tires when, during World War II, our usual supplies from Southeast Asia were cut off. The hardened sap has been used for chewing gum as well, but that's not recommended because we now know that milkweed contains a number of toxic substances!

Many plants known to have medicinal properties are also poisonous when consumed in high enough doses. Although common milkweed contains substances that even now are in use in human medicines, the plants are labeled toxic or poisonous in wildflower guides. We occasionally hear of range animals hungry enough to ignore the bitter taste of milkweeds dying after eating milkweed. Books on foraging for edible wild plants describe ways of fixing milkweed shoots or immature seed pods, describing them as tasty and delicious! Now, I don't eat poke greens; I'm leery of eating anything you have to boil and pour off three times to make it safe. The same goes for a dinner of milkweed: Why do it unless you're starving in a wilderness somewhere?

But it's an entirely different story if you happen to be a monarch caterpillar, or one of the several other milkweed groupies out there. That toxic sap doesn't affect monarchs, and indeed, they use it to their advantage in the serious game of survival. The story goes like this: Monarch butterflies lay their eggs only on milkweed plants, a relationship that has evolved down through the eons. And those voracious eating machines, the caterpillars, devour many times their own body weight in toxin-rich milkweed leaves. They somehow incorporate the poisons into their body cells without suffering any ill effects. Then when the caterpillars become adult butterflies their bodies still contain the toxins, which are so distasteful or sickening to their potential predators that they quickly learn monarchs are awful to eat!

With our monarch butterflies in sharp decline, scientists urge folks to consider adding milkweed to their gardens. A perennial that needs little tending, milkweed is both unusual and attractive. Like your daylilies, it grows back each year with minimal effort on your part. In addition to being essential in the lives of monarch butterflies, you will find that the nectar of the milkweed is an excellent butterfly attractor for numerous other species as well. And get this: the monarch caterpillars that hatch on your milkweed plants? They're guaranteed not to eat anything in your garden *except the milkweeds.*

In addition to gardens, it is critically important that we encourage milkweed cultivation in fields and along roadsides. Some states have curtailed roadside mowing until fall, to allow insects and other critters to use those resources till they are ripened and gone. To continue to survive, the monarchs must have a continuous supply of milkweed all along their migration routes from Mexico to Canada. Please help them out.

UNUSUAL SPRING GOINGS-ON

Some pretty unusual things go on out there in the spring. We've had our share here in East Tennessee lately. First, it was the cardinal, pecking incessantly, hour after hour, on our dining room window. He was determined to eradicate that other showy red bird that was challenging him for his rights to his territory . . . his reflection. It went on for weeks.

That was a couple of years ago. Last year, it was the robin. Flutter, flutter, peck, peck. This time it was the living room window. And it was a female. While the male perched proudly in our magnolia tree and watched, the really disturbed mama bird tried tirelessly to drive away the reflected hussy, who she must have thought was vying for her man. Same result: bird slobber all over the window, Spouse out with the window cleanser and the squeegee.

Then, just when we thought we were safe, this year a hormone-crazed eastern towhee began attacking his reflection, again in the living room window. Ordinarily fairly secretive and feeding out of sight under the bushes, in spring the towhee will sit up on an exposed perch and sing his "Drink your teaeeeee" song for hours on end. But we hadn't had one attack our house before. Now, let's see . . . where did I leave that squeegee?

A different sort of experience, but part of the same process: Last Monday was Memorial Day, and it was memorable at our house because it turned out to be the Big Fledging Day for a nest full of young Carolina wrens. They were being raised by two overachieving parents, in a nest up under the eave just outside our kitchen door.

Spouse and I were sitting peacefully on the back porch—I was severely spent from a full day of yardwork—when we had a wren explosion.

Suddenly, we had the two parent birds singing and calling, and new fledglings with little short tails and frizzy hairdos squawking and crashing into bushes and walls. Although there were only three or four of them, it seemed as if at least 40 new birds had burst out of that nest! It was quite an event.

The experience was made a bit calmer this year because our ever-faithful pet Kitty passed on to her reward last year. (Just by being present in the backyard, she always took Fledging Day to a whole new level of drama and excitement.) Anyhow, the parents managed to get the fledglings gathered up and out of sight before a big gullywasher rolled in about eight o'clock. I wonder what those wide-eyed baby wrens thought of that! We wish them well.

When it comes to some really out-of-the-ordinary spring goings-on, I'll bet most of you have never heard of Wray, Colorado. Wray is a small ranching town in northeast Colorado, way out in the dry, fairly flat, sagebrush-and-grass high plains, almost in Nebraska. And there lives the greater prairie-chicken. Spouse and I were there as part of a very nice organized birding tour of spring in Colorado. Because most of us were there to see the five species of grouselike birds, all sharply declining in numbers and some called prairie-chickens, the trip was affectionately called the Chicken Run. We had been successful so far, and Wray was to be our last stop, and our last species of "chicken."

Greater prairie-chickens, which I will call "chickens" from here on to save wear and tear on my two index fingers, look sort of like a big grouse or a chicken. They're brownish, with a barred pattern to them, to help them blend in with the dusty soil, sagebrush bushes, and patchy tall grass they like to live in.

But then comes spring, and staying out of sight is forgotten. Triggered perhaps by the lengthening days and warming temperatures in their high plains habitat, the male chickens begin gathering before daylight in groups in selected large open spaces, maybe half a football field in size, called "leks."

They are not there to read the morning paper and talk about politics. This is a designated courting ground, where they fluff out their feathers, inflate big orange air sacs on each side of their neck, and spread their tail feathers into a fan like a turkey. Then, with a bevy of fairly unimpressed-looking females observing, they dance around, stomp their feet, turn the other way, and do it again.

All this is to dazzle the girl birds into believing that they would be the best mate possible. Sometimes actual fights occur, complete with flapping and chasing. A pecking order develops, with the year-old male birds looking on forlornly from the sidelines. Remind you of the high school sock hop?

We got to see this amazing performance in mid-April, from an unheated trailer on a cattle ranch outside of Wray. You had to be sitting inside before daylight, settled down, very still and quiet. And it was cold—26 degrees that morning—and there were still patches of snow on the ground outside. Finally, our hosts opened the shutters that looked out over the lek, and as daylight came, there the chickens were, calling, stomping, fluffed up, and showing the girls their best stuff.

We sat there and watched quietly for over 2 hours, so as not to disturb the birds. But once the birds were done and we were out, our reward, in addition to seeing the lek spectacle, was a huge breakfast back at the ranch, put on by the folks in Wray, very friendly hosts and hostesses. They are proud of their chickens and are trying to raise interest in them, encouraging people to come out and see them and learn about the many issues concerning the birds' conservation. Hot coffee, thick bacon, scrambled eggs, biscuits, and gravy. Bird watching can be a great pastime!

HICKORY CHICKENS

Springtime here in our part of the world moves each year from south to north and from lower to higher elevations in a fairly predictable fashion. And as it moves along each year, it produces a series of events as it goes by . . . some exciting, some beautiful, and some, well, interesting.

Exciting, for example: how about that first rose-breasted grosbeak on your birdfeeder or the first blue-winged warbler singing on Sharp's Ridge? Beautiful? Ah, that first clump of bloodroot bursting forth, or a hillside of trout lilies or big purple trilliums. But then, today's subjects—hickory chickens—are beautiful and exciting mostly in the eyes of their beholders; however, they're definitely interesting.

Hickory chickens are not a Southern female vocal group; nor are they a recipe for barbecued legs and wings. Hickory chickens is a mostly upper East Tennessee–southeastern Kentucky name for a somewhat different group of organisms more properly known as morels. Also known as dry land fish, merkels, molly moochers, and a hundred other names, they are mushrooms!

Now before you give a small snort of disdain at the thought of a lowly mushroom, allow me to point out that a half-ounce package of dried morels is going for about $12 at your local supermarket, which figures out to be about $384 per pound! I found their price listed on the internet ranging from $185 to $315 per pound. Somebody must think they're pretty good. And, indeed, they are delicious, and the good news is that if you know how, you can forage around and find some for yourself . . . for free.

Fungi in general and mushrooms in particular are an important part of nature. Out there in the woods, they go about their business unseen, making

74

use of their zillions of microscopic rootlets known as mycelia. They grow into and digest all sorts of organic material, like leaf litter and dying and dead trees, turning them back into good rich soil.

When it's time to reproduce, this out-of-sight network of rootlets makes a fruit which appears above ground somewhere, often seemingly overnight, which we recognize as a mushroom. We've all seen shelf fungi on tree trunks, fairy rings of white mushrooms in a yard, all sorts of shapes and colors of 'shrooms beside a path or in the woods. The mushroom has been described as similar to an apple on a tree; it is the fruit of the plant. But instead of seeds, it produces tiny microscopic spores, so small that they can float away on the air currents, to hopefully start a new batch of mycelia somewhere else.

Well, our morels do their fruit-bearing thing in the spring. Morel hunters wait for them as eagerly as the birders look for that first returning migrant. The morels first appear around the middle of March here in East Tennessee and work their way north as spring progresses. They show up in Michigan by the first part of April and can be found in northern Michigan by late May.

Identifying morels is not difficult. With just a moderate amount of care, morels are, as mushrooms go, pretty unmistakable. They are usually around 2 to 4 inches tall with a short white stem and a conical-shaped cap covered with sharp ridges and pits. A most important clue to be sure you have a morel: They are completely hollow! As with all foraged wild edibles, caution must be used to rule out lookalikes, some of which can cause serious illness and even death. Such is the case with a variety called false morels; some folks can eat those, too, but they have caused fatalities, even in a few unfortunate people who have simply inhaled the cooking fumes. Consult a good field guide or go out with an experienced person.

Lots of people are out there hunting morels. Every year, professionals foraging for market collect morels worth up into the tens of millions of dollars in Washington, Oregon, and Idaho. But the everyday people have the most fun. They range from the stealthy lone forager to groups of friends to several large local and statewide get-togethers and festivals. Some of the larger gatherings happen in the upper Midwest and feature morel-hunting competitions, morel-related crafts, friendly hosts dressed up as morels going around shaking hands, and the sharing of many stories, and possibly even a tall tale or two.

But what good is a morel, after all? Well, they're a rare delicacy with a hard-to-describe luscious flavor. Once picked, they can be eaten fresh or dried for later use. Drying can be accomplished by stringing them up for a few days in a cool, dry place, or by giving them a few hours in a food dehydrator. Once dry, they will keep in a sealed glass jar for years. The dried morels can be reconstituted by a brief soaking in water, making them as good as new; some cooks think they're even better that way.

Many folks like their morels just rolled in flour or cornmeal and fried in butter. Even better to many people is to simmer them in some butter, add some heavy cream and a dash of cooking sherry, and use that as a wondrous sauce for a nice beef tenderloin. Pardon my salivating!

Morels are another of nature's remarkable curiosities. Check them out in your field guide and cookbook, but don't expect any morel hunters you might encounter to tell you where their secret places are; that's closely held information. And for the less adventurous, you don't have to go tromping around the damp, cold spring woods to find morels; you can just grab $12 and head for the supermarket. Bon appétit!

HARD TO SEE

About 3 weeks ago, a birding friend and I spent a remarkably good birding morning at our newest state park, the Seven Islands State Birding Park, out past Strawberry Plains along the French Broad River. It has a beautiful bunch of habitats: hilly woods, riversides, and big fields planted with an abundance of vegetation that birds love to make a meal of. Although it was late spring, the birds were all singing and hopping around in the treetops, including a number of them that you ordinarily hear but seldom see.

Amongst all the songs we were hearing was that of the elusive yellow-billed cuckoo, the old rain crow. Its sharply declining numbers make its song an even more welcome sound these days. My friend wanted to not only hear, but also see, the cuckoo, so we made a stab at it, with my offhand warning, a product of many years' experience: "They're hard to see."

This outing got me thinking later about how hard it can be to see some of our most common birds. Those folks familiar with lots of bird songs can just listen and know which of our feathered friends are around, and be happy with that. But if you're faced with trying to show someone a particular bird—maybe a newer birder or a person who hasn't seen that particular species before—you're quickly reminded that some of those birds can be frustratingly, maddeningly, impossibly difficult to see!

Lots of birds are easy. Think robins, bluebirds, mockingbirds, and hummingbirds. They all go about their business as if they have things to do and need to be getting on with it, and we're just part of the surroundings. Pigeons, doves, crows, starlings—not particularly warm and friendly, but as much a part of the scenery as the cars and buildings.

Then there are those that are only easy to see in the spring when the birds' hormones kick in, with territory, mate, and nest as high priorities, and personal safety, not so much. Indigo buntings, which we met earlier, offer a good example. In May, when you hear Mr. Indigo singing, you automatically scan each nearby treetop. He'll for sure be up on one of them. Ditto for the brown thrasher, invisible for most of the year scratching around in the dense underbrush, but singing atop his favorite tree for hours in the spring. All this partly, at least, explains why you see your birding friends also behaving in peculiar ways in the spring—up before daylight, choosing binoculars and field guides over food and drink, and leaving chores undone.

But for now, I'm thinking about those species, mostly common ones, not rare at all but rarely seen, that intrigue and frustrate all those who would like to see them, veterans and novices alike.

The late Roger Tory Peterson, artist, field guide author, and dean of the whole present-day birding scene, was famous for, among other things, his succinct, one-line or even one-word summation of a given bird species' appearance or personality. "A cigar with wings," "a pale owl of open country," "a tight-sitting bog-wader"—such phrases stick in your mind better than any photographs or long, detailed descriptions.

And so it is also with his descriptions for where our sneaky and difficult birds hang out. If you read such telling words as "brush," "weeds," "thickets," "undergrowth," or "dense cover," you can assume there will be some difficult bird viewing ahead.

A good example is the word Peterson uses to describe the aforementioned yellow-billed cuckoo: "secretive." Absolutely true. You may occasionally be lucky enough to get a glimpse of one flying from tree to tree, but once there the bird slinks and slithers through the leaves and branches as skillfully as a snake. If you can ever spot one and follow it along, you'll find that about all you'll ever see of it at one time is a single beady eye, peering warily out from the leaves at you. Incidentally, we never saw the one calling at Seven Islands that day!

Peterson also uses "secretive" to describe the little grasshopper sparrow; correct again. Occasionally, you'll be lucky enough to catch one up on a stem of grass, giving its quiet, insectlike song, but then it drops onto the ground and disappears forever. The sparrows in general are a difficult lot, and many in that family fall into the "hard to see" category. Peterson uses one of his more graphic phrases for the Lincoln's sparrow, a bird that we see here only in migration, and then very rarely. He describes it as "a skulker, afraid of its shadow." Good luck on seeing that one!

But there are others to torment us. Try showing a group of hopeful birders a singing white-eyed vireo, a common bird here. Peterson's description of its favorite habitat: brush, brambles, dense undergrowth. Or the spectacularly yellow, yellow-breasted chat? A common bird here—we actually saw some at Seven Islands the day we visited—but Peterson says to look for it in "brushy tangles and briars." Both of those two birds can sing happily for hours in a 4-foot bushy tangle 10 feet in front of you, but you might as well take a snack break or go scan the sky for hawks; you'll not likely see either one unless you're there at spring hormone time, and only *maybe* then.

But after all, consider this: If they were all as easy to see as robins, birding wouldn't be half the fun, or half the challenge. The hard-to-see guys make us learn the songs and calls. They throw down the challenge to learn more, work harder, and be better birders. And, once in a while, they pop up out from their cover and give us one of those wonderful "oh, WOW, look at that!" moments that we all get up early and stomp around for countless hours in the wet grass for. Most birders can remember the exact place and the day, hour, and minute they finally got a really good look at each of those hard-to-see thicket-singers. It gives you a great sense of hard work paying off, and also makes for some great winter conversations around the fireplace.

So, don't let a few briary tangles discourage you! Learn who that is singing in there, and sooner or later you will see the varmint. After all, anybody can see a robin. Well now, let's see: I wonder what's going on in the brushy tangles along the back fencerow this morning.

HAWKS IN THE YARD

We're sitting on eggs at our house. We've been at it for about 2 weeks now, since late March. My Granny Collier would have called it "setting." Actually, Spouse and I aren't doing the setting; it's a big mama red-shouldered hawk and her helpful mate doing the work. But we're watching and waiting right along with them.

They have been raising a family in our woods every spring for 7 years now. It's like having a nest of wrens or robins, but on an industrial scale. Sometimes they remodel and reuse the previous year's nest; however, this year they decided (undoubtedly the mama bird decided) to start over on a new nest.

They began a month ago, high up in a big wild cherry tree. I first caught on to the fact that the birds were building their new accommodations when I saw one of the birds out in a spruce tree in the side yard near the house. I thought she might be checking on our feeders for a possible quick snack, but no, she was plucking selected green-needled twigs from the tree. With her beak full, off she flew. Aha! Nest building.

Once we found the nest construction site, we trained the old 20x spotting scope on it from our foyer and just left it there, to watch the daily progress and goings-on whenever we passed by. In addition to big and small sticks fussily placed, positioned, and arranged, there were lots of evergreen sprigs woven in, spruce and cedar. I've heard that the aromatic twigs might help keep bugs away, like in your cedar-lined closet. Maybe so.

But now comes the boring part—setting. At least incubating human mamas can get out and about while the neat little package is developing. If you're a bird, though, you have to watch those eggs like a hawk, so to speak. Crows, blue jays, and squirrels just love unattended birds' eggs. And, the eggs have to be kept constantly warm in the chilly, damp March and April weather.

It takes 28 days for the rascals to hatch, and the parents share the setting duties. We've seen the changing of the guard! One bird will fly in, they will shuffle around for a minute or two, then the setting one will fly away, and the relieving one will settle down on the eggs. We watched a poor, faithful, determined bird on one stormy evening as the heavy winds blew and the rain poured down. You could almost read its mind: something like "who said having eggs is a blessing?"

All this setting does eventually come to an end, and as in human families, that's when things really get lively. It takes 6 weeks for the fluffy, goofy, and nearly helpless hatchlings to become full-sized, feathered creatures, ready to be taught the skills of flying and hunting for a living. All that growing happens in just 6 short weeks (imagine growing a newborn infant to a high schooler in 9 months!) and requires lots of feeding. A *whole lot* of feeding.

So, then you watch the scope every day to see what delicacies the parent birds bring in for lunch—lizards, rats, big snakes—yummy stuff. At first the parents carefully nip off bits of meat and poke it in the little fluff-balls' mouths. But as the young ones grow and get stronger, hungrier, and more quarrelsome (sound familiar?), the parents just toss the prey into the nest and let them go at it.

And then one fine day, amidst a lot of calling and shrieking and flapping, off the nest they come, out into the big world. You can only wonder what it must be like to take your first leap off that nest, and feel the air holding you up as you look around at everything you've been watching all the 6 weeks of your life, now going by beneath you.

Young raptors aren't born knowing how to hunt. They have to be taught by their parents. And estimates by the experts are that only about one in four succeed in learning their skills well enough to survive. That's evident in the ones we've observed; some seem to get it, and some don't.

One year we had two full-sized young hawks in our yard who apparently thought they were robins. They would sit around on the lawn, watch the robins, and pick around looking for worms, much to the dismay of their parents, who would hop, flap, and call, trying to get them to come and learn lizard catching, or some other useful hawk skill. Goodness knows what became of that pair.

As I write, one of the birds is settled down in the new nest, looking around, seemingly glad that the sun is shining today but longing to be soaring in the blue morning sky. Take heart, bird, they'll be off the nest in just 2 months. We wish you good fortune with your new family!

A BIRDING HOTSPOT

South Texas is different. If you are able to travel around our huge and amazing country, there are lots of places that stick in your mind as different: the rocky coast of Maine, the endless flatness of Kansas, and the grandeur of Glacier, Yellowstone, and Death Valley national parks.

But for serious, total "differentness" you would have to pick south Texas as a top contender. The geography, the weather, the food, the people, the language they speak, and how they drive—it's all different. And the wildlife? How about roadrunners, peccaries, and armadillos, just for a start. You sure won't see any of those scurrying across the road in Halls or Powell.

And south Texas is especially different—or I should say outstanding—from a birdwatcher's point of view. Spouse and I just finished a 5-week-long birding loop across the United States, with notable stops in western Colorado, southern California, and southeast Arizona. Beautiful birds and interesting places. But if you asked us to pick the place that was the most "different" overall, names like McAllen, Mission, Pharr, Raymondville, and Riviera would likely come to mind. This area, at the lower end of the Rio Grande River Valley, is known simply as the Valley by the locals and birders alike.

There are two parts of Texas with special appeal to birders. One is Big Bend National Park. Far to the west of the above-mentioned Valley area, Big Bend is in west Texas. In remote, sparsely populated Brewster County, it is over 500 miles from the lower Rio Grande Valley and McAllen (did I mention that Texas is big?). While the Valley is bustling with people and traffic, Big Bend is enormous, quiet, and alone.

Big Bend National Park has two large campgrounds, right on the Rio Grande River. Few people cross the river there other than the locals. It's just too far from anywhere to make it worthwhile. There is a lodge up at 7,000 feet in the Chisos Mountains, pleasant even in the summer. The park has deserts, mountain forests, and even hot springs. And its bird list is phenomenal. Its most sought-after species is the Colima warbler, found nowhere else in the United States. Birders hike miles to see one. Another special bird that makes its home there is the Lucifer hummingbird, with a brilliant violet throat; it is occasionally seen in Arizona and New Mexico as well. Big Bend National Park easily makes it to near the top of my list of favorite places.

However, McAllen, Texas, doesn't. McAllen is the central city of the Valley. It is growing like a mushroom—over 100,000 people, a big four-lane throughway, consuming its former neighbors into suburbs. But it's in a unique location. As far south as Miami, instead of being at the tip of a peninsula, it has more land below it: the high mountains and big deserts of Mexico, continuing on south into the tropics of Central America. And McAllen is very near the ocean. It's only about 75 miles from South Padre Island, of Spring Break fame, and the Padre Island National Seashore.

Just to the north of McAllen is King Ranch. The largest ranch in the world at 825,000 acres, it occupies two counties, King and Kenedy. Kenedy County doesn't have any cities in it because it's made entirely of huge ranches. I said this place was different, didn't I?

Anyway, all this geography adds up to a remarkable variety of habitats and good places to find a large number of bird species, many of which you're not likely to see anywhere else in the United States. And it's pretty hot in the Valley; it's a true subtropical area.

Noisy flocks of red-crowned parrots and green parakeets live in Brownsville and McAllen. Spectacular green jays, bright orange-and-black hooded orioles, and raucous yellow-and-brown great kiskadees are everywhere. And then there are the birds that only a birder would love, like the groove-billed ani, the plain chachalaca, and the olive sparrow.

The wide-open spaces and abundant food make south Texas hawk heaven. There are the tawny brown Harris' hawks that hunt in packs, white-tailed hawks, gray hawks, and lots of black-and-white crested caracaras, also known as Mexican eagles.

It's hummingbird heaven, too. South Texas is home base to 10 species in addition to various transients. The special local hummer in the Valley is the little buff-bellied hummingbird, which has a green back and chest and bright red bill.

In addition to the long list of birds that you would expect to see on a visit to the Valley, one of the big attractions for birders is the possibility of glimpsing rarities. A diligent birder will usually find at least one, sometimes several, unusual, rare, or never-before-seen-here birds. They usually hop over from Mexico, but sometimes they come from farther south in the tropics. Blue mockingbird, white-throated robin, and black-headed nightingale-thrush—these and many others have been seen in McAllen.

And if you're into butterflies instead of birds, the North American Butterfly Association (NABA) has recently established a 100-acre butterfly park in Mission, Texas—continuous with McAllen—that has gardens, pond, and fountains, all to attract the zillions of subtropical butterflies that inhabit the Valley and northern Mexico.

There are too many people packed into the southern tip of Texas, but you can still escape to the wildlife refuges and parks and drive the country roads in search of hawks and orioles. It's always warm, often hot; if you don't like cold, it's a good place to go. But unless you like a steady diet of beef barbeque and Mexican food, you'd better bring your own peanut butter and jelly sandwiches to the Valley. The birding, though, is great!

SUMMER

BIG SKY SPRINGTIME

Unless you possess a time machine, there are only a couple of ways I know to prolong springtime—go higher, or go north. But why prolong springtime? To continue enjoying all those exciting spring birds and wildflowers, that's why, and to do so in nice crisp weather before the oppressive heat of summer has set in. To spend a few more mornings surrounded by singing and courting birds and just-sprouted and abundant blossoms, all too soon gone again.

Thus, as spring was drawing to a close, with hints of summer upon us, Spouse and I needed to find a place where it was indeed spring again, after the one in Tennessee was done. And we found just such a place in north-western Montana, which is indeed higher than East Tennessee, and farther north than northern Maine. The place? The Nature Conservancy's 18,000-acre Pine Butte Swamp Preserve and its adjacent Pine Butte Guest Ranch. Located just where the high rolling shortgrass prairie that occupies the eastern two-thirds of Montana meets the first row of craggy, snow-capped Rocky Mountains, the property rises abruptly from 4,500 feet above sea level out on the plains to over 8,500 feet up on the mountain peaks.

One could expect a late spring there, with lots of different birds and lots of flowers. And then the clincher: The program that week at the ranch was to be led by famous field guide author and bird artist David Allen Sibley. Sibley, from Massachusetts, was to be joined by a co-leader, Keith Hansen, another bird artist and author, from the coast of California. It sounded like an excellent team, and they proved to be just that, expert and very enjoyable.

The program was scheduled for the first week of June, so Spouse and I headed out the last week of May, and birded our way to western Montana.

87

Along the way, we enjoyed some great history lessons. We crossed the path of the Lewis and Clark expedition (1804–1806) several times as we proceeded along the Missouri River from St. Louis to Great Falls, Montana. There are numerous parks, monuments, and exhibits along their route, and the magnificent Lewis and Clark Interpretive Center in Great Falls, where we spent an entire day.

Finally, a couple of hours northwest of Great Falls and 2,300 miles from home, we found the Pine Butte Guest Ranch nestled among big, rugged, and still snowcapped mountains and sitting beside the rushing, snowmelt-filled South Fork of the Teton River. And just down the road and out onto the prairie is the Pine Butte Swamp Preserve itself. Now, you wouldn't expect to find a swamp in Montana, and although the Pine Butte Swamp Preserve is wet, it isn't really a swamp—it's a fen. That means that rather than having a big area of dark, slow-moving water with big cypress trees standing around, there are lots of seeps, springs, and little streams filled with clear, cool groundwater from the mountains, which creates an interesting wetland in an otherwise sparse and arid countryside.

That in and of itself attracts all sorts of plants and animals. However, the wetlands turned out to be bad for the original ranchers. They had hoped to drain the "swamp" and grow crops and cattle, only the swamp wouldn't drain! The ranch failed and was later put up for sale, and the Nature Conservancy bought it. Score one for nature! Now protected and with plenty of water, it is full of wild things: deer, elk, moose, bobcats, golden eagles. And, gulp—grizzly bears.

Lewis and Clark were the first to describe the grizzly, at that time unknown to science. They vividly described them in their journals as "verry large and turrible" . . . and they were. Their band of explorers had some very close calls with grizzlies in Montana, though fortunately, no one got eaten. (Nowadays, all the ranch hands carry a can of bear spray on their belts, and we were all warned to stay aware of our surroundings and not wander around alone.) The area surrounding the Pine Butte Preserve has the largest concentration of grizzlies in North America. The mama grizzlies bring their new cubs down from the mountains in the spring to feed out in the wetlands below. We got to see only one, but it was very active.

Ah, but the birds. The state of Montana may have only 9 people per square mile, but it boasts a bird list of nearly 400 species. We were hoping to see considerably over a hundred on this trip. At the ranch each day, we birded for an hour before breakfast, and then we were away, either out onto the prairie or up into the mountains to see what we could see. Our searches for prairie birds out on the grassy hilltops showed us why Montana is called

Big Sky Country. You could see nearly forever in every direction, and the sky did indeed look bigger than any I had ever seen.

Out in the arid West, as you can imagine, lakes attract large numbers of birds. We spent one day at a huge lake, appropriately called Freezeout Lake, as it was 43 degrees that day. Big rafts of birds were everywhere. We observed 15 species of ducks, 4 species of gulls, 3 species of terns, and more than a dozen other water-related species—white pelicans, grebes, herons, marbled godwits, and yellow-headed blackbirds.

Up in the mountains we spied numerous bird wonders, small and large, from tiny male calliope hummingbirds doing their big swooping courtship flights to majestic prairie falcons and golden eagles, nesting high up on the sheer cliffs above us. We saw birds that only a true birder could love, with names like MacGillivray's warbler, Townsend's solitaire, and gray jay. A famous high country bird is the Clark's nutcracker, named for the Clark of Lewis and Clark. There is also a Lewis' woodpecker, named for that Lewis; they are scarce, and we didn't see one on this trip.

My favorite bird of the trip had to be the amazing American dipper, a little gray bird that gathers its food by actually walking under water along the bottoms of rushing mountain streams, searching for aquatic bugs and larvae as nonchalantly as if it were pecking around in my yard. We stood on a bridge over a small rushing Rocky Mountain stream, miles from anywhere, and watched a dipper forage for food for the hungry mouths in its nest located under the bridge.

Not to be outdone by the birds, the wildflowers were spectacular. They were out in their finest spring array, mostly flowers that we had never seen before. We burned many pixels photographing those high mountain meadows full of blossoms, against the constant backdrop of patches of snow on craggy hillsides.

Our bird species list grew and grew, and when at last we had to bid the ranch goodbye, we had tallied up 142 species for the 5 days we had spent there. That along with a whole array of new wildflowers, lots of scenery and history, and some of the best steaks you ever ate, made for a trip that we would gladly repeat any year, except that there are a lot of other places out there where we hope to prolong springtime again in the years ahead.

IT'S SUMMER, GO OUTSIDE

You may not have noticed it yet, but the days started getting shorter a couple of weeks ago. That was the first day of summer, and it seems to work that way every year. Alas, sooner or later the sun will be setting at six o'clock again.

But apart from that one little hitch, it looks to be shaping up into a fine season. They don't all go so well. You may remember the year we had the Easter Freeze, followed by the Spring Drought, leaving summer a dry and dismal affair? This year, though, there's been no big late freeze, and most of us have had enough rain to make summer a lush, green, and fruitful time, the way summer is supposed to be. There have been cherries to pick, and fresh cherry pie. Strawberries were abundant, and the apples are coming on. And, thankfully, everyone is mowing a bunch of hay.

But I think summer was made especially for kids. If you could have seen and heard about a thousand of them squealing and screaming under the big ladder truck's fire hose down at the Powell Methodist Church Vacation Bible School a week ago last Friday, you would have had to agree.

For kids, summer used to be the time when, after enduring the last miserable weeks of non-air-conditioned school—knowing full well that they'd learned everything the fourth grade could possibly teach them—at last they were free! Out into the wonderful world of summer, 3 glorious months of no plans, no schedules—only the yard, the fields, and the woods. Limitless possibilities, unknown wonders to be discovered, and adventures to be had.

But, maybe a little overwhelmed by suddenly switching from totally structured life to the wonderful gift of 3 months of "nothing scheduled," the words "we don't have anything to do! What can we do?" were heard early on in the summer vacation. To which came Mom's immediate and unblinking reply: "Go outside and play." Translated, that meant, "Go run through the fields and woods, have fun, get dirty, use your imaginations and make discoveries, and enjoy the world around you. And come in when it gets dark!"

Back then, soccer was being played only by people across the water; not even T-ball had come to our neighborhood in the Greater Inskip area just north of Knoxville. And though it's hard to imagine, there was no internet, no video games, not even computers. More mature citizens might even admit to spending summers without a television set in the house. Primitive times!

But kids seemed to have a good time. Forts and treehouses were built, bugs and frogs were collected, and dragons and monsters were slain. Kids found cloud-shapes in the sky, picked flowers in the fields, and were fascinated by turtles and repulsed by spiders. Do you ever wonder if those summers are gone, or, maybe, just hiding somewhere? Could they be brought back, or should they? Those questions lurk in the back of my mind, more so as I grow older. I myself still go outside and play every chance I get, but I see and hear about a generation of kids coming up who don't seem to know what "outside" is, or more especially, *what's* outside.

My ears perked up when a veteran schoolteacher I know from California told me about a book by Richard Louv, who works and writes a lot about children and nature. He received the 2008 Audubon Medal for his work, a medal previously won by the likes of conservationist Rachel Carson, actor/activist Robert Redford, former President Jimmy Carter, and biologist/writer E. O. Wilson.

The book is entitled *Last Child in the Woods*, and its subtitle sums up the message: "Saving Our Children from Nature-Deficit Disorder." The author points out that 80% of Americans now live in an urban environment, and lots of kids never even walk on grass or touch a tree as they grow up. It does leave an empty space in a child's life experience to be disconnected from nature; nature experiences even at an early age have lifelong benefits. Louv quotes naturalist Robert Michael Pyle at the beginning of one of the chapters: "What is the extinction of a condor to a child who has never seen a wren?"

It turns out that there are a number of unhealthy things that hinder a child's development when he or she is completely ignorant about, and out of touch with, the natural world. And this doesn't apply just to city kids. Suburban and rural kids can have nature-deficit disorder, too, if all their afterschool hours and days off are filled by watching TV, playing video games, and downloading music on a computer.

Louv lists many good things that come from kids' having free, unprogrammed time outdoors to explore, imagine, and discover: increased awareness of their surroundings, better self-esteem, more confidence in learning and problem solving, even increased opportunities to develop spiritually.

Parents are important in all this, of course; giving kids enough freedom to play and explore without micromanaging, and providing time off from coaches with whistles for a little quiet time along a stream to watch a frog or a bug can be extremely beneficial. And Louv stresses the importance of parents planning family outdoor-related activities. Many well-adjusted adults cite family hunting, fishing, camping, and hiking trips as some of the most memorable and formative times in their growing-up process.

We have plenty of opportunities in our communities to provide meaningful and fun outdoor experiences for our kids. We have local greenways, parks, fields, and woods. We have nearby farms, natural areas, and hiking trails. How about a zoo or a botanical garden? Just getting out into the yard (without an electronic device) is a great first step.

And some sage advice for all you big grownups—mom, dad, grandparents—that really good outdoors I'm talking about? It's not just for kids. It's summer. Go outside and play!

THE LIGHT SHOW

Yogi Berra is supposed to have said "you can observe a lot by just watching." A lady named Lynn Faust, by just watching an event and then realizing that it was a globally unusual, rare, and amazing thing, has brought it to everyone's attention for our collective study, enjoyment, and wonder.

It seems that Ms. Faust's family owned one of the old summer homes in the Elkmont community, in what is now the Great Smoky Mountains National Park. She can remember when, every year in early June, at about nine o'clock or so her mama would call for everybody to drop whatever they were doing and come outside to watch the "Light Show."

The Light Show, as they called it, was truly a show. Thousands of fireflies began to appear in the darkening deep June woods, later in the evening than ours seem to first appear here at the lower elevations. At first, they just blinked off and on as usual. Then as the evening darkened on into night, a remarkable thing began to happen: The fireflies blinked more and more in unison!

By ten o'clock or so, the show was in full swing. There would be total darkness for about 10 seconds, and then a couple of leaders would go flash, flash. And then, incredibly, hundreds, thousands of fireflies up and down the dark, wooded hillside blinked in unison—flash, flash, flash, flash, flash, flash. Then, total darkness again. And in about 10 seconds, it all happened again. And on and on into the night.

Ms. Faust then read about synchronous fireflies in Southeast Asia being studied by a professor of neurobiology from Georgia Southern

University, a Dr. Jonathan Copeland. Convinced that she had observed a similar phenomenon in the Smokies, she wrote to Professor Copeland in October 1992. He was intrigued enough by her description to drive up to Elkmont and check it out. He was amazed at what he saw, and after some serious scientific study, the Smokies fireflies were proven to be demonstrating synchronicity. Elkmont was on the world map of firefly behavior!

All this information and much more was provided to 25 of us eager nature types on the afternoon and evening of June 5th by Professor Copeland and a Townsend naturalist named Wanda Dewaard. We were enjoying a half-day session of the Smoky Mountain Field School appropriately titled "The Light Show in the Smokies." We spent a couple of daylight hours in the lecture room at the Sugarlands visitor's center, and then after a supper break, headed out for Elkmont.

About a quarter past nine we set out up the Little River Trail, an old railroad bed left from Little River logging days. It is wide and gentle, good for walking in the fading evening light. The fireflies began twinkling on and off about 15 minutes into our walk. Along with the ones soon to be synchronizing were occasional small, single fireflies with a bluish light, that wandered about with their lights always on, not blinking—the "Blue Ghosts."

We learned that evening that there are some 120 species of fireflies in North America, each with its own Morse code of flashing signals, to attract the females of only their specific type. Only two of those species are known to ever be synchronous, one along coastal Georgia in the Savannah region, and our Elkmont species, known officially as *Photinus carolinus*.

And as advertised, the fireflies really did put on a show for us. As the deep woods darkened to nearly pitch black, they came out in the thousands. We'd see six to eight flashes, then total dark again.

Sometimes huge groups of fireflies would blink all together, while other times different groups along the mountainside seemed to form a wave of light going from right to left. Sometimes a wave would start higher up and move down the mountainside towards us. Then total darkness again for 10 seconds. Up the trail and back down again, the fireflies were everywhere and still going strong when we left them about eleven o'clock and headed back for civilization.

This amazing spectacle usually occurs the last week of May and the first 2 weeks of June. By then, the fireflies have mated and laid eggs, and this year's adults, which haven't eaten anything since they emerged, have died away.

Spouse and I are very fond of spectacular natural sights, and we've had the privilege of enjoying our share. The Northern Lights in Churchill, Manitoba; the Great Falls of the Yellowstone River; and more than 100,000 snow geese on the wing in New Mexico, just to name a few. For us the light show at Elkmont ranks right up there with the best. You should put it on your calendar for next year!

FIREFLY DRAMA

People say that Memorial Day weekend is the unofficial start of summer. It apparently was this year, with blue skies, white clouds, and temperatures around 90 degrees. And that evening, we had a perfect Memorial Day surprise ending, a fitting sight for the start of summer.

After cleaning up from the day's activities of planting and mowing, I paused to admire my exceptionally good mowing job. It was dusk, around half past eight, and there appeared the most remarkably large bunch of fireflies I guess I've ever seen, short of those thousands of synchronous fireflies whose performance in Elkmont we've just recounted.

They were coming up out of the grass and blinking their lights, scores and scores of them. I don't know what called them forth—the earlier, warmer temperatures, or the half-moon shining directly overhead, or the Signs—but they certainly all had the same idea at the same time. The scene was so impressive, I rustled Spouse out to see the show with me. Summer must truly be here, we said, and reminisced about warm and luscious summers past, with fireflies and jarflies and suppers on the back porch.

The Smoky Mountain synchronous fireflies get a lot more press, but our local and ordinary fireflies are no slouches when it comes to having an interesting lifestyle. It turns out that those amazing little off-and-on flying lightbulbs are out there flashing their lights with something more in mind than just enhancing our lovely summer evening experience. Those are the guy lightning bugs out there flying around; the girl lightning bugs are down on the ground, watching and waiting. When a lovely, unattached girl bug sees a flash that looks right for her, she flashes back, and the guy bug zooms down to introduce himself and establish a relationship.

Now, there are many species of fireflies, with sometimes three or four kinds out and about on any given night. So, how do you tell if you're courting the right species? It's all in the timing. The length of time from the male's flash until the female responds with her flash is different and specific for each species. So, a single male of a certain species recognizes a single flash at just the right time interval from his and heads down for a romantic rendezvous.

It all sounds nice and summery and romantic, right? But alas, everything in nature is far more complicated than usually meets the eye and that holds true for the love life of the firefly. You may not want to watch this next part, folks, because there are scenes that contain instances of graphic violence!

The two common firefly genera involved in this drama have confusingly similar names, *Photinus* and *Photuris*. I certainly didn't pick those names. I would have called them "A" and "B" if it were up to me. Anyhow, think of *Photinus* as the happy-go-lucky good guys, and *Photuris* as the dark, evil femme fatale.

So, sometimes on a lovely summer evening a Photinus guy goes flashing along, and lo! There below is the flashing signal of a female, and down he goes. Only, it turns out to be a female *Photuris*, who can give a *Photinus* signal should she want to. And when our *Photinus* suitor arrives, bouquet in hand, the *Photuris* female pounces on him and devours him, leaving behind only a few scraps of legs and wings. Burrrp!

What a revolting development! Being hungry is understandable, but why not just get some handy little morsel on the ground for supper, instead of all that deception and drama? Wouldn't you know, the entomologists have that one figured out, too. Using some really sophisticated science and a lot of lab time, they have unraveled the story. They have discovered that the *Photinus* firefly's system can manufacture steroids called lucibufagins from the cholesterol molecules they get in their diet, just as human livers make all sorts of essential things from the cholesterol we eat. These chemicals are toxic to other animals and help protect the *Photinus* fireflies from such predators as birds, spiders, and lizards. People who own pet lizards are aware of all this and know not to feed their pets fireflies. There have been fatal pet lizard outcomes!

Just to show you how everything is interrelated, we have learned that the chemicals that the fireflies use for protection are similar in nature to the cardinolides found in the milkweed plant that the monarch butterfly caterpillars eat and use for protection. And a similar poison is found in the foxglove plant, but it is a useful one for people; we call it digitalis.

But back to deceit and murder. The lucibufagins that make the *Photinus* fireflies distasteful or poisonous to would-be predators? The *Photuris* fireflies can't make them! And so, down through the eons, instead of developing a system to produce their own poisons, the *Photuris* fireflies have adapted to a different, and certainly more dramatic, way around the deficit: Eat two or three *Photinus* bugs and fill your own system with beneficial, protective poison. (Incidentally, that poison also serves to protect the eggs of the *Photuris* from such predators as ladybugs, once they are laid!)

Pretending to be a lovesick bug in order to lure a suitor to the grisly fate of being devoured for his toxic juices is a script fit for a Halloween movie! The next time you're watching fireflies magically light up the summer dusk, enjoy them for the amazing little lights they are. But you might want to wish them luck in the choice they make of a date for the evening.

THE RAIN CROW

Some of the best memories of summer are the sounds that we associate with it. Who isn't instantly carried back in time by the sound of an ice cream truck in the distance? Summer memories can be brought back to us by fireworks, parades, or thunderstorms. For me, I think the summer sounds that really take me back are nature's outdoor sounds—the early morning chorus of the birds, the lazy afternoon sawing of the jarflies, and the nighttime singing of a thousand katydids.

It's definitely no longer April or May out there, but there are a surprising number of birds holding forth, now singing their summer songs. One bird in particular is known for its habit of singing on a hot, humid summer day, especially if there is some likelihood of a rain shower.

Way back in the middle of the last century, my Granny Collier pointed out the mysterious "kow kow kow kow" of the rain crow to me, coming from somewhere in the dense green leaves of her big maple trees, and she evidenced little doubt that the bird's prediction of an approaching rain shower would be correct. It was a strange and haunting sound, something a person would store away and remember the next time it was heard.

Looking back, I wonder now why I didn't try to get a glimpse of the bird. We just accepted that sound as a normal part of nature, knew where it was coming from, and, of course, expected it to rain. The rain crow has always been one of my favorites, partly because of nostalgia, I'm sure, but also because they're just plain interesting.

The rain crow's proper name is yellow-billed cuckoo. It belongs to a big family that includes the bird of cuckoo-clock fame, the Europe- and

Asia-dwelling common cuckoo. Then there's their weird cousin, the road-runner of the American Southwest, famous for its exploits with the hapless Wile E. Coyote.

We have three cuckoos in North America. The yellow-billed cuckoo summers in most of the eastern part of the United States, the black-billed cuckoo, ditto, but with a little more northern tendency, on into southern Canada.

And the mangrove cuckoo, a Caribbean bird, is found only in the Keys and southern coast of Florida. Though their songs are different enough to be distinguishable by voice alone, they're all three very similar in appearance. A look at your favorite field guide will show you what I mean by "similar." It takes a bit of study, but they can be told apart as long as a person can get a decent look at one. Of the three, you are much more likely to see a yellow-billed cuckoo in the lower elevations of the Southeast.

I spoke of getting a decent look at a rain crow: that's not an easy task. Patience and luck are both helpful here. Cuckoos are lanky, slithery birds that usually fly short distances from one perch in the dense foliage to another, and then become invisible in their new tree. They tend to forage by sitting quietly and waiting for a food item to give itself away by moving just a tiny bit. Once you spot where a cuckoo is in a tree and watch for a while, you will see it moving slowly along, looking for food, but all the while keeping leaves and branches between itself and you, with only a single eyeball or tip of tail visible to the frustrated birder.

Our cuckoos also nest in thick cover, in a loose platform of twigs lined with grass and leaves. How many eggs they lay depends on how much food is available to them in that particular season. They tend to feed on larger insects, like cicadas and katydids, than many of our songbirds, and are one of few birds that will eat tent caterpillars. If the right food is abundant, cuckoos tend to produce more eggs than they care to look after, and then they may lay a few in another cuckoo's nest or even leave a few in a robin's or catbird's nest. Such behavior is the norm for the European cuckoos; they lay their eggs *only* in other birds' nests, like our cowbirds, but this behavior is unusual for our rain crows.

One other interesting feature of a cuckoo's life is that, like a very primitive South American bird called the hoatzin, young cuckoos leave their nest about 7 to 9 days after hatching, long before they can fly. They spend the next couple of weeks clambering around the shrubbery, exploring their surroundings, still being fed by their obviously very patient parents.

We don't hear the song of the yellow-billed cuckoo nearly as often as we used to. The experts tell us they have declined in numbers by 1.6% per year over the last 30 years, a loss approaching 50%. But out west in British Columbia, Washington, and Oregon, that number has been a dreary 4.6% decline per year. Doing the math, we see they've declined past zero out there, and that is indeed the case. The cuckoos out there are what the biologists term extirpated, meaning "gone"—they aren't there anymore. That sad situation is believed to be mainly due to the loss of their favorite nesting sites—cottonwood and willow thickets along the streams of that

more arid part of our country. Dams, development, and irresponsible grazing along streams have all added up to a lack of habitat . . . and no more
yellow-billed cuckoos.

Thankfully, our eastern yellow-billed cuckoos are not quite as picky about
their nesting requirements, and we haven't been able to destroy as much
of their suitable environment. Although they're declining significantly in
numbers, they are still hanging on. I'm certainly glad. I heard the song, and
then saw a pair of cuckoos, out north of Knoxville in Union County back
earlier this season, apparently nesting. I wish them well. Hearing that song
makes me smile just as much as the music of that approaching ice cream
truck.

Summer is a pretty good thing, and the call of the rain crow is icing on
the cake.

JARFLIES AND LOCUSTS

As far as country sounds go, what noise can do a better job of bringing back the vibes of good summers past than the droning of the jarflies in the afternoon trees? They are just tuning up for the season; I heard my first one about six o'clock last Monday afternoon, the first week of July. It was a loud, long, steady hum that went on for many minutes, a sign that, sure enough in spite of everything, the seasons were progressing along in their dependable, endless way.

Now, I'm talking about our good old regular yearly cicadas here, not that rowdy crowd of 17-year locusts that have just come and gone from these parts. The 17-year guys have been widespread, but seem to occur in dense, loud, but rather localized concentrations. Over at the home of some friends, only a few miles from us, we noticed scores of dangling tips of tree limbs on several different types of deciduous trees, their leaves brown and withered. That was the work of the female 17-year locusts, which make slits in the bark of twigs where they lay their eggs. This results in the twigs' dying and often dropping to the ground, where the small locust larvae emerge and go into the ground. There they feed on root sap and wait for another 17 years to go by. They don't cause permanent damage to big trees, but enough of them can kill a small one.

Our common cicadas have a similar life cycle, as do most all of the approximately 75 species of cicadas in eastern North America. The grubs just don't stay underground as long, emerging in 1–3 years. They burrow out of the ground and climb up on trees in their thick brown shell, which splits open along the back. Out comes the big, greenish cicada, ready to sing to us on summer evenings. The male cicadas are the only ones that sing, and each species has a slightly different sound, at least to female cicadas. When the singing starts, you can send the kids out to hunt for the abandoned jarfly nymph shells on tree trunks and fenceposts—a great summer game.

The name locust causes some confusion. You will remember the Biblical plague of locusts in the Book of Exodus, chapter 10, which "covered the face of the whole Earth" and "did eat every herb of the land." Well, they were still a plague into the 1800s in the American West. They swooped down in such great numbers that the trains couldn't run on their tracks, due to the massive numbers of crushed bugs on the rails. They completely devastated all the crops, and they even ate the clothes off the clotheslines!

It turns out that Pharaoh's locusts, and those of the Great Plains farmers, weren't cicadas, but grasshoppers. They were insects in the same family as our common types of grasshoppers, and looked pretty much like them, only hungrier. Although they still show up in Africa from time to time, the ones out West have apparently all died off now, for reasons not totally clear to scientists. But everybody's glad.

A book I found several years ago entitled *Locust,* by a biologist named Jeffrey A. Lockwood, gives a lot of history about the heyday of the western locusts and how they reduced hundreds of frontier families to starvation. Among the many interesting facts related by Lockwood, we are told that North American locusts, scientific name *Melanopus spretus,* were a species distinct from locusts anywhere else in the world.

And as to how millions of insects could swarm for hundreds of miles and then just disappear, sometimes for years? The answer didn't come until the 1960s when scientists finally discovered that between swarms, the locusts assumed the shape of nice, peaceful grasshoppers that hung out, munched grass, and didn't swarm or bother anybody. Then, when the right conditions returned, they were triggered into raising the next brood with larger bodies, longer wings, a strong urge to swarm, and a monstrous appetite.

Finally, extensive field research and field testing seem to confirm that *Melanopus* is truly extinct, not just temporarily phased out. But, just like any good horror story, the author says they have found little hints that the locusts may still be present in small pockets in the high Rockies, their ancestral home, waiting . . . great, *just* great!

At any rate, it turns out that our common cicadas—jarflies, of summer music fame—as well as the 17-year locusts (there are 13-year locusts, too) are really cicadas, not locusts at all. Fortunately for us, cicadas aren't a plague, and they cause little damage of economic importance.

They provide a tasty summer treat for blue jays, cuckoos, and other birds. And along with crickets and katydids, they burst into summer song just in time to replace all the spring bird song that's rapidly fading away. So, this weekend, settle into your lawn chair in the shade, and let the serenade begin.

MOUNT LECONTE

Mount LeConte is one of my top favorite places to be outdoors. A few steps up one of the many trails, and you're as alone in a quiet, green forest with streams, waterfalls, birds, and wildflowers as if you were in some remote wilderness. So, I get considerable comfort from seeing Mount LeConte, framed by the sides of Sharp's Gap, as I drive down Interstate 75 south toward downtown Knoxville from the Powell community.

I also get a serious yearning to just keep on driving south till I pass by all my chores and errands and arrive at the mountain, and find myself trudging up a trail or hanging out in one of the big rockers on the LeConte Lodge porch, looking down on all the frenzy in the valley below.

In real estate, they say, location is everything, and Mount LeConte has a unique location. All the other high mountains that form the backbone of the Smokies lie half in Tennessee, and half in North Carolina, divided by the state line and the Appalachian Trail. Not so with Mount LeConte: It lies 6 miles north of the state line entirely in Tennessee. It is connected with that main high ridge and the Appalachian Trail by the Boulevard, a 5.4-mile ridgetop trail, a total distance of just over 8 trail miles from Newfound Gap.

Mount LeConte rises more than a mile in elevation from its base near Gatlinburg, around 1,200 feet above sea level, to its highest point at High Top, at a height of 6,594 feet, a big mountain by Eastern standards. At that altitude, it creates its own weather. Often on a sunny day down here, you can look up and see a huge shroud of storm clouds gathered around where Mount LeConte is supposed to be, dropping rain or snow on those high rocks and woods. It is the wettest place around, with nearly 90 inches of rain a year, twice Knoxville rates.

And it's cool up there. The weather station on top has never recorded a temperature over 85 degrees. The weather can change quickly, too. Often a sunny morning will turn into an afternoon of high wind and thunderstorms; a crystal clear night becomes a fog-draped, wet, dripping dawn. One late May weekend we set out in the sunshine, ate sandwiches at Trillium Gap, and then within minutes a snowstorm arrived and accompanied us the rest of the way up the mountain, every balsam tree a perfectly flocked Christmas decoration.

Besides the Boulevard, there are five other trails going up Mount LeConte: Trillium Gap, Brushy Mountain, Rainbow Falls, Bullhead, and Alum Cave. They all vary in length, steepness, number of waterfalls and stream crossings, views, kinds of birds and wildflowers, and so on. They can be back-and-forth hikes, or taken in various combinations for loop trips. We generally prefer to go up Trillium Gap in the spring, for great wildflowers and numerous birds, coming back down either Rainbow Falls or Bullhead. In the fall, we hike up and down Alum Cave for spectacular views and a 2-mile shorter route.

Although little human history took place up on Mount LeConte before the mid-1800s, it has a long history of names since then, names of places and names of people. The place names are many: Huggins Hell, Inspiration Point, Arch Rock, Peregrine Ridge, Grotto Falls, Myrtle Point. Once you've been there, often at the cost of a many-mile hike, each name brings back recollections of the day—the weather, who was along, and lots of great pictures in the memory banks.

One of the intriguing people names is that of the person for whom the mountain is named. Every source that I consulted had a different twist on it, the confusion compounded by the fact that there were two John LeContes, said to be cousins, or John and Joseph, said to be brothers. Some accounts have one of the Johns and the Joseph as one and the same person.

The consensus seems to be for Professor John LeConte (1818–1891), a teacher of physics and chemistry at Franklin College (later to become the University of Georgia). In 1858 a scientific expedition was launched to determine the heights of several of these mountains, and Professor LeConte assisted in the work, and the mountain was then named for him. The professor, by the way, supervised a munitions factory for the Confederacy during the Civil War and then went on to teach for years at the University of California in Berkeley.

A couple of other names must be mentioned. Paul J. Adams—who as a young man explored the mountain and observed its plant and animal life extensively and knew it as well as anyone ever did—in 1925 built a camp atop Mount LeConte at the request of the Great Smoky Mountain Conservation Association. There he introduced many famous and influential visitors to the wonders of the Smokies, a key effort in making the national park become a reality.

The other was Jack Huff, who in 1926 began where Adams left off and built and managed what was to become LeConte Lodge. He is famous for hiking to the top of the mountain with his elderly mother in a ladder-backed chair strapped to his back, when she became too old to hike it herself.

Mount LeConte is a wonderful, special place. For me it carries memories of snowstorms and thunderstorms, of waves of migrating warblers and mama grouse with her babies, of night skies filled with the Milky Way. I'm very grateful that it is our good fortune to have it preserved for us. And I'm certainly glad that I can see it, even briefly, on the way to town.

FLEDGING SEASON

You may be seeing and hearing some unusual bird activity in your neighborhood this time of year. It's the beginning of fledging season. Fledging is when the newly hatched eggs become feathered things that can fly (more or less) and leave their nest. Surely it's a time of great excitement and anxiety from the parent birds' point of view. I would imagine it's sort of like having four or five clueless teenage children all walk out of your house forever on the same morning.

There are two big categories of young birds, based upon what they can do when they hatch from their eggs. There are the ones called precocial, which means they can see, walk, and eat on their own, even if they're not ready for flying yet. One great example is the wood duck. As soon as they all get hatched, out of their tree cavity they go, plunging down to the ground to line up behind Mama Duck and march off to the nearest body of water. And they can swim right away, too, forming a line of little swimming fuzzballs heading down the creek.

The shorebirds have precocial young also. Little newly hatched killdeer chicks look like regular fluffy chicken chicks up on spindly long legs, but there they are, out there scurrying around trying to catch food and ready to run for cover whenever the always-watchful mother killdeer gives a danger sign.

The other main category of young birds, which includes all your usual songbirds, is called altricial. These babies hatch out blind, featherless, and helpless, wretched-looking little things that only a mother could love. The parents go into a frenzy of feeding that often lasts for 2 full weeks, until the babies fledge and learn to find food for themselves. The parents feed and feed and feed, and the babies grow and grow and grow. As they get bigger, the babies grow feathers and begin to flutter about in the nest.

And then finally the big day comes. After a lot of encouraging chirping and calling back and forth by the two parents, the young fledglings take the big leap, one by one, flying shakily off the nest, often crashing into trees or walls on their first try.

Fledglings are usually fairly close to the size of their parents when they leave the nest, but with a lot of shorter, fluffed-up, and often out-of-place feathers. They usually do not have fully grown tail feathers, and they present themselves to the world with short little tails and often very questionable flying abilities.

Hopefully, they make it up into a tree and away from the family cat, now in a state of heightened alert after hearing all the chips and chirps going on. Then the parents continue to watch and feed the youthful flyers for another week or two, until they are finally fully independent and out on their own.

In the meantime, it's really fun to watch (and hear) the goings-on. Spouse and I watched two different newly fledged batches of dark-eyed juncos in the Smokies last week. Little shorttailed copies of the adult birds were taking brief, random flights from bush to bush, while the very nervous parents flew all around, chirping and chipping their alarm calls.

It's always a big event when our wrens or bluebirds fledge off a new batch of birds. We see the bluebirds especially, for several days afterward, with their fluffy spotted unkempt youngsters, lined up side by side on a tree limb where the parents can keep an eye on them and feed them.

The visual goings-on are accompanied by unusual noises. Newly fledged baby birds give pitiful begging calls, the likes of which you will never hear any other time of year. Crows, in particular, converse in a language of whines and squawks that people sometimes don't even realize are coming from crows.

For birds of prey, the process of becoming independent takes much longer. The young birds have to be taught serious flying and hunting maneuvers. Being a successful hunter is a learned skill and a life-or-death matter. As mentioned earlier, some estimates are that only about 25% of young hawks learn hunting well enough to survive!

Peregrine falcons are mighty hunters and awesome flyers. They have been clocked at speeds of 200 miles per hour in one of their power dives, and they make their living by knocking other birds out of the sky. When young peregrines fledge off the nest, they must be taught the utmost in flying skills. While they are still being fed and taught under the watchful eyes of their parents, they engage in free-wheeling aerial acrobatics and dogfights, all aimed at teaching them the skills they will need to survive as high-speed hunters. All this exciting activity is accompanied by an array of screaming and screeching, from parents and young alike.

So it's an interesting season right now. Strange-looking new birds are bumping around doing strange flying and making strange sounds. Keep your eyes peeled, and you may get to observe a bird family in the process of trying to get their kids off on the right foot. Or wing.

MR. NO-SHOULDERS

On one recent Saturday morning, I looked out my dining room window to see if anything was happening at my goldfinch feeder. A row of thorny shrubs grow up to window level along that end of the house, and that morning I noticed something different about the shrubs.

Comfortably stretched out across the tops of the branches was a shiny, black, 4-foot-long black racer. He looked at us looking at him, and when he figured that we weren't going to try to catch him or eat him, he continued carefully on his way, easing through the branches without causing the slightest movement. This particular snake had shiny, smooth scales and a uniform, gray-brown colored belly, typical for the black racer. They are easily confused with the most commonly seen snake in these parts, the black rat snake.

For those of you sufficiently intrigued to look at one closely, you will find that black rat snakes have little ridges, or keels, on each of their scales, and they have a black-and-white checkerboard pattern on their belly. And in cross section, the rat snakes are flat on the bottom, like a loaf of bread, while black racers are round in cross section, like most other snakes.

Both of these species lay eggs, and when the babies hatch, they are quite different in appearance from the adults. The young snakes are brownish and patterned with alternating dark splotches down their backs. Because of this, they are often thought to be copperheads and immediately pounded flat with the nearest blunt object.

Both of these species are excellent climbers and are often found foraging around in shrubs and trees, searching for insects, tree frogs, lizards, and bird's eggs. They are active as long as the weather is warm enough, and then they den up during cold weather in some protected place, often in the company of copperheads and rattlesnakes.

Probably no creature on Earth is as feared and disliked as poor Mr. No-Shoulders. Snakes have been getting a bad rap ever since Eve said, "The serpent beguiled me, and I did eat." It seems that the first urge everyone has upon encountering a snake is to kill it—"Get the hoe, Ma, there's a snake in the garden!" Never mind that it's out there eating the insects and rodents that are eating the garden!

Snakes are indeed beneficial to us, eating mostly rodents such as mice, voles, rats, chipmunks, and squirrels and insects, frogs, lizards, and other snakes including venomous ones. Occasionally, they will eat birds' eggs and nestlings. Sometimes they will indeed raid a songbird's nest, or eat a hen's egg or two, but on balance they eat a lot more troublesome things than good ones.

For years, my Granny kept a longstanding, somewhat uneasy truce with a really big black rat snake that lived in her barn. It would occasionally eat a chicken egg, but she never had to deal with a single barn rat, and she felt like she was getting the better end of the deal.

There is no end to the fables and tales about these snakes. Here's one example: Black racers have a stinger in their tail, and can put their tail in their mouth to form a hoop, and roll downhill chasing people. This explains one of their folk names, "hoop snake." If the racer doesn't catch the person, it will sting a tree in frustration. And when it does that, the tree always dies.

One story about black rat snakes is that they will cross breed with copperheads, producing offspring that look like black snakes but are venomous—the legendary poisonous black snake. They have been said to be able to suck milk from cows, and to charm birds and children. And they are believed to be able to guide copperheads and rattlesnakes to safety, from which story they earned the local name of "pilot snakes."

With no arms or legs, snakes are different. They are mysterious, and the venomous ones can be dangerous. But all in all, they are a big part of our outdoor environment, and an important cog in the wheel of our ecology. If you will just observe them for a while at a little bit of a distance, you will find that they are interesting and fun to watch. Do them, and all of us, a huge favor. Don't kill the next one you see.

JUST ORDINARY BIRDS?

There aren't too many folks out there who would turn up their nose at a big skillet of fried chicken. Or how about a nice plump turkey with all the trimmings? Ducks make good eating—they taste sort of like chicken with extra fat—and a lot of people like the wilder flavors of dove and quail.

But what about squab? Once a popular dish for special occasions in Victorian England, Irma Rombauer's *All New Joy of Cooking* says they are also highly regarded in France and that their meat is dark, rich, tender, and succulent. Rombauer then gives four different recipes for preparing your squab.

Squab are farm-raised young pigeons that have not yet learned to fly. They dress out at a pound or so and are available in this country if you know where to look.

Now, I doubt that Col. Sanders and Chick-Fil-A are worried about competition from the squab industry. I was just trying to find something good to say about pigeons. And wouldn't you know, I needn't have worried; a little digging in the books brought forth all sorts of interesting things about pigeons!

The proper English name for our common city pigeons was, until recently, "rock dove." Now it is officially "rock pigeon," to correspond with what they've always been called in the Old World. Over there the wild ancestors of our pigeons typically nested on rocky cliffs, hence the name. People who study such things have determined that pigeons were the first animal ever to be domesticated by human beings. John K. Terres in his *Encyclopedia of North American Birds* tells us that terracotta figurines of domestic pigeons have been found in Iraq, dating back to 4500 BC, while chickens weren't fully domesticated by the Chinese until around 2000 BC.

Although first raised for their meat, they later were prized for an unusual, genetically programmed skill they were found to possess: a fierce homing instinct. These same, common, city pigeons are also the famous "homing pigeons" or "carrier pigeons." It turns out that when a domestic pigeon is taken some distance from its home loft and released, it almost invariably finds its way back home again, navigating by the sun, magnetic fields, and visual landmarks in ways still not clearly understood. Homing pigeons are trained by taking them farther and farther from their home roost and releasing them to return. They are powerful flyers and have been clocked at speeds above 85 miles per hour and known to return home from distances as great as 1,000 miles.

By attaching a message to the bird's leg, you had yourself a biological airmail service that was fast, dependable, and essentially unnoticed by human eyes, or, later, by radar. Carrier pigeons were used by Julius Caesar to report back to Rome the news of his conquest of Gaul. Alexander the Great used them in his military operations, as did Hannibal.

Carrier pigeons were used by the ancient Greeks to spread news about the results of the early Olympic Games. When Napoleon was defeated at Waterloo on June 18, 1815, a carrier pigeon took the news to England 4 days ahead of the same news carried by horse and ship, the fastest conventional means of communication in those days.

Amazingly, military use of the carrier pigeons continued up into recent times. Terres tells us that some 5,000 homing pigeons were used in World War I, and 36,000 pigeons served the US armed forces overseas in World War II. One famous pigeon named GI Joe was decorated for gallantry after saving an Allied-occupied Italian village from bombing!

The story goes like this: Plans were made for the Allies to bomb the Italian village of Calvi Vecchia, thought to be occupied by German troops. It was later learned that Calvi Vecchia had just been taken by friendly troops from the British 169th Infantry Brigade. With no other means of immediate communication available in the situation, the American homing pigeon GI Joe was dispatched with this critical information and arrived just as preparations to launch the bombing run were being made.

It was estimated that over a thousand lives were saved by GI Joe's speedy and accurate mission. The bird was decorated in a ceremony at the Tower of London with the British honor, the Pickin Medal of Valor, the first non-British recipient to receive that medal. Back home after the war, GI Joe lived in retirement with several of his fellow feathered heroes. He died in 1961, at the ripe old age of 18.

Rock pigeons were introduced to the New World by settlers very early on, probably in Nova Scotia in 1606 and Virginia in 1621. They are fruitful birds, sometimes producing as many as five broods of young in a year, and now are abundant and common across America.

They are especially abundant in cities, where they are often looked upon as a nuisance. The big problem is their large numbers and innumerable droppings around public buildings. But lots of people like having them around and enjoy feeding them in parks.

Pigeons also provide an excellent food source for that master bird predator taking up residence more and more often in the cities, the peregrine falcon. Its power dive at nearly 200 miles per hour can make short work of a bird going only 85. No doubt the military guys in charge of the homing pigeons worried a lot about falcons!

So, notice the pigeons and don't disparage, but tip your hat; their ancestors have proudly played important roles in human history for thousands of years. And other than being a little messy, they're really not much of a bother to anybody. Squab, anyone?

VARMINTS AND FRIENDS

One recent morning, I was out in the yard early to get ahead of the heat, seeing about the grass and so on. I had just congratulated myself that the deer didn't seem to be eating my hostas and shrubs this year and was taking a spin on the lawnmower. As I zipped by one of the walnut trees along the way, something on one of the branches caught my eye. Closer inspection revealed that one whole leaf, made up of over a dozen leaflets and their stem, was engulfed in furry caterpillars.

Well, now, I didn't think anything would eat a walnut tree. As I mowed along and pondered that discovery, I came upon another, smaller walnut tree that had been completely defoliated, not a leaf to its name! And a couple of other nearby trees had masses of caterpillars either on the leaves or in a big clump on the trunk. Houston, we have a problem.

I called for help where I usually go for pest and varmint help, the county Extension Agent's office. A nice, calm-sounding young lady—whose walnut trees were apparently not being consumed by alien beings—asked me for a description of the critters. I told her they were hairy, an inch long, mahogany colored, with no webs or tents and she immediately declared them to be walnut caterpillars. She allowed that I was the first person to be reporting them this season, that the usual spray would take care of things, and that the defoliated tree would probably recover.

As I was talking with her on the phone, I gazed out into the backyard, and there strolled a mama doe and new fawn, the mother undoubtedly showing her baby the location of the tastiest hostas in the neighborhood. Some days just seem to go like that, varmints large and small.

But back to the walnut worms. The episode left me reflecting upon the whole caterpillar situation. We're all familiar with the tent caterpillars that decimate the leaves of our cherry trees in the spring, and the fall webworms that similarly attack various trees in the fall, defoliating entire limbs and sometimes whole trees. Sawfly caterpillars prefer meals of pine needles and smell like turpentine when you squash one. And then there are those huge 2-pound tomato worms that strip the foliage off your prize tomato plant in one night's work.

So, here's the paradox: One of nature's loveliest creatures, the butterfly, comes from a caterpillar. Caterpillars are the larval form of all butterflies and moths. They are eating machines, designed to convert foliage into caterpillar flesh from tiny egg to adult, ready to become a butterfly or moth. And then, in a process still not fathomed by modern science, they are transformed into beautiful, harmless creatures that fly, sip nectar from flowers, mate, lay eggs, and die.

So, it's the same dilemma as determining what's a wild flower and what's a weed. Caterpillars eating my tree are bad; butterflies flitting around my field are good. Maybe we can sort it out, at least partially.

There are over 11,000 species of butterflies and moths in North America. Some of them occur in numbers that, along with their appetites for particular crops, make them a serious problem for the farmers producing our food crops. We can appreciate the scope of the problem when we discover our garden suddenly infested with potato bugs or cabbage worms. Imagine finding 100 acres of potatoes or cabbages that your livelihood depended upon infested by worms!

The larvae of sawflies and gypsy moths can wreck stands of timber that would otherwise be destined to become lumber for houses or wood for furniture. And the battle against the larvae of the clothes moth, munching on our favorite sweaters and blankets, has been going on ever since the first piece of woolen cloth was woven.

These problems have to be addressed on a large scale. It turns out that the majority of them are being caused by the larvae of moths, not butterflies; there are many more species of moths than butterflies. Moths are generally nocturnal, less colorful, and a lot less familiar to most of us than butterflies. The larvae of butterflies are eating machines, too, but they occur mostly as scattered individuals, not big hungry masses. Butterflies have a lot going for them.

As is so often the case these days, they also have a lot going *against* them. A number of species are getting scarce, even endangered. Several have gone extinct. Destruction of habitat, insecticides, climate change, and a general lack of awareness of butterflies and their needs are all part of the problem.

One group of folks involved with the protection, enjoyment, and awareness of our butterflies is the North American Butterfly Association, NABA. Headquartered in Morriston, New Jersey, they publish a quarterly journal called *American Butterflies*, which provides information on different species in different areas of the country, how to attract butterflies to your garden, where to go butterfly watching, and how to photograph them. As previously mentioned in "A Birding Hotspot," they have built a National Butterfly Center in Mission, Texas, near the Rio Grande River. It features a big, information-filled visitor's center and acres of butterfly-friendly gardens that attract scores of common, as well as rare, butterflies.

On a more local note, there are a lot of things we all should learn about and do to protect our local butterflies. There are a lot more species out there than you might realize, over 600 kinds of butterflies alone, found in North America. And those eating-machine caterpillars? Well, one thing I've come to realize is that if you want to attract lots of butterflies, you don't just plant flowers for the adults to sip nectar from; you need to plant things that the caterpillars like to eat. And then keep in mind that it's OK for those worms to eat part of your garden!

A majority of our local butterfly caterpillars eat stuff you'll never miss—tree leaves, weed and grass leaves, and the like. But some are a lot pickier. They like specific plants to feed on, and if you want certain butterflies, you plant things their caterpillars like to eat. Once you get to know them, caterpillars are fascinating critters, too! They come in an amazing assortment of shapes, sizes, and colors, fun to find and observe. So, you may end up planting garden plants that are the favorite food of some of your favorite caterpillars, just so those worms can eat them! A lot of people are doing that these days. It's probably something your grandmother would be shaking her head over.

Butterflies, like flowers, are one of nature's ways of decorating the world for us. Learn more about them, and you may find yourself enjoying them even more than you would have thought.

DOLLY WHO?

Name recognition is a part of our modern-day lives. Around East Tennessee, for example, if you should mention the name Dolly, everybody knows exactly who you mean, even without a last name. And you'd be right, most of the time. We've recently become acquainted with another Dolly; this one is named Dolly Sods. This one happens to be a place, not a person. While it's amazing and memorable, it probably lacks quite a bit in the household name recognition department. Maybe we can help with that.

I had read about Dolly Sods in a copy of *West Virginia Magazine* some time ago and had been curious to see it ever since. Since we were scheduled for a birding tour of Minnesota and North Dakota beginning in early June, Spouse and I decided to bird watch our way up to Minneapolis by way of Virginia, West Virginia, Ohio, and Michigan so we could visit Dolly Sods along the way.

We're talking West Virginia here, about 350 miles from Powell, Tennessee. It's really not all that long a trip. We have friends who go up there for trout fishing, and our youth group goes skiing up there in the winter, at Snowshoe. In spite of the modest distance, once you're there it seems to be a place long ago and far away, with lots of mountains, views, trees, and few people. Not a bad combination!

Eastern West Virginia is high, rugged country with lots of hills, valleys, and streams. I've noticed that there are no straight stretches of roads longer than a quarter-mile. The plants and animals are ones often found much farther north, in New England, say, or in southern Canada.

We picked what we thought would be four of the most interesting features in this most interesting area for our attention, and we were certainly not disappointed. They are all found mostly within the huge Monongahela National Forest.

At the southern end, we found the Cranberry Glades Botanical Area. (Don't ask what it's near; like the rest of them it's not near anything!) The 750-acre wetland and bog is the largest area of its kind anywhere south of the bogs in Canada. The ground underfoot is a spongy mass of peat—partially decayed vegetation. A half-mile boardwalk wanders through the bog so that you can see all the unusual plants and critters without getting mired up. There are wild orchids, acres of cranberry vines, and the carnivorous plants—sundews and pitcher plants—that snack on flies and bugs.

Then, we drove north from the bogs along spectacular West Virginia Route 150, the Highland Scenic Highway. Open only in the summer, the highway rolls along the mountaintops, with panoramic views looking as far away as Virginia. There are big scenic turnouts with picnic areas, hiking trails, and meadows. We saw bald eagles, singing mourning warblers, and ravens. It was so impressive we did part of it twice!

About 90 miles of scenic highways and byways north of the Cranberry Glades, you come upon Canaan Valley. Named for the Biblical Promised Land, it is pronounced ka-NANE by the locals. Back in the nineteenth century, it was very remote; it wasn't settled until the late 1800s. It is the largest high elevation valley east of the Rockies. Once a wild land of dense hemlock, spruce, and hardwood forests, the Canaan Valley proved to indeed be the Promised Land for the timber barons. It suffered the same ravages by the timber industry that our Great Smokies did. By 1925, every marketable tree had been cut. The brush burned in great wildfires, and the soil washed away. The land has recovered very slowly.

Then in 1994, the Canaan Valley National Wildlife Refuge was established, the 500th for the United States and the first for West Virginia. It now covers more than 16,000 acres, including some 5,600 acres of unique bogs and wetlands. The Refuge houses the Canaan Valley State Resort Park, with such amenities as golf, pool, a nice lodge, and hiking trails to its south; and the scenic waterfalls and gorges of Blackwater Falls State Park to its north. And it has a bird list of nearly 200 species!

With all the scenery, lodge, and birds to enjoy, it was hard to leave the Canaan Valley, but we knew that just on the other side of the mountain our fourth target area, Dolly Sods, awaited. So, on a nice, blue-sky June morning, we headed up a very rural (read: steep, narrow, and winding) road to the beginning of the Dolly Sods Wilderness Area. The elevation at the entrance sign was 2,700 feet; from there a better-grade dirt road took us to the top at 4,700 feet, for the 15-mile drive bordering the edge of the wilderness, along Forest Road 75.

Dolly Sods was named for a family of German settlers, the Dahles, who grazed their cattle on the vast open grassy areas that developed after all the trees were cut in the early 1900s, areas the locals called sods. A designated wilderness area within the Monongahela National Forest, it is open only to foot traffic and backcountry camping. Forest Road 75 along the eastern edge of the wilderness gives us less-bushwhacking types a wonderful glimpse of the wilderness, as well as great views off the top of the escarpment to the east.

We saw lots of birds along Forest Road 75, many of them of more northerly species. We saw winter-storm–tortured evergreens, luscious pinkster azaleas, and the feature for which the Sods are most famous, untold thousands of acres of blueberry bushes. I think every blueberry bush everywhere wants to go to Dolly Sods when it dies— blueberry Heaven. They weren't even blooming when we were there, but the locals told us that in late summer you can go up there and pick blueberries forever—if you don't mind sharing them with the bears!

Dolly Sods exceeded our expectations. It's up near the top of the world in those parts. It's one of those rare places where there aren't any cars, ATVs, or dirt bikes. It belongs to the birds, the bears, and the blueberry bushes. It's a place to look and to listen. We human beings need places like that. This particular human being does, at least. I'm glad I met Dolly Sods.

MOSQUITO HAWKS

Ebony jewelwing, swamp speedwing, twin-spotted spiketail, black-shouldered spinyleg. Are these creatures from the latest special effects, aliens-consuming-the-world movie at your local theater? Nope, they're dragonflies, another really remarkable group of flying insects out there besides butterflies. And, as an added bonus, they love to eat mosquitoes . . . but more on that in a moment.

For sheer numbers of people in the field, I'm sure nothing surpasses the phenomenon of bird watching, or birding, as birders call their sport. Millions of individuals are out there, observing, counting, and making lists. But sometimes birders run out of winged friends to see. In offseason, on hot summer days, on just bad days, there may not be much shaking birdwise. So, some birders don't just go home, they look for something else to watch.

The next thing on nature's plate for them would be wildflowers, if it's the right time of year, or butterflies, if they're in the right place at the right time of day. And butterflying is now a booming hobby. Well, now, butterflies are amazing and beautiful, with lots of appealing features, but for this birder, and a growing number of enthusiasts, there is another group of flyers out there that will really test your eyesight and reflexes: those dragonflies. Let's train our binoculars on them here for a minute!

Dragonflies have been around for a long time, a whole lot longer than possums and dinosaurs, right up there for longevity with everybody's favorite, the cockroaches. There are beautifully preserved fossils of dragonflies (and roaches) going back to the Carboniferous period, roughly 300 million years

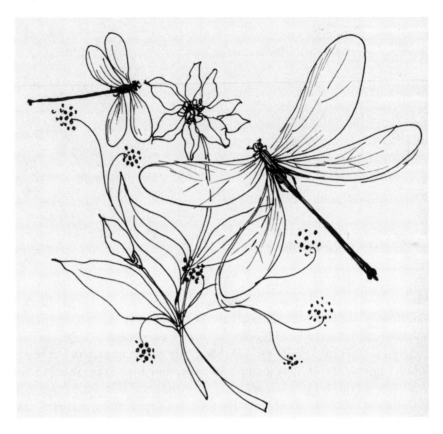

ago. In fact, there were some really big insects flying around the swamps in that era. Some fossil dragonflies from those times sport wingspans measuring a whopping 28 inches!

To have survived this long and prospered, you'd think they must be well equipped for getting along in the world, and they are. Unlike possums, which have made it through the eons by eating anything and having zillions of babies, the dragonflies survive with speed, quickness, excellent eyesight . . . and scary, predatory larvae.

Fly fishermen and other close observers of life in nice, clean, rocky streams recognize dragonfly larvae. They live in various spots in the water—in the bottom sand, on vegetation, behind rocks. But they all have a common weapon: a big, hinged lower jaw with graspers at the ends, that folds up against their face and then shoots out in a fraction of a second to nab their prey. They eat other aquatic critters, insects, and the like, and can even grab small minnows. After terrorizing the stream where they live for varying periods of time, depending on species, the larvae metamorphose into adult dragonflies, ready for some *real* predation.

For vision, the dragonflies have a pair of huge, compound eyes made up of as many as 56,000 transparent lenses, perfect for detection of tiny (mosquito-sized) bits of movement, from as far away as 30 yards. They have a neck, like a praying mantis. As they sit or fly, they very quickly, and constantly, look up, down, sideways, ever alert for a possible meal on the wing. And flying? They zoom around at speeds of up to 20 miles an hour and border on the impossible for a person to catch.

As they fly, the dragonflies hold their legs down beneath their body to form a basket, which they use to capture small flying prey. Then the tasty morsel gets passed up to the jaws, where it is chomped up and eaten, frequently on the wing, without missing a wingbeat. They eat millions of mosquitoes, keeping bogs, ponds, and marshes habitable for the rest of us with their healthy appetites. They may eat critters even larger, though, including other dragonflies – they are indeed fierce predators.

We mentioned a few of the many interesting common names for various species of dragonflies. The old folk names for dragonflies are even more interesting. Folk names for things are catchy, descriptive, and easy to remember; that's why they survive and get handed down through the generations. The name "dragonflies" itself certainly fits their personality and behavior. They've been called many other names in various places.

"Mosquito Hawk" is as accurate as a name can be. Dragonflies really are mosquito hawks, zipping through swarms of mosquitoes and harvesting them straight out of the air. This certainly is a big service to us humans who prefer to have our blood remain in our bodies as we enjoy being outdoors.

"Horse Stinger" comes from the fact that dragonflies were often observed out in the fields with the horses, some of which were seen to have bleeding wounds on their backs. The wounds were actually inflicted by voracious horseflies, and the dragonflies were hanging around to eat the horseflies, not the horses. But the name stuck.

"Devil's Darning-needle"? Apparently, this name comes from their long, pointy shape and the way they hover and zip around. And legend has it that they would sometimes sew up the lips or ears of misbehaving children!

There are seven families of dragonflies in North America, plus three of their cousins, the damselflies, and over 435 separate species. They come in a huge variety of colors and patterns. Often, like the birds, the males and females of a given species will sport completely different colors—confusing until you learn a bit more about them. A nice pond or marshy area is prime dragonfly territory since they lay their eggs in or near water, but you can find them in pastures, parks, and fields of wildflowers as well.

I'm finding that digitally photographing them is really fun, if challenging. With luck and patience, you can move up much closer to dragonflies than you can to birds, and they will sometimes cooperate for a nice still closeup. Then, you can take them home on your memory card, look them up, and identify them at your leisure!

With increasing interest in dragonflies, there are some good field guides out there to help with identification. Try the Stokes' *Beginner's Guide to Dragonflies*, or Dunkle's *Dragonflies Through Binoculars*. And by the way, a pair of close-focus binoculars are a big help with your observations, too. There are good models now that focus nicely on objects as close as 7 feet or better.

So, there you are: another good reason to go out the door, folks. Spring flowers gone? Birds not singing? Try some dragonflies on for size!

PURPLE MARTINS

Purple martins are birds that many people wouldn't even notice. With their curved, swept-back wings and dark coloration, at a casual glance they could easily be mistaken for starlings. As they gather in groups on powerlines this time of year they suggest a flock of generic "blackbirds," but there is a lot more to these fast-flying aerial bug-zappers than a bunch of starlings.

Of six species of swallows that can occur in the Knoxville area, purple martins are the largest and the darkest. The males are deep purple with black wings and tail; females and first-year birds are dark with grayish undersides. They feed almost exclusively on flying insects, which they catch by the zillions on the wing, often 500 feet or more in the sky.

Purple martins are migratory birds. Their wintering grounds are primarily in Brazil, but some winter on up to the north coast of South America. They spend half their year there, then half in North America, from Florida north to southern Canada. Their average date of arrival in Knox County is around March 8th to March 12th, though it can be weeks earlier than that.

And that arrival date is eagerly anticipated, speculated, competed for (like having the first ripe tomato), compared, and recorded by a whole army of folks across eastern North America, who are the enthusiastic hosts for the colonies of these birds.

One memorable Saturday, I spent a very pleasant couple of hours with my favorite martin fanciers, Charlie and Percy Freeman, out Strawberry Plains way, a few miles east of Knoxville. They lived on a little creek that watered Percy's excellent garden—tomatoes, okra, 12-foot-high corn. And peering

out from a good-sized patch of low-growing vegetation: big, green martin gourds. Natural gourds only last 2 or 3 years, according to Charlie, and he should know. He said the new plastic ones will last indefinitely, but the birds prefer the real ones. Charlie and Percy put up their first six martin gourds in 1982. That year was a record for the martins' earliest arrival date; they showed up on February 12th! Charlie and Percy called J. B. Owen, Knoxville's beloved long-time bird guru to report the date, and he was duly impressed. Percy recalled him asking, "Are you sure?" She was *sure*. That date is still on record in a compilation of arrival dates for Knox County birds!

The Freemans' colony had grown to 30 gourds and a six-apartment house. That year they were hosts to about 30 pairs of birds; the birds showed up on March 9th, and they raised a big bunch of new purple martins. Like most martin people, Charlie and Percy spoke of their birds as if they were members of the family from way out of town, in for a treasured visit. They talked of their habits and behavior, of their successes and their problems.

Hundreds of thousands of purple martins spread out across eastern North America every year, and that requires a lot of housing to make nests in. The most fascinating thing about martins is their almost complete dependence on human beings to provide their nesting facilities. Apparently because humans have been providing houses for them for hundreds of years, the martins, at least those east of the Rocky Mountains, nest only in houses and gourds provided for them by people. Indeed, it is so unusual to find martins nesting in a natural cavity that one such occurrence was written up in a bird publication in an article entitled "Purple Martins Discovered Nesting in a Florida Tree Snag."

Martin people are passionate about their tenants and their housing. Some colonies number in the hundreds. There are never-ending discussions about the best designs for housing, the best safeguards against predators, and the best ways to provide extra food or nesting materials.

It turns out that martins are fairly picky about location. Since they require tons of flying insects to eat, especially when raising their four or five young birds in the nest, they need a good-sized area that has bugs, such as a huge open field or meadow area, a lake, or a marsh, within a mile or two of their home. And they like housing with no big trees or bushes close by, so they have a good clear shot at their nest hole as they come zooming in at high speed; this helps them evade hawks that may be lurking around in hopes of nabbing a slow-approaching bird. Accustomed to humans as they are, though, they insist on housing that is located within 100 feet of a manmade structure such as a house, barn, or shed.

When the martins arrive, they pair up, select an apartment, build a nest, and lay eggs. After the eggs hatch, the parents get busy in earnest. They swoop back and forth, bringing ever-larger mouthfuls of food to their fast-growing young. (You folks with teenagers in the house will understand this stage in the birds' lives!) Charlie and Percy took me out to a friend's house a couple of years ago. He had a colony of 300 or so pairs of birds, and it was the height of feeding season. It is hard to describe the intensity of the comings and goings, and the chirping and conversation, as that zooming swarm of dark swallows filled his yard!

The young birds are on their own in 5 weeks, and then, like having a house full of visitors who all go home, it's over. The birds drift away, small groups at a time, to join up with the big flocks heading south, July through October. They're usually all gone from here by August.

There are a couple of famous places where purple martins gather into enormous roosting flocks before they head across the water for South America.

Two sites, at either end of the Lake Ponchartrain Causeway in southern Louisiana, may host as many as 250,000 martins in June and July. Another huge gathering of martins can be found on an island in Lake Murray, west of Columbia, South Carolina. It is estimated to have a whopping 750,000 martins at the peak of the season!

Interested in having a purple martin colony? You can get a lot more details from Don and Lillian Stokes' nice book *Stokes Purple Martin Book*. Or log onto the website of the Purple Martin Conservation Association (http://www.purplemartin.org). With patience, energy, enthusiasm, and some luck, you could be host to a thriving colony of those wonderful, swarming dark swallows.

Charlie and Percy's purple martin season was winding down when I was there; only a few lingering birds were still around as reminders of another busy season. But it was always a joy and a blessing to visit the Freemans, hear their stories, and see their birds. And, those big bags full of okra, tomatoes, and fresh-picked corn weren't so bad, either.

THE COAST OF MAINE

Spouse and I were on the road again for the second time in June, this time on a trip to Maine and New Hampshire. Our primary objective was birding, naturally, but people have been traveling to the coast of Maine to escape the heat of summer ever since there were roads to enable them to get there, and finding a cool place had been a consideration in our travel plans as well.

The Maine coast has been a summer refuge for generations of folks of all walks of life. There are summer houses everywhere, tucked into the wooded shorelines and coves, from modest to magnificent. A lot of them have been converted now into quaint and comfortable inns and bed & breakfasts.

If the lodging is good, the eating is even better. You can get a pound-and-a-half of fresh steamed lobster with all the trimmings for about $10, but you'll have to wear some shoes and a shirt.

When you first see the coast of Maine, you'll know right away that you're not in Myrtle Beach. For one thing, there aren't that many people, or at least they're so spread out that you don't see very many of them at a time. For another, there's not much of a beach—just evergreen forest, rocky cliffs and shores, and ocean.

The coast is full of inlets and coves, so there are hundreds of miles of shoreline. You can access the coast in lots of places, especially in the numerous, lovely state parks all along the way. The weather is generally mild in summer, but if it gets too warm, just get out on a boat ride and you'll be pulling on your Polartec woolies within the first mile or so. The ocean water in Maine is like ice water, and the wind coming off it is like a super air conditioner. Don't plan on frolicking in the surf in Maine!

Birding isn't the only thing you can do in Maine. There is enough scenery and shopping for any dedicated vacationer. The tourist destination Bar Harbor is surrounded by the spectacular Acadia National Park, and the legendary L. L. Bean Sporting Goods store is open 24 hours a day, 7 days a week, closed only on Thanksgiving and Christmas. And the road warrior can drive to Quoddy Head, the easternmost tip of Maine, the first place the morning sun hits the United States each day.

But, as I said, it was the birding that took us to Maine on this trip. The northern latitudes, the gloomy, dense spruce woods, mossy wet bogs, and fogbound rocky coast all make for diverse and excellent birding. And it was! We saw 133 species of birds in the week we were there, many of them northern specialties such as common loons, giving their haunting call across the lakes; gray jays, flying down out of the spruce trees to eat a peanut out of your hand; and the rare Bicknell's thrush, singing at dusk, high on a Mount Washington mountainside that still had lingering patches of snow.

One of my favorites on this trip stands out in my birder's memory. I'll share it with you because you will never *ever*, unless we have a sudden Ice Age come upon us, see them anywhere near Tennessee.

The bird is the elusive spruce grouse. Now, we have ruffed grouse here in Tennessee. Some of you may know, or be, grouse hunters. You know that our grouse are few and far between, hard to see until they explode up in front of you in the—up until that moment—still, quiet woods, and then they're gone. About the only good looks we get at a ruffed grouse is in the Smoky Mountains in the spring, when the mama grouse are tending a batch of a dozen or so fluffy babies, calling to them constantly and fussing over them to keep them together.

But compared to our ruffed grouse, the spruce grouse is one of those eccentric relatives that you hear your friends talk about on occasion. They live in dense, dark spruce forests so thick you can hardly walk through them . . . moss on trees, moss on the ground. And they are widely dispersed, only a few per square mile.

Unlike the ruffed grouse, the spruce grouse, once you find one, are almost tame. They will take to a spruce tree and just sit and watch you, even if you get up almost directly under them. Reportedly, the Native Americans would harvest them by just hitting them with a stick. The only thing that saves them from being hunted to extinction is their taste; they feed mostly on spruce buds and twigs, which makes their meat taste like turpentine. So, nobody much cares for hunting them. Who wants to spend a day looking for a bird you can kill with a stick and that tastes like turpentine?

Anyway, after days of off-and-on attempts, we finally ran across a spruce grouse. It was on Campobello Island. Actually a part of Canada, the island is connected to Maine by a short bridge. Franklin and Eleanor Roosevelt had their summer home there. The Roosevelts' summer home, a pleasant, rustic place, is open to the public. I found it to be an interesting place, with a glimpse into the personal family life of a world-famous couple.

But the spruce grouse was even more interesting. Out in the spruce woods, it performed as advertised. It ran along the ground for a ways, then up it went into a tree, and there it sat while we took photos and murmured in admiration. It was one of those wonderful birding experiences where you finally get to see a long-sought bird, and you get to observe it as long as you care to, and then go away with the bird still sitting there, as if to say, "So, what's the big deal with you people? You act like you've never seen a spruce grouse before."

We had lunch that day at a little place recommended to us by the locals, that didn't even have a sign out front. We ate a selection of lobster stew, fresh-caught haddock fish and chips, and homemade pie. There were pictures on the wall of the family that owned the place, three generations of which had been involved in the fishing/canning business. One of the patrons, a young man, began explaining what the photos were all about. It turned out, he was the husband of our waitress, who was the granddaughter of the owners. Birding has its many unforgettable moments.

FLEDERMAUS IN TROUBLE

On August 14th, I had called it a day and was heading into the house just at dusk, when I was stopped in my tracks by a sight I hadn't seen all summer long. There, over our side yard of newly mown grass, zipping back and forth with their amazingly agile fluttering flight were two bats!

They were very busy at what bats do, scooping up mosquitoes, moths, and gnats from the darkening sky. Bats, of course, are the only mammals on Earth that can fly. And they don't just flap along somewhere; they arc speedy, dodgy masters of the air, able to turn on a dime and leave you nine cents change. And with each feint and turn, there's a good chance that one more pesky insect has been eliminated from your evening sky.

There are a thousand or so species of bats around the globe, most of them living in the tropics, where they find a good, steady supply of food year round. There are about 45 species in North America; we have some 16 kinds in Tennessee. The majority of them, like the ones we see in these parts, eat mostly insects, but there are also species of bats, larger ones, that eat mostly fruit. The large fruit eaters include the largest of the bats, the huge flying foxes of Asia, Africa, and Australia that weigh in at 4 pounds and have a wingspan of 6 feet. Imagine a few of those roosting in your attic!

A few species of bats have adapted to eating fish. They swoop down and catch a fish off the surface of a tropical stream and fly off to a perch somewhere to munch on their catch. And then there are the vampire bats, which, as everyone knows, like a snack of blood now and then. (They bite and lap it up; they don't really suck it out of their victim's veins, like Dracula).

Bats have some science fiction–like features that have a lot to do with our fascination with them. Their amazing bat wings consist of thin membranes of skin stretched across their greatly elongated forearms and fingers, plus more membrane between their hind limbs that help navigate their erratic flight. And seeing in the dark? While the big fruit-eating bats do see well in the dark, our small insect-eating bats use an amazing system called echolocation. Just like a submarine listening to the pings from its sonar in search of an enemy, the bats put out a constant stream of chirps of such high frequency that human ears can't hear them.

The bats' ears are so sensitive that they must automatically close with each sound, so their own noise doesn't deafen them. Then they open their ears to hear the sounds bounce back from rocks, trees, power lines, and prey. They automatically compensate for the speed and direction of a flying mosquito, calculate its exact location, and unerringly nab it at high speed, in the dark. And all this happens in milliseconds. Remarkable, indeed!

Through the ages, bats have been given many names around the world, mostly relating them to mice. The old English name was "flittermouse," a pretty apt description. People of many other languages called them names with "mouse" in mind also. My favorite has always been the German name for them, *fledermaus* or "flying mouse." Johann Straus wrote an opera in 1874 called *Die Fledermaus*, featuring a villain who at one point wears a bat costume to a ball. I understand the opera runs for 3 hours or so; I won't be attending, but I do love the idea that a bat could be a flying mouse!

The aforementioned vampire bats, with their habit of sipping blood, have given bats a bit of a bad reputation. Zipping low over people's heads in the dark and living upside down in caves probably hasn't helped either. And bats occasionally carry rabies and a couple of other bad diseases (never pick one up!), but overall, they are of immense benefit to us all. For example, a bat consumes half its body weight in insects every night—around 3,000 bugs per bat! That adds up to a lot of mosquitoes; a group of 1,000 bats can eat 4 tons of insects a year. It is estimated that bats save our agriculture folks up to $50 million per year in insect control services.

But, there is big trouble in paradise. Although bats can live up to 15 years in the wild—extremely long lives for such tiny animals (shrews seldom live 15 months)—our bats are dying off by the millions. A fungus thought to have arrived from Europe on tourists' shoes was first identified at a public attraction called Howe Caverns in southern New York in February 2006. It causes a disease in bats called white-nose syndrome that is nearly always fatal. The fungus grows on the bats' noses, rousing them from hibernation and causing them to use critical amounts of stored-up fat before spring, and they starve to death.

Since so many bats live together in very close quarters in a single cave, sometimes in the thousands, and since many of our bats migrate widely, the disease spreads quickly from one bat to innumerable others and is carried far and wide. The disease has now been found over most of the eastern United States and Canada and seems to be moving out west.

Some of the bat species affected by white-nose syndrome were already on the threatened or endangered list, and they will probably face extinction. If most or all of our bats were to die off, think of the tons and tons of insects bats eat nightly but in their absence would be left up there in the sky to reproduce at their regular enormous rate. The biologists predict a real insect problem for the farmers and the rest of us if the worst happens. They are comparing the situation to what happened to our chestnut trees or the colony collapse syndrome devastating the honeybees.

A lot of serious scientific work is under way to study the fungus and how it spreads. In Europe, the bats survive white-nose syndrome because they have been living with it for eons, but American populations are vulnerable. A number of possible remedies are under study, but so far nothing has been proven effective enough for widespread use. Many caves have been closed to the public in hopes of slowing the advance of the fungus, including caves in the Smokies and other parts of Tennessee. We can only support our scientists and hope that they, and Mother Nature, will find a solution.

In the meantime, if you are so lucky as to see a bat or two around, note them well and remember what you saw. It may be a long time until you see another one.

BETTER THAN YOU THOUGHT

People who are used to being outdoors give them some space but don't pay them much mind. Indoor folks often dread even going out, ever on the watch for a possible attack. Terrorists? Politicians? No, no. It's all those things flying around out there armed with stingers! They are dreaded probably second only to the critters bearing eight legs and poisonous fangs. But then, they are a part of this story as well. It's a story that would make for a good Halloween column, but the main actors will all be gone by then. Here in August, though, they're lurking everywhere out there . . . so let's proceed!

Now, I'm not thinking bees here. We all think bees are good, useful, and important. And although some people are so fearful of bees that they design their gardens to discourage them from even being around, most of us know that bees leave us alone as long as we leave them alone.

I'm thinking wasps. And a huge family they are. Over 17,000 species live in North America in the order *Hymenoptera*, the social insects—the wasps, bees, and ants. Like the Smiths or the Joneses, or any large family, they come in all shapes and sizes. And they come with lots of different personalities, too, from benign to fearsome—from our peaceful and businesslike mud daubers to the awesome tarantula hawks of the Southwest. If we had those around here, *nobody* would go outside.

But, back to East Tennessee. We probably find the yellow jacket our most common wasp family annoyance, whether invading our can of soda at the picnic or zapping us when we accidentally mow over, or even too near, one of their nests with our riding mower.

Even more threatening are the bald-faced hornets. Faster fliers, stronger stingers, they are the ones that build those big paper football-sized nests in trees and shrubs. Although they generally don't bother people unless they're bothered (think of a 10-year-old boy chucking a rock into a hornet's nest as he utters those famous words "hey guys, watch this"), even hummingbirds avoid them. On numerous occasions I've seen a hornet chase an otherwise feisty and aggressive hummingbird away from a feeder.

Then there are those big, furry red-and-black "ants" called cow killers for their famously powerful sting. They are actually wingless female wasps, out looking for their favorite prey, other wasps and bees, to feed to their young. The male velvet ant has wings like regular wasps and is seldom even noticed.

So, they build nests on our houses, make us nervous, and occasionally sting us. Is there anything good to say about them? Actually, there is a whole lot. In contrast to some of our other piercing and biting friends like mosquitoes and ticks, those wasps out there do us far more good than an occasional sting does harm. For one thing, adult wasps do considerable good as food crop and flower pollinators because they feed partly on flower nectar and, in the process, help pollinate flowers, fruit, and vegetables. But far and away their main service to us, one that goes mostly unnoticed, is that of pest control.

So, here's the deal: While our most famous social insect, the honeybee, feeds all those hungry larvae in all those thousands of hexagonal cells a vegetarian diet of pollen and honey, all the zillions of wasp larvae are eating meat. "Mostly carnivorous" as the field guides say.

And what is meat to a mama wasp? Insects and spiders. All day, every day, those hundreds of yellow jacket larvae in their underground paper cells, and those hornet larvae 60 feet up in a tree in their paper football nest, are being fed chewed-up, emulsified meat from a daily hoard of insects and other such critters captured by all those worker wasps out there scouring the countryside, and your yard and garden, for prey.

Who would have thought? An even more specific and focused job of pest control is being done for you, daily, by some members of a big group called the solitary wasps. Instead of making a large nest attended by an ever-growing number of workers, solitary wasp females go it alone. Most of them make burrows in the ground, but some species attach individual nest cells to buildings and other sheltered places. Those cells look just like little clay pots. In fact, it is believed that some of the early native peoples copied the design of those cells for their pottery. A great case of art imitating nature!

A lot more familiar to all of us are the nests of our common mud daubers, more properly called pipe organ mud daubers for the tubular mud nests they build on the sides of sheds, barns, and houses.

The nests of these solitary wasps all consist of a series of individual cells. Each cell contains one wasp egg and is stocked with the meat the hatched larva will feed on until it is ready to become a flying adult wasp. Different species of solitary wasps supply their nest cells with different meat; some use only crickets, or grasshoppers, or cicadas. But to me, the heroes are the mud daubers and a group called spider wasps. For them, the only meat that's acceptable is spiders! If you've ever examined the contents of a mud dauber nest, you have seen that each tube is divided into cells, each one with a big, unmoving, but alive spider.

In a story truly fit for Halloween, the female wasp searches out a spider and stings it. This does not kill the spider, only paralyzes it. Then she drags it or carries it, depending on its size and hers, to the nest. She puts this living "zombie" spider in with an egg and seals it up, to await the hatching of the hungry larva. Once hatched, the larva finds itself closed up with a big, delicious chunk of living meat, to gradually consume as it progresses toward becoming an adult wasp. One source even said the wasp larvae selectively eat away on the spider, leaving such vital parts as the heart and nervous system till last so the spider remains alive until almost completely consumed. . . . Yuck!

While certainly unappetizing to us, each species of spider wasp has its favorite spider prey, from tiny crab spiders on up to big wolf spiders larger than their wasp predators, and to the monster tarantulas harvested by the fearless tarantula hawks mentioned earlier. There are a lot of spider wasps, and they and the mud daubers carry off a whole bunch of spiders every day. Those, plus the millions of other wasps that eat everything from aphids to horseflies, make a huge and unappreciated dent in our pest populations. Think about it: Would you rather risk an occasional sting, or have a zillion more spiders in your surroundings? And I sort of like the zombie part. It's made a lot of horror shows, often with people as the prey.

VINES ARE WILDFLOWERS, TOO

Maybe vines aren't the first thing to pop into your mind when you're thinking of wildflowers. But consider this—the official wildflower of the state of Tennessee is a vine. The passionflower, *Passiflora incarnata*, is a vine if there ever was one. It uses its many tendrils to latch onto whatever support it can find and climb up into good sunlight, then produce its spectacular 3-inch lavender and white blossoms.

The passionflower's status as state wildflower has been on the books since 1919, but it hasn't always been there on solid legislative ground. We're dealing with the Tennessee State Legislature here, so naturally the story is a convoluted one. It goes like this:

Back in 1919 someone decided that Tennessee needed a state wildflower, and that it would be nice if the state's schoolchildren chose it. Out of a number of worthy candidates the children selected the passionflower, also known as the maypop, and the legislators apparently voted it in. All was well until 14 years later, when the garden clubs of the state got together and decided that the cultivated garden iris would be much more appropriate as their state flower. They even came up with the argument that the passionflower hadn't been actually, really, *properly* approved anyhow!

After the usual lobbying and political manipulations, the legislators decided to make the iris the official state flower. The die-hard maypop people refused to back down, so for 40 years we had two state flowers, more or less. Then in a piece of legislative genius, and to resolve this critical impasse, in 1973 the legislature solved the issue (or so we thought) by declaring the passionflower as our state wildflower and the iris our state cultivated flower.

Well, fine, then. It was settled. But uh, oh. . . . An intrepid, wonderful lady conservationist, Dr. Elsie Quarterman, rediscovered the purple Tennessee coneflower, *Echinacea tennesseensis*, growing in some cedar glades in middle Tennessee. It was a native wildflower and also had the mystique of having been already officially declared extinct, and now it was found again. Leaping once more into action, the legislature in 2012 proclaimed the purple coneflower as our second state wildflower.

So, there you have it. Our original, native, beautiful, and widespread official state wildflower is the passionflower. It now serves alongside the iris, which is actually a native of central and southern Europe but is nonetheless our official state cultivated flower. These two are joined by purple coneflower, our second official state wildflower—a native to be sure, but only found scattered in some very special habitats in three of the 95 counties in the state.

Well now, so much for the politics of state flowers. Let's go on to something perhaps more interesting about our passionflower, which is both a wildflower and a vine. It is a member of a mostly tropical family. The species we know in Tennessee, like the others in the family, produces an unusual and complex flower with lots of parts, surrounded by a purple and white fringe. Way back in the fifteenth and sixteenth centuries, Jesuit missionaries to this part of the world adapted all the structures of the flower to the story of the passion of Jesus. Parts of the bloom were thought to represent the nails, another, the hammer; the fringe stood for the crown of thorns, and so on. All of this tradition actually gave our state wildflower its Latin scientific name, *incarnata*.

The Cherokee Indians called the maypop the Ocoee, from which the Ocoee River and its valley got their names. And another common name for the plant is wild apricot, because of its 2-inch oval green-to-yellow fruits, which have a peculiar pungent odor and are considered by some people to be edible. Edible, maybe, but the plant has indeed been used since the 1800s as a supposedly reliable remedy for cases of what people at that time called "nervous anxiety."

As far as edible goes, though, there is a bright orange butterfly called the Gulf fritillary that chooses to lay its eggs only on the tendrils and leaves of the passionflower and thus feeds its caterpillars only on that plant. Where you find passionflowers, you will likely also find Gulf fritillaries.

There are many other wildflowers out there that are vines, too. Some are so common that we scarcely notice them. We all see the purple, blue, or white blossoms of common morning glories and seldom think much about them, but when you're out and about look for their showy, little red cousins, the small red morning glory, another widespread citizen of fields and meadows.

There are the trumpet creepers, with their big clusters of bright orange trumpet-shaped flowers. Both those, and the cross vines, which sport similar-shaped orange trumpets that have yellow fronts, are big favorites of bumble-bees and hummingbirds. The Virginia creepers are sometimes mistaken for poison ivy; they have five leaves rather than three. They climb high into the trees, and their tiny yellow flowers are generally overlooked. But then in the fall their foliage turns a nice autumn red, and they produce a prolific number of berries that are an important source of food for wildlife as winter approaches.

The Dutchman's pipe, or pipevine, larval food plant for the pipevine swallowtail butterfly, is a vine with one of the most unusual blossoms, a tubular curved affair that resembles an old Dutch Meerschaum smoking pipe. The vines can be seen growing to enormous, Tarzan-sized junglelike adornments climbing high into the trees of the Smokies.

And we have two natives that may be shunned at times because of their overwhelming invasive alien cousins, honeysuckle and wisteria. Our native honeysuckle, called red or coral honeysuckle, is a nice perennial that does not spread everywhere to become a serious pest. It is another favorite of bees and hummingbirds. And our native American wisteria makes a nice covering for your garden arbor, unlike the Japanese and Chinese wisterias, which look the same but will climb 30 feet into the trees, often strangling them.

Vines, sure. Wildflowers, you bet. And many of them have varieties developed for the home garden. You can enjoy them out in the fields and woods, and if you like, you can grow some of them right there at home. You'll find that they make an interesting addition to a mailbox post, a fence, or an arbor—a lot of plant and flowers for only a small amount of gardening effort!

NEW THINGS IN SOME
REALLY OLD MOUNTAINS

The Great Smoky Mountains National Park, or "the Smokies" as we refer to the place around these parts, just sits there. The park watches all the busy little anthills of human activity around its feet—Gatlinburg, Townsend, Cosby, Cherokee—as patiently as a wise old grandmother tending a flock of 2-year-olds on a nursery floor. And why not? Geologists tell us the Smokies have been around for at least 250 million years, maybe the oldest mountains in the world. And even at that, they're built of rocks that were made from the remains of previous mountain ranges. Some of the oldest rocks, over on the Cataloochee side, are dated at around a billion years old.

A Saturday course offered by the Smoky Mountain Field School a couple of years ago and led by University of Tennessee geology professor Dr. Don Byerly, ranged from the Sugarlands visitor's center up to Indian Gap on the crest of the Smokies. An enthusiastic storehouse of knowledge, the professor showed us how some of the basement rocks of the Smokies, called "grey-wacke," have small blue quartz pebbles in them. You can find big rocks full of them in the tumbled boulder fields along State Highway 441. Anyhow, the blue color comes from little microscopic zircon crystals embedded in the quartz pebbles. Geologists have studied the zircons with electron microscopy, and they tell an amazing story. Each time the zircons have been involved in the fiery, high-pressure process of mountain building, they are altered in certain identifiable ways. These Smoky Mountain zircon crystals are not only part of the present mountains, they have been part of several generations of mountains before them. They had already been the building blocks of three or four mountain ranges before the present Smokies were pushed up, originally as high as the Himalayas are today, to start the slow, inevitable process of eroding back to hills again.

Dr. Byerly explained to us how a knowledge of the local geology can have practical applications, sort of like reading the directions before putting something together. He showed us pieces of a blackish rock called Anakeesta shale. It is found in widespread deposits all across the upper mountains. There in the shale glistened innumerable tiny cubes of iron pyrite—fool's gold. When you bulldoze through Anakeesta shale and then fill an area with it to build a road, rain water releases sulfuric acid. Engineers did that at Indian Gap, to build the new road to Cherokee. And guess what? Above the road at Indian Gap, they found that after the construction was done, the water-dwelling insects and plants, salamanders, and fish in the little stream there all lived happily on. But below the big fill of acid-bearing rock? Four-and-a-half miles of dead stream: no trout, no critters. Even years later it's not back to normal and likely will never be.

But we spoke of oldness. Hundreds of thousands of years here, a billion there. What difference does that make to a picnicker at Elkmont or a hiker on Gregory's Bald? For one thing, great age shapes the landscape. The mile-thick glaciers of the last Ice Age were enormously powerful earth-movers, but they didn't travel farther south than the Ohio River Valley. To be sure, though, they shaped the Smokies. It was as cold on Mount LeConte 20,000 years ago as it is in northern Canada today. The icy winters, with all that freezing and thawing, cracked the rocks, and they tumbled down the mountainsides. And later the rains and snows continued to make things rounder, softer, covered with gravel, then soil.

All of this happened over and over, every 100,000 years or so, for 1.5 million years. Each time, cold weather forests, plants, and animals advanced ahead of the ice to the Smokies. With each warmup, the southern forest partially returned. So, in the Smokies we have the remains of northern forest: red spruce, Fraser fir, yellow birch trees, and northern flying squirrels. We have Canada warblers, black-throated blue warblers, and least flycatchers, all birds that live and nest in New Hampshire and Ontario. And biologists tell us that because the Smokies have been there so long, and yet were never covered with glacier ice, there is an unbelievable mix of living things that have used all that time to adjust and adapt and become more numerous and varied—biodiversity, they call it.

And the Smokies are champions of biodiversity. Take 1,500 kinds of flowering plants, for example. Each April, hundreds of people from every state in the union come to Gatlinburg for a week of exploring our 500,000-acre flower garden; we call the event the Spring Wildflower Pilgrimage. Or how about 31 species of salamanders, more species than in any other area of its size in the world. One of them, the red-cheeked salamander, is found nowhere else except here in the Smokies! And trees. There are 100–135 species of trees in the Smokies, more species than in all of Europe. Our old-growth forest here, occupying about 25% of the park's area, represents an amazing 95% of all old-growth forest east of the Mississippi River! If you've been feeling unusually big and important lately, try a stroll through a grove of 400-year-old poplar trees to ponder your place in the world and put things into perspective.

And because of our biodiversity, we have the All-Taxa Biodiversity Inventory (ATBI). The first study of its magnitude anywhere, the ATBI aims to discover and inventory every living thing in the park, hopefully within some reasonable number of years. This remarkable far-reaching program was under way in fall 2000, and the results so far have been spectacular. In the nearly two decades since the project was launched, scientists and volunteers—"citizen scientists"—have discovered more than 9,000 species previously unknown to the park and an amazing 900-plus species formerly unknown to science! It has been so successful that other national and state parks and various nature preserves, both here and abroad, have started similar inventory programs based on the Smokies Park model.

How does it work? They started with the basics: the underlying geology, the soil types, the amounts of rainfall in various areas. Then they began to find and identify all the living things. Over 1,000 scientists, college students, and volunteers have been involved in the program. They do focused collection activities—fern forays, beetle blitzes, and so on—and then invite specialists from around the world, more than 20 countries so far, to sit for hours and days, microscopes at the ready, identifying all the plants and critters that have come in.

There are a lot of things living and running around up in the Smokies that nobody knew even existed. As you would expect, they find lots more *tiny* new things than *large* new things. While they have identified 11 birds new to the Park, along with 6 new fish and two new reptiles, they have found over 1,900 beetles, 580 mushrooms, and 143 slime molds new to the park. They've logged over 1,100 species of butterflies and moths, some 37 of them previously unknown to science, and over 260 spiders, 40-plus new to science.

The list goes on, but I must share one of my favorite discoveries from the ATBI, a species previously unknown to me—water bears. Water bears are animals, tiny creatures that live in wet moss. Properly called tardigrades by biologists, they are slow-moving, pudgy little things that lumber along on four pairs of stubby, jointless legs ending in two claws. Some species have only females. The reason you probably haven't seen any water bears lately is because most are only half a millimeter long. A "giant" water bear may be one millimeter long. And their most remarkable feature? When things go bad in their environs—a serious drought, for example—water bears can stop all signs of being alive, no metabolism at all . . . dead, you might say. And then when things are better, you guessed it! They come right back to life. Pretty much unbelievable sci-fi kind of stuff. . . . So far, the ATBI people have found 82 species of water bears in the park, 21 of which are new to science.

Nowadays in the early part of the twenty-first century, we seem to be so busy covering everything with buildings and asphalt that we forget what an amazing, abundant, and considerably unknown world we have around us. The Smokies do indeed have an abundance of life, but you will find that your backyard, your garden, and your local park are full of life as well. It's interesting and fun to get to know more of it.

APPLES

Apples, you say? That's a fall subject. Apple cider, bobbing for apples at Halloween, that sort of thing. And, apples get ripe in the fall. Well maybe so, but just cast an eye at the fruit section of your local grocery store, and you'll see bins of big, perfect, red, yellow, and green apples ready and waiting. However, those Red Delicious and Granny Smith apples didn't necessarily grow and ripen this year, folks. They're brought to us through the magic of twenty-first-century science and agriculture. But more of that in a moment.

To me, apple trees and summer seem to go together. Every summer, my brother and I would climb our Granny Collier's favorite old apple tree, the one she made pies from. It had nice low horizontal limbs to start from, and we could disappear up into the leaves and be completely cut off from the world below.

Many Americans have fond memories involving old apple trees, regarding them with strong feelings of nostalgia. Witness the words of Henry Williams, penned in 1905: "In the shade of the old apple tree, Where the love in your eyes I could see." Williams' poem goes on considerably longer, in pretty much the same vein.

Besides tree climbing and romance, the memories seem to concentrate on eating: warm apple pie, apple stack cake, apple butter, and apple dumplings. The fact that so many of us can recall apple memories points to just how much apples have enriched our lives.

Apples have been around for a long time, considerably longer than people, actually. They have been prized as table food since antiquity, eaten by the Egyptians, the Romans, and all those Asian and northern European heathens

148

that were our ancestors—the Germans, Scandinavians, French, Spanish, and English.

Serious scientific study over the last 60–70 years places the origin of apples in central Asia. There, it was discovered, grow vast forests of apple trees instead of stands of oaks and maples. Tall, wild, gnarly forerunners of today's domestic orchard trees, they bear lots of small, hard, bitter fruits.

Apples, we find, have an unusual system of reproduction. When the seed of any given apple manages to grow into a tree and produce its own apples, they are almost never like the one the seed came from. They are usually small and sour. Occasionally, though, one produces a rare, special, large, and tasty variety. Through the ages, the locals kept an eye out for these special trees, and if they found one, they could then perpetuate it not by planting its seeds, but by grafting its buds or shoots onto another apple rootstock.

So then, as these peoples moved westward into Europe, they would bring both the seeds, to plant and grow into sour cider apples, and cuttings of the special ones that they wanted to grow true each time. The more northern groups and tribes tended to use the small, sour cider apples, while the larger, sweeter dessert or table apples were favored in the warm, sunny Mediterranean countries.

The story of apples goes on, full of history. Many of the best varieties were preserved by monks through the Middle Ages in carefully tended walled gardens. One such apple, known by the 1300s as a favorite in formal French gardens and called Paradise, is a dwarf yellow apple whose rootstock is now known as Malling 9. It is the leading dwarfing rootstock in the United States and probably dates back to the Romans.

Those hard, sour cider apples? It seems that hard cider was once the main alcoholic beverage of the masses, and there are still places producing true, fermented, sparkling apple cider today. These days, however, from the United States to China, Europe to Saudi Arabia, the big, tasty, blemish-free table apples are where the action is. China is the world's largest producer of apples. In the United States, New York state and Washington state turn out the most apples.

It takes legions of scientists, working at university laboratories and agricultural research stations, to keep us ahead of the curve in apple production. There are scores of pests and diseases that enjoy apples as much as we do, and it's a never-ending battle to hold them off. Other workers spend countless hours continually trying to come up with better strains of apples—more frost-resistant, more colorful, more tasty, better for cooking, and on and on. We should continue to have plenty of good apples to eat and bake with.

Another bit of history, this time local: In the 1920s, up in Cherokee Orchard above Gatlinburg, in the area that the Motor Nature Trail now winds through, there stood Mr. M. M. Whittle's apple orchard and plant nursery. It contained over 6,000 fruit trees but was abandoned when the Smokies Park was established. Its legacy lives on though, in the nice orchards still in business in the Cosby area today.

Putting great apples on our tables all year long is big business, very big. Unimaginable tons of apples are grown every year; stored for remarkable lengths of time in refrigerated warehouses, often in an atmosphere of nitrogen which delays ripening and stops spoilage; and then shipped just about everywhere. We've come a long way from the times when the New York apple growers lowered barrels of apples through the ice into frozen-over ponds for the winter, to preserve them for sale in the city the next spring.

Our present-day apples have a very long heritage. They are the most-eaten fruit in the world. The list of foods made with apples, by nearly every nationality and ethnic group around the globe, is limitless: meats, soups, stews, cakes, pies, dumplings, and tarts. As for me, I wouldn't mind having one more piece of my Granny's warm deep-dish apple pie, made with apples from her favorite tree. With a big glob of hand-cranked vanilla ice cream!

SUCCESS STORY

Spouse and I don't get to the Big City very often, but when we do, we always try to make time to visit a museum or two. As far as I am concerned, having huge museums and great restaurants are about the only good reasons for having a Big City.

Anyhow, this April we had to go to Chicago for a couple of days, so we went a day early and spent it at the Field Museum of Natural History. The Field Museum is an enormous, city-block-or-two-sized building looking out past the Chicago Aquarium and on over the waters of Lake Michigan in one direction, and at Soldier Field in the other direction.

Being a museum of natural history, it has all the birds, rocks, plants, and bones I could want to linger over in a museum. It has huge halls of exhibits, but one in particular caught our eyes on this particular visit. A temporary traveling exhibit shared with several other large museums across the country, it was called "Dinosaurs: Ancient Fossils, New Discoveries."

The Field Museum has long been famous for its dinosaurs. It houses Sue, the largest and most complete *Tyrannosaurus rex* skeleton known, and a brontosaurus that is so huge they have to keep it outdoors. But the exhibit we were enjoying that day displayed new discoveries focused on using technology to learn new things.

For example, using the science of biomechanics, along with CT scans and computers, scientists are figuring out such things as how fast *T. rex* could run (probably a maximum of 25 miles per hour) and how high a brontosaurus could raise its head on its incredibly long neck (probably not straight up, maybe only 20 feet high). And the depictions of new discoveries included a big, life-sized diorama of life around 125 million years ago in northeastern China's Liaoning Province.

A whole crowd of new dinosaurs has been discovered there, and they are remarkably well preserved. So well, in fact, that we can see their skin and feathers. Yep, a whole bunch of dinosaurs with *feathers*! The scientists are beginning to conclude that feathers developed originally as downy filaments to keep the dinosaurs warm, and only later developed into features enabling the marvelous present-day miracle of flight. They think that our birds descended directly from some of the theropods, meat-eating dinosaurs. Said one: "If you want to see a creature pretty close to a *T. rex*, just look at an ostrich."

We checked out all the permanent exhibits of dinosaurs, too; we stood there, gazing up at all those giants that ruled their world in their time. But then, as the Discoveries exhibit explained, a funny thing or two happened to their world. A large meteor hit the Yucatan Peninsula and a series of huge volcanic eruptions occurred in what is now western India, both of which gave rise to clouds of dust and ash and heat, blocked out the sun, and caused the mighty beasts' extinction. These events, 65 million years ago, killed off 50% of all living species, more animals than plants. No more dinosaurs.

However, I'm going to let you in on an evolutionary success story that we can all feel good about, one that is a part of our lives even today. Now, it's not universally beloved; Janet Lembke covered it in a chapter in her book *Despicable Species*. But renowned and revered as cartoonist Walt Kelly's Pogo, it's everyone's—well, probably *someone's*—favorite animal, the possum!

What has a possum got to do with dinosaurs? Well, sir, back in the Jurassic period, some 200–145 million years ago, when all those huge lizard things were stomping around all day, eating everything in sight, there appeared some little, furry, mouselike creatures that hid from the big lizards during the day, came out at night, and had live babies instead of eggs—the first of what became the mammals we know today.

Early on, primitive mammals laid eggs, too, like the present-day duck-billed platypus that lays eggs but then nurses its young with milk. But live birth gave this new line of beasts a better chance for survival, and the next evolutionary step from eggs was to have underdeveloped babies crawl into their mother's pouch to suckle until they were big enough to face the world. It worked, and you had the marsupials—pouch animals—kangaroo, koala, and possum!

One of the earliest live-birth mammals was a furry critter that emerged in China named *Eomaia*, which means "dawn mother." It had a long tail and opposable first toes, and it climbed trees. It looked a lot like a mouse-sized possum, from 125 million years ago. Fossils that are essentially identical to present-day possums have been dated to around 65 million years ago. What in the world is there about a possum that would let it succeed for all that time, see the Terrible Lizards come and go, see people build cities and roads and drive cars, and keep right on being a possum?

A few possum facts are in order. You will find possums always listed first in the field guides to mammals, because they are the most primitive mammals we have in North America. Possums are the only marsupials we have in North America, and they have the most teeth—50 in all—of any of our mammals, the source of their charming smile!

They can open their jaws to wider than a right angle, and they can live most anywhere and eat most anything, plant or animal, living or dead . . . one of the big secrets to their success.

Their gestation period is only 13 days, and a litter of a dozen tiny newborn possums will fit into a teaspoon! They crawl into the mother's pouch, attach themselves to a teat, and suckle there for 2 months. By then they are big and strong enough to come out and ride around on mama's back as she goes about her daily chores. Possums have two, sometimes three litters a year. They are thought to live an average of about 7 years.

Possums have opposable thumbs on their feet, and that along with their scaly, prehensile tails makes them great climbers. They can also use their tails to carry stuff, such as a bunch of grass for a nest. They are usually active at night (recall those big daytime lizards). They do "play possum" when sorely threatened, becoming limp and apparently lifeless for as long as 6 hours before shuffling away to safety.

Stupid? How could you call an animal that has been around for 65 million years, through thick and thin, from dinosaurs to the space age, anything other than amazing? A colleague of mine, who had the occasional tendency to talk down to people, once had an elderly patient tell him, "Doc, I'm not as dumb as I look." I'm sure that if possums could talk, that's exactly what they would say to us today.

WE HAVE ROBINS

Spouse and I have a lot of robins at our house. They are all over the place. Three or four of them meet me in the driveway every time I pull in. Six or eight are foraging for worms out in the side yard most any time of day, and a couple of them are still singing to me even in this hot weather.

I guess we shouldn't be surprised, if you do the numbers. They've had 3 months now, since they arrived in the spring, to pair up, nest, and raise a couple of broods, usually of four youngsters each. So, for every couple of robins you start with in April, there might be around a dozen of them now, in that one single family. That can add up to a lot of robins when all those spring eggs hatch!

The American robin is likely our most familiar songbird, known to nearly everyone who has ever looked out their windows. They are instantly recognizable by their red breast, upright stance, and their typical stop–look–nab foraging technique. Their loud "cheerily, cheer-up, cheer-up, cheerily, cheerily" song begins by dawn and can last on into the evening hours. They continue to sing for us now, and thankfully, will go into the fall.

Their name "robin," originally being a reference to any familiar family member, was given to them by the earliest settlers because the robins' reddish-brown breast reminded them of the European robins, a similar but smaller and unrelated bird of their homelands.

Robins are also one of our most widely distributed songbirds, nesting from Alaska across Canada and the United States into Mexico. They do migrate. The whole continent-full of them shifts southward in the fall, becoming more concentrated in the southern half of the United States, so we have a lot of northern robins that winter here with us each year.

Although they have fared much better than most species of birds since we humans moved in and took over, robins haven't always had smooth sailing. Back before they became protected by the Migratory Bird Conservation Act of 1918, they were trapped and kept as caged songbirds, like canaries. And much worse than that, they were shot by the untold thousands by southern market hunters.

Our most famous observer and painter of birds, John James Audubon, painted a nest of robins as his plate no. 131. In his corresponding commentary about robins in *Ornithological Biography*, vol. 2, he said, "From the middle of November until March, in the southern states every gunner brings them home by the bagfuls, and the markets are supplied with them at a very cheap rate." As to how the wintering robins rated as table fare, Audubon comments that "they are then fat and juicy, and afford excellent eating."

The robins took another big hit back when DDT was being sprayed abundantly on trees, ditches, even crops. I recall a film clip shown on the evening news of a crop-duster airplane spraying a field of vegetables, the cloud of poison enveloping the crew of migrant workers tending the crop. The large chemical companies assured everyone that their product was harmless to everything except their target insects, but then strange things began to happen.

In 1954 the city of East Lansing, Michigan, home of Michigan State University, began a program of spraying DDT on their stately elm trees, which were under attack from Dutch elm disease. A year later, when spring returned to the Michigan State campus, people noticed robins everywhere, on the ground, having seizures, dying, or dead. Biologists from Michigan State found they had been killed by neurotoxins. The robins had, as usual, been eating their favorite food, earthworms. But the earthworms, after having fed over the previous fall and winter on fallen DDT-laced elm leaves, had become toxic; just 10 or 12 worms could kill a robin.

The city of Bloomfield Hills, Michigan, put out a call for anyone who found a dead robin they suspected of having been poisoned to bring it in for study. They had to cut off their request when, after a week, their freezers overflowed with a thousand dead robins. Whole towns were calling the experts for help, asking why there weren't any songbirds anymore.

And so, in her monumental 1962 book *Silent Spring*, Rachel Carson wrote that "the story of the robin might serve as the tragic symbol of the fate of all the birds" in our chemical-soaked world. Her book, along with the growing public alarm at all the dead and missing birds, turned the tide, at least to the extent that in 1972 DDT was finally banned in the United States and Canada.

But back to our robins. Today they are alive and well and as familiar a part of our daily lives as kinfolk. They serve as a standard for bird study: Other birds are "about the size of a robin" or "a little smaller than a robin." Birds are described as singing their songs like "a robin with a sore throat" (scarlet tanager) or "like a robin with voice lessons" (rose-breasted grosbeak). You know them at a glance by their "robin-red breast," and they lay robin's-egg blue eggs.

And they are nothing if not industrious. Over the 2-week span that the young birds are in the nest, the two parent robins will make over 300 feeding visits to the nest a day, ultimately delivering over 3 pounds of worms and caterpillars to their babies' hungry mouths. One studious biologist has noted that on its last day in the nest, a single young robin, by then the same size as its parents, will eat 14 feet of earthworms stretched end to end!

Earthworms? Robins love them. And just so you know, some serious study has gone into resolving the debate over how robins find their worms. It turns out that they find them by sight, peering closely with that cocked eye, rather than hearing them, smelling them, or feeling vibrations. Interestingly, in late summer the robins do an unusual thing. Over a couple of months, they switch their diet from almost all meat—worms and caterpillars—to almost all fruit. They eat fruits and berries most of the winter. They go for tree fruits such as apples, serviceberries, hackberries, and mulberries, as well as grapes, blackberries, and pokeberries. But a few of those is a small price to pay for having our faithful, familiar, friendly kinfolk, the robins, living with us day by day.

"Cheer-up!"

OUR EIGHT-LEGGED FRIENDS

One morning a couple of weeks ago, I flipped on the light in my shop, and there on the wall below the window was the mother of all spiders. It was hairy, had a body about three-quarters of an inch long, and a legspan of over 3 inches. After my initial shock, and after I convinced myself that it couldn't jump 6 feet or go for my jugular, I nabbed the brute in a jar and put it on the workbench until I could see about looking it up.

Instead of any panic or fear, the giant calmly sat there in its jar, watching me work at the workbench. It methodically cleaned each of its hairy legs, pulling each one through its big fangs. Its eight eyes had the same friendly gaze you get from a polar bear or a great white shark. I imagined it was thinking, "I wonder how you would taste with your insides digested and sucked out? If only I were just a little bit larger!" I looked it up and discovered that it was a wolf spider. I turned it loose in the garden so it would quit staring at me, and I hope it is cleaning up all the pesky critters out there.

What about spiders? Well, for one thing, they're not insects, because they have eight legs, not six. They're kin to the horseshoe crabs, scorpions, ticks, and chiggers. There are over 37,000 known species of spiders, and the experts say that may be only a *fourth* of all there really are out there. They live from 22,000 feet of elevation up on Mount Everest to the heat of the world's deserts and most everywhere in between. Some can fly through the air on their silk, and some can swim and dive. Some are large enough to eat bird nestlings and small snakes.

And numbers—there a lot of spiders! A number I recently found for spiders in a grassy field really caught my eye. Some poor soul, probably a graduate student, had tabulated 2.2 million spiders on 1 acre of land! Now that's a lot of spiders, folks. And they're not just out there in the field. They're in your yard, and in your basement, and yep, they're in your house. Author Adrienne Mason begins her fascinating book *The World of the Spider* this way: "Wherever you are, there is a spider within a meter of you." A really comforting thought.

Of the thousands of species of spiders, less than 30 are harmful to humans, and most of those live in the tropics. Two species, the black widow and the brown recluse, are well-known threats to human health and can kill, but generally spiders are very beneficial to us. With their exclusively carnivorous choice of diet, they help the birds keep our hordes of insects in check, as well as being excellent bird food themselves.

There are two general groups of spiders, the wandering spiders and the web spiders. They all produce silk, the amazing signature material of their clan. The wandering spiders, such as my huge wolf spider, range about freely, chasing down prey and eating it on the spot. The web spiders are the ones that usually come to mind when we think of a spider. They spin webs in a great array of shapes and sizes, some strikingly beautiful.

And that silk is amazing stuff. It is light and strong, with half the tensile strength of steel, and so strong that a strand of it could be played out for a distance of 50 miles before it broke under its own weight.

Spiders produce different silk for different purposes. One major use is for what's called a "drag line." Spiders extrude a line of silk as they go about their daily lives, so that if any emergencies arise, they are always attached to something, or can attach to something else, like laying out a safety line all day long.

Spiders use special silk for wrapping prey, for enclosing their eggs in tough silken sacs, and for lining burrows and hiding places. And about that flying thing. . . . Some spiders use their silk for flying by climbing up on a plant stem or other launching point and playing out some silk into the breeze until there's enough to lift them off. Away they go, presumably to greener pastures. This is called ballooning, and sometimes there are so many spiders ballooning that they make up a significant amount of the diet of the swifts and swallows, which as you recall harvest the flying insects from the air.

But those beautiful, symmetrical webs with their strong, dry radial support lines and their stretchy, sticky circular lines are what the web spiders are famous for. They're nicknamed "orb-weavers" . . . an evocative term for another one of nature's wonders. Think of the big webs of the common black-and-yellow garden spider, with a white zigzag pattern woven onto the center, presumably to warn birds not to fly into them and destroy them. The orb-weavers are programmed to produce their amazing webs by following a precise order of laying down support lines, then radial lines, and then a spiral of temporary circular silk. Finally, they turn and go in the other direction, eating the temporary silk as they go, and laying down the carefully spaced, specialized sticky catching silk.

If you take the time to watch this process, you will see how the spider very daintily and carefully feels the next radial strand, and then places the circular strand at exactly the right spot as it goes along. The result is an awesome bug trap, ready for business.

Spiders as artists? Some early summer morning, try to visit a foggy meadow full of hundreds of dew-covered spider webs, or find a single big orb web bejeweled with individual drops of dew. They make some of nature's most striking, intricate art—hard to improve upon. I'm glad we have spiders.

TWO NOT-SO-FRIENDLY EIGHT-LEGGERS

In North America, nearly all spiders are harmless to humans. Even the huge tarantulas of the western United States, which some people keep as pets, are reluctant to bite people, and when they do, their bite is no worse than a wasp sting. Nevertheless, it remains a fact that there are two species of North American spiders, actually southeastern US spiders, which are of serious concern to us humans.

The first, and the one best known to most people, just looks like trouble. Round, shiny black body, long skinny black legs, and tell-tale scarlet hourglass-shaped spot on its belly—the infamous black widow. Named for its unpleasant habit of sometimes eating its mate for a post-lovemaking snack, the black widow makes a poorly organized cobweb, usually under something, and then typically sits upside down on the underside of the web, waiting for prey. They like dark, moist places. We have a black widow that lives on the underside of the metal lid of my water meter out in the yard. It's been there for years. Never seems to bother anyone; the meter guys all wear heavy gloves!

The bite of the black widow itself does not amount to much, is not especially painful, and may go unnoticed. But then in a few minutes to an hour, the nerve toxin that the black widow produces causes severe muscle spasms, especially in the abdominal muscles. These are often so severe that they are mistaken for appendicitis or a perforated stomach ulcer. Fortunately, these distressing symptoms can be relieved fairly promptly by administration of appropriate intravenous medications. Of considerable comfort is the fact that less than 1% of black widow spider bites are fatal.

The second bad actor in our spider family is a more significant medical hazard, that interestingly was recognized as being the source of some serious medical problems as late as the 1950s. People had been exhibiting ugly, ulcerated, slowly healing wounds suspected of being some sort of bites, but it was some curious and dedicated scientists named Atkins, Wingo, and Sodeman, reporting in the journal *Science* in 1957, who definitively connected the brown recluse spider with these wounds.

Brown recluse spiders are more of a problem to us than black widows because, for one thing, they like to live in houses, lurk amidst stacks of things in closets, and get in towels and bedclothes, so they encounter humans more often. Second, the bite of the brown recluse can have serious local, as well as generalized, results. In contrast to the bite of the black widow, the brown recluse bite causes a local reaction of pain, redness, and rash or blister formation. The area may break down due to the enzymes in the spider's venom, causing an ulcer to develop. And if this gets secondarily infected with bacteria, the wound may continue to get larger and deeper.

Generalized effects include alterations in the body's blood-clotting mechanisms, sometimes leading to gangrene of fingers or toes, or worse. The wounds caused by brown recluse bites often take 3 weeks or so to heal, and in the more severe cases, 3 months or more, and they may require surgical excision and skin grafting.

Brown recluses are light brown, somewhat hairy, with a body about a half-inch long, with longer legs that give them a legspan of about an inch and a half or so. Their tell-tale identifying mark is a clear-cut, obvious darker brown fiddle- or guitar-shaped spot on their head and thorax.

It is important if you or someone you're with gets a suspected spider bite to catch the spider if possible and take it with you to the doctor. Most of the time, the cause of bites can only be guessed at, and positive identification of the perpetrator can be of immense help in deciding on appropriate early treatment. And speaking of early treatment—unfortunately, medical personnel often see these bites days or weeks later, after they have become chronic and infected, making the bites much more difficult to treat. In the majority of cases, early treatment can make a significant difference in the time it takes to heal, and in lessening possible complications.

Along with copperheads and rattlesnakes, these two spiders present humans with significant risks to health, and even life. The best defense with any of them is to be alert and aware of your surroundings and whatever might be sharing your space with you. Avoid putting hands in dark corners without looking first. Turn back the sheets before turning out the lights—you just might have a new bedmate! And, as with most other things in life, carry around a steady supply of good luck. Sleep well!

THE BROODING PROS: CAROLINA WRENS

Heading up Clinton Highway one pleasant summer morning, going to the now-defunct Camper's Corner RV place with my old travel trailer in tow, I was feeling some anxiety about how I was going to get the big new fifth-wheel unit that I was trading it in for across four lanes of busy traffic and safely back to Powell.

At the RV place, one of the staff and I were checking things out, and we took the fiberglass cover off the two propane tanks at the front of the trailer. And gadzooks! There was a nest-full of nearly grown Carolina wrens, mouths wide open, assuming that the RV guy and I were going to stuff worms into them. Not really what I needed at that moment!

Well, I put the nest of birds in the backseat floorboard and went about my business. The RV staff helped me switch trailers, they showed me how to work stuff, and we did all the paperwork.

Finally, they got me out and across Clinton Highway in one piece, and I breathed a sigh of relief as I headed for the safety of Powell. Suddenly, as I stopped for a traffic light, a chorus of loud and insistent cheeping arose from the back. My pin-feathered passengers had been away from home for nearly 2 hours, and they were really hungry! Finally back home, I grabbed a 5-gallon plastic bucket, placed the nest-full of birds in the bucket, and set it up in a bush that was 20 feet or so from where the old trailer had been parked, doubtful about the youngsters' prospects for survival.

Carolina wrens are serious and industrious builders of nests and raisers of broods. Both birds in the pair share the nest-building duties, then the female lays about five eggs and does all the setting, for about 14 days. Then when they hatch, the male helps to feed the hatchlings, a full-time, daylight-to-dark proposition, for another 12–14 days.

In our part of the country, Carolina wrens raise two, and often three, nests full of babies per year. They are very efficient in their family responsibilities. The male finishes raising the first brood while the female begins another nest and lays another batch of eggs. Then, when the male has sent the first brood on out into the world, he starts helping the female with that next bunch of hungry mouths.

Carolina wrens are one of those species that have adjusted well to human beings and their buildings and activities. Out in the wild, they build their nests in brush piles and thickets and stay pretty well out of sight. But, given farms and neighborhoods with their outbuildings and garages, they have shown a great deal of originality in where they locate their nests . . . under eaves of houses, in hanging baskets, in wreaths on doors, in water pumps and mailboxes, even in pockets of old coats hanging on the back porch or in old hats and boots!

Carolina wrens are wonderful singers. They are one of a small number of birds that sing just about all year long. In fact, they reminded me to write about them this week with an outpouring of late summer music this past weekend! The bird song you enjoy through summer mostly comes from Carolina wrens and mockingbirds, with some less melodious vocalizations from the blue jays, crows, and chickadees.

Carolina wrens have as many as 40 variations to their song. They are all loud, clear, and musical. One commonly heard song sounds like "teakettle-teakettle-teakettle" repeated over and over in threes, often just outside the bedroom window early in the morning. And they use a whole array of fussing and scolding notes, which you have undoubtedly heard if you have a cat in your yard.

What about the hijacked bird's nest returned finally to the big white bucket? Lo and behold, both wren parents showed up within 10 minutes, worms in mouths, scolding me loudly. They immediately set about playing catchup on supplying food to the over-hungry gaping mouths in the nest. In the bucket. In the bush. The young birds flew off the nest 4 days later, to add more voices to the chorus of wren song I enjoyed that summer, and am probably still enjoying this summer.

If you hear a loud and persistent songster outside, grab the old binoculars and take a look. The Carolina wren is a small, perky, brown bird with a prominent white streak over the eye and a cocked-up tail. You really should get acquainted with your local wren, if that hasn't already happened yet thanks to its attempted nesting in your garage or its pre-dawn lusty singing outside your bedroom window!

NIGHT LIFE

Everything is scarier at night. Especially something that is already scary during the day. So, it was a spine-tingler when, one dark summer night, we paddled our canoes out into a big cove in the Okefenokee Swamp in south Georgia to shine gators.

What you do is, you have a headlamp strapped to your forehead so that whenever the light shines in the right eyes, it reflects back into yours. So, out there in the dark swamp and feeling pretty vulnerable at water level in a tippy canoe, you watch your beam of light slowly sweep over the surface. Then, if you're lucky, the beam catches the reflection of two deep red, glowing coals, just out of the water.

And that's a gator. Those red-hot coals are the eyeshine of two big reptile eyes that have been watching you since you first put into the water. You can gauge the length of the gator by the distance between the eyes—6 inches between the eyes, and you know you've got a 6-foot gator. Poachers have shined gators in the Okefenokee Swamp for generations. Sort of like our less-than-sportsmanlike neighbors who hunt deer at night with a spotlight, to blind and confuse them.

But gators aren't blinded or confused. When those glowing coals disappear, it just means they've eased under the water, and it's up to you to decide which way they're headed.

We don't have gators to shine in Halls or Powell . . . at least one thing I'm glad I don't have to worry about! But "shining" works for a whole bunch of other critters, and can be a fun thing for Mom or Pop and the kids to do on a nice warm, dark summer's evening, even in East Tennessee.

Different creatures have different colors of eyeshine. Only the gators have those fiery-red coals. But you can shine raccoons, possums, deer, and coyotes, as well as cats and dogs. And there are a bunch of more unusual and numerous things to shine. Probably the most fun are the spiders. Most spiders have eight eyes, and your headlamp beam will reflect bright green, surprisingly bright, little green sparkles all over your lawn. When you close in on one of the reflections, you will be surprised at how such a little spider can reflect a bright green little flash. Or occasionally, what a huge wolf spider it is that's doing the shining!

If you have access to some really clean, clear water in a shallow stream, like in the Smokies—clear water is getting very hard to find these days—you can add to the game by shining into the water. It turns out that crawfish eyes reflect a bright white light, like a pair of tiny car headlights proceeding along the bottom of the stream.

The secret to successful shining is to have the light source as near to your eyes as possible. Having the headlamp low in the middle of your forehead is ideal; a handheld flashlight won't reflect back the eyeshine nearly so well.

So, if the kids are tired of chasing fireflies this summer, and you're tired of having them hanging around the house, get a headlamp or two and head out into the wilds of your yard, or better still, a nice big nearby field, and see what you can shine!

THE OUTER BANKS

The mountains or the beach? The beach or the mountains? It's summer, it's hot—where should your family go for a break? The mountains have cool air and lots of cold mountain stream water. It's hot at the beach, but there's plenty of cool ocean water to immerse yourself in, and waves. Then, we reason, the mountains are here all year long, and everybody knows that the beach is only there in the summer.

So, it's decided: We're heading to the beach. So are lots of other folks. A summer-months issue of *National Geographic* magazine contains an article entitled "Our Coasts in Crisis." It has some surprising statistics. It says that over half of the US population lives in places that border on our coastlines—Atlantic, Pacific, Gulf. And 53% of the US population lives within 50 miles of the coast. Everybody wants to be near the water!

And with good reason. People have always been attracted to the sea. It's huge, boundless, powerful, always moving, and always changing. People are awed, mystified, inspired, and just plain fascinated by the sight and sound of the ocean and by what lives near it and in it. For most of us, being beside the sea is an exciting, or relaxing, or inspiring experience, depending on who we are, or maybe depending on how old we are. Building sandcastles is really cool, but a comfy chair in the shade and a good book become more appealing to me each year.

There is an awful lot of coastline in America. So, where do we go for some beach time? That depends on what you plan to do when you get there. If life at the beach for you means playing golf and wrapping around a few fried seafood platters, and Mom and the kids don't mind the crowds and need plenty of entertainment, probably your best bet will be one of the household-name beaches that everybody already knows about. That same issue of *National Geographic* had an aerial photograph of summer at Coney Island, New York, taken around 1950. The article alleges there are 1.3 million people in the photo, in that section of beach alone. Fun, huh?

Some of us prefer to go someplace where we can see a half-mile of sand with nobody there but us. Well, almost nobody. For total solitude you'll have to go to harder-to-reach places, such as the beach in Olympic National Park in Washington state. The only footprints you'll see in that sand belong to shorebirds, bears, and moose. But for a nice compromise between accessibility and isolation, we've come to love the Outer Banks of North Carolina. The old part, where you hang a right at Kitty Hawk, and head south, away from most of the clutter of civilization.

The Outer Banks are way out there, about 600 miles from Knoxville as the crow flies. On a North Carolina road map, they appear as a narrow strip of islands running north to south, with water on both sides. To the east of them lies the Atlantic Ocean (next stop, England); to the west lies the huge, shallow Pamlico Sound, so big you can't see the mainland from the Banks.

Whalebone Junction is the place where North Carolina Route 12 turns south, and you find you're really on the Outer Banks. It's nearly 60 miles of scenic, two-lane road from there to the end. One of the first nautical sights you'll see are the horizontal black-and-white stripes of the Bodie (pronounced "body") Island lighthouse on the right; across from that area, on the ocean side, is Coquina Beach, named for the thousands of tiny, multi-colored seashells called cocquinas that litter the beach at that particular spot. That area has a nice wide beach with bathhouses and the big wooden skeleton of one of the scores of shipwrecks for which the Outer Banks are famous.

A bit farther along you get your first good look at the ocean, as you cross the Herbert C. Bonner Bridge, a high, curving feat of engineering crossing Oregon Inlet. Fishermen used to line the water's edge below, before the tides washed most of those beaches away and the Park Service closed the rest. The big deep-sea fishing boats come and go beneath the bridge from the busy nearby marina. A US Coast Guard Station and the marina are located at the south end of the bridge; the Coast Guard Station had to move from the ocean side to its present spot because the ocean was about to wash it away as well.

South you go, through long stretches of dunes and marsh, low trees and open spaces. You'll go by Pea Island National Wildlife Refuge, with a great visitor's center (books, information) and excellent bird watching (dykes, ponds, observation tower, innumerable birds). And you'll go through a series of little villages, where most of the people are—Rodanthe, Waves, Salvo, Avon, Frisco, and, at the end, Hatteras Village, where the ferries come and go to parts south and west.

You won't see any high-rise buildings on the whole stretch, unless you count the lighthouses. Most of the accommodations are individual houses, built up on one-story pilings due to lots of past experience with high water. They vary in size from modest to large. Down near Cape Hatteras, there are a few vintage motels, all within a block or two of the beach. And for the more adventurous, there are several RV parks scattered along, and three national park campgrounds that accept tent campers and trailers.

The national park is the reason the Banks still look the way they do. Most of the land here besides the villages belongs to the Cape Hatteras National Seashore—the beaches, the lighthouses. The National Park Service protects and monitors the nesting areas on the beaches used by black skimmers, least terns, the endangered piping plovers, and dozens of sea turtles. The villages crowd right up to the edge of the park, but there they stop. And the rest—thankfully, most of it—is sand, shrubs, and sky.

The Outer Banks, like most barrier islands, are under the influence of the ocean—the currents, the tides, the weather. The ocean giveth, and the ocean taketh away. As time goes by, the islands slowly inch southward and westward. Every year, the ocean creeps closer to the highway. It overwashes parts of it in big storms. A couple of sections of the highway have had to be moved westward in the last few years, to keep them on dry land. In addition to the big Bonner Bridge being replaced by a more westward-located bridge, a second smaller bridge farther to the south on Route 12 is being built to carry the traffic over an entirely new inlet, recently created by one or more of the Banks' fierce winter storms. And the Cape Hatteras Lighthouse, at 198 feet the tallest brick lighthouse in the world and built in 1870, was moved inland more than 1,000 feet in 1999 to save it from the waves. Over the lighthouse's nearly 150 years, the coast had moved west so much that the surf was pounding on that structure's very foundations.

So, the Outer Banks won't be there forever. The experts predict that the Banks will be broken down into a series of smaller separate islands in a matter of decades; sooner, if just the right hurricane comes along. And, they say the Outer Banks may be completely gone in the next few centuries. You'll be OK out there, but they may not look the same when your great-grandchildren visit them.

From the North Carolina Aquarium in Manteo to the Native American Museum in Frisco, there is plenty to see and do on the Outer Banks. Besides lying immobile on the beach, there is great surf fishing, deep sea fishing, wind surfing in the sound, parasurfing, and sea kayaking. There are some excellent seafood stores, where the crabs, scallops, and fish are caught minutes before you buy them. And there are plenty of eateries for those who flatly refuse to cook while on vacation.

From Whalebone Junction to Hatteras, you'll find dunes, beach, marsh, sunshine, and fresh-caught fish. People, too, but not too many. There's plenty of space between you and the next family on the sand. And an infinite number of waves coming in, one after the other, to just sit and contemplate. Wish it was there all year round.

OUR FORGOTTEN FRUIT

Let me tell you the tale of a butterfly and its favorite food, set in motion in the swamps of East Carolina but with a couple of surprising connections to our East Tennessee. It begins with Spouse and me trudging along a trail in the Pocosin Lakes National Wildlife Refuge, over in the hot and steamy swamps of East Carolina—which the locals assure me is a different, and much better, state than either of those other two, the North or the South Carolinas. It's a different kind of place, tabletop flat, with endless fields of corn, soybeans, and cotton separated by nice patches of woods, and with people few and far between.

We had already seen a bear amble out of a cornfield and rear up on its hind legs to study us and our car; a nice big coiled-up red-bellied water snake had posed for some photos, and we were awed to see a thousand purple martins along the way, gathered in a grove of trees and nearby lines, poised for migration soon to begin.

Our half-mile trail ran from the dirt road out to a good-sized body of water called Pungo Lake, which we were thinking might be a good potential winter trip because of its role as a wintering site for 80,000 snow geese and countless thousands of ducks. In August, though, there were few birds in the woods and none on the empty water of the remote lake. Along the way, however, there was a noticeable abundance of one species of butterfly, the striking black-and-white-striped zebra swallowtail. They are not all that commonly seen, yet there they were, one after another after another.

Now, it happens that most butterflies can live on the sugary nectar of many different kinds of flowers. Their caterpillars, though, can be a different story. Some species of caterpillars are really picky eaters, eating only the leaves of a single species of plant. Our most famous example of that is the caterpillar of the monarch butterfly, which will eat only the leaves of the milkweed plant. No milkweeds, no monarchs.

In similar fashion, the zebra swallowtail caterpillars will eat only one kind of leaf— those of the pawpaw tree. And so the lightbulb went off when we saw all those zebras, and we surmised, "There must be a pawpaw tree around here somewhere!" And when we started looking for pawpaw trees, they were everywhere. The swampy Carolina woods were full of them, their big, oval, magnolia-sized leaves standing out like green flags, their odd green fruits on a few.

So, what might zebra swallowtail butterflies and pawpaw trees in a swamp in East Carolina have to do with East Tennessee? Well, for one thing, the zebra swallowtail butterfly happens to be the official state butterfly for the state of Tennessee. So designated by our legislature back in 1995, it was inaugurated as an official state symbol along with the cave salamander (official state salamander) and the box turtle (official state reptile).

With zebra swallowtails as our state butterfly, you would think there had to be pawpaw trees to be found in Tennessee. And sure enough, there are. Always have been, for millennia; pawpaws are native trees, all across the state.

Probably the best way to learn about pawpaws is to ask an old person, preferably one who grew up in a family that went out in the woods to gather edible things like chestnuts, walnuts, hickory nuts, muscadines, morels, and ramps. They know what they taste like, where to find them, when to harvest them, and how to fix them. But here are some of the facts: Pawpaws are widespread in the East, from the Atlantic coast to the Mississippi River, and from Michigan south to central Mississippi, Alabama, and Georgia. They seem to be centered more or less in Ohio. They grow as small understory trees in reasonably moist woods; they like shade, with big trees towering over them. Most of their relatives are tropical trees and fruits, and pawpaws stand out once you learn to look for them, with big, oval, drooping, tropical-looking leaves.

The experts tell us that pawpaws are North America's largest native fruit. They are peculiar bananalike oblong things, green before they're ripe, and then with a purplish, overripe-banana look to them when they become ripe. They are full of big seeds and have a custardlike pulp that tastes like a cross between a banana and a mango. Sort of. That pawpaw flavor is an acquired taste, but people who love them, really love them.

Around these parts, pawpaws ripen in September. And pawpaw lovers keep a close eye on their favorite patch. If you pick a pawpaw when it's still green, it won't go on and ripen like a banana will. And if you wait a day or two late, they drop on the ground, to be immediately gobbled up by deer, raccoons, possums, turkeys, and squirrels. They're best when they drop easily with just a little shake of the tree.

By coincidence I found a nice fact-filled book on the very subject of pawpaws on the "new book" shelves at the Powell Library. Authored by a young fellow by the name of Andrew Moore, the book is entitled *Pawpaw: In Search of America's Forgotten Fruit*. Moore is a student of the pawpaw and a big promoter. It turns out that a lot of people are working to bring them up to date, growing them orchard style, with improved and dependable varieties. Several states hold annual pawpaw festivals, and they are the official state native fruit of Ohio. They are sold at farmer's markets and grocery stores and are made into pudding and ice cream.

Toward the end of his book, Moore cites an outstanding pawpaw event that has taken place here in our area: The runner-up for the Peoples' Choice award at the 2014 International Biscuit Festival in Knoxville, Tennessee! It was a pawpaw pecan buttermilk biscuit, topped with Tennessee whiskey and sorghum caramel! Sorghum? Whiskey? Caramel? Pawpaws? Maybe it should be our Official State Biscuit!

The "forgotten" pawpaw? They'll be getting ripe soon. You should try one for yourself; you might become one of those avid pawpaw people. Especially if you can manage to find somebody who will tell you where to find some.

FALL

TALL FALL FLOWERS

Well my goodness, it's Labor Day! It seems like it was just a few weeks ago that we were excitedly looking for the first blossoms of spring, those delicate little white and yellow things that rush out of the ground at the first moment they can, before the tree leaves overhead shade them out of existence. Those were the Spring Ephemerals, ephemeral meaning "fleeting." And fleeting they were. The bloodroots, hepaticas, anemones, toothworts, and trilliums. Soon after the woods leafed out, they were gone, almost without a trace. A shriveled brown leaf here, a seed pod there, but mostly, gone.

And now in September we have a new batch of flowers that provide us with quite a different scene than the ones we enjoyed in early spring. They are big, robust, and substantial. Instead of being nestled in the leaf litter on the forest floor, these tall, tough plants fill the roadsides and abandoned fields, waist high, shoulder high—the Tall Fall Flowers. They aren't hard to find. They like unmowed pastures, drainage ditches, and woodland edges; you'll find them anywhere out of reach of a mowing machine. You may see any of the ones discussed here by just watching out your car window as you drive around each day.

Now, there is a four-letter word you and I need to discuss. It's the "W" word—"weed," that is. Gardeners define a weed as anything that is growing somewhere that you don't want it.

Farmers mowing the unwanted plants from their pastures, or county workers trying to keep our roadsides clear this time of year, likely will consider some of our fall flowers to be weeds. In fact, some of them have "weed" in their common names; take for example ironweed and Joe-Pye weed. A number of these weed families have been bred and groomed and "improved" to where they have achieved an accepted place in the seed catalogs and flower gardens. So, "weed" depends on your point of view; in other words, you can decide for yourself what is a weed and what isn't.

Perhaps the king of the fall wildflowers is the goldenrod. There are over 100 species in North America, about 30 types in Tennessee. All of them are golden yellow except for the single white variety called silverrod. Bright golden yellow and 3–4 feet tall, with innumerable tiny flowers displayed in clumps up and down the stem or in graceful sprays near the top, goldenrod distills the late summer sun and shines it back for all to enjoy.

A widely held misconception about goldenrod is that it is the cause for all those nasty hay fever symptoms that beset mankind just as it blooms out. Not so! Less than 2% of the pollen in the air this time of year is from goldenrod. The real culprit? Achoo! It's ragweed. How can we say that with such assurance? Let's look at the lifestyle of the two plants.

Ragweed has small, inconspicuous green flowers. You don't see any insects on ragweed. It doesn't attract them, because they are not needed for its pollination. Its pollen grains are tiny, dry, and carried on the wind. Ragweed depends on the air to move its pollen to another plant. And into your sinuses.

Goldenrod, on the other hand, has bright, showy flowers; makes nectar that attracts a shopping list of insects; and has sticky, heavy pollen designed to stick to the bugs so they will carry them to the next goldenrod plant—not in the air, not in your nose. And because they bloom at the same time, and the goldenrod is bright and showy and the ragweed is drab and unnoticed, the goldenrod often takes the blame for the flying pollen.

Speaking of lots of insects, goldenrod is a very interesting little mini-zoo when in full bloom. You may see honeybees, bumblebees, and a variety of wasps and flies, large and small. Many of the insects attracted to goldenrod flowers are safe to catch and get a closer look. There will be colorful little guys such as soldier beetles, longhorn beetles, and ambush bugs. Check them out in your handy field guide. There will usually be a crab spider lurking somewhere, most often the color of the flowers it is hiding among. And there will be ants and treehoppers and butterflies.

It's fun to take a white cloth, like a sheet or pillowcase, out into the field and shake a couple of goldenrod heads into it. You will find all sorts of beasties to watch and identify, and it's a great way to introduce a bunch of inquisitive kids to some exciting things that they didn't know even existed.

A couple more of the tall fall flowers that are blooming out there are in the purple department, the two with "weed" in their names. They both have big clusters of color made up of large numbers of tiny individual flowers at the top of a tall stalk. Ironweed has deep, royal purple flowers. Joe-Pye weed, named for the nineteenth-century herb doctor who used the plant to treat fevers, kidney stones, and other maladies, is almost like a shadow of the ironweed, with a pale, ghostly shade of purple. And Joe-Pye weed favors moister places to grow, such as roadside ditches and drainage areas.

I checked out my personal clump of Joe-Pye weed recently and found it to be the center of activity, much as its cousin the goldenrod. In addition to a bumblebee and several unidentified kinds of little bees and wasps, there were several individuals of a couple of species of butterflies, called skippers, visiting for a sip of nectar. Joe-Pye weed has stout red stems with whorls of leaves, and on the leaves I began to notice a dead skipper here and another one there.

That led to a search for the assassin, and aha! There she was, a big green crab spider, lying quietly in wait for the next unwary skipper. She doesn't make a web to catch her meals; she just nabs them when they come within reach, oftentimes catching things much larger than herself. She poisons them with an injection, sucks them dry, and tosses the empty husk over the side. Sometimes you'll come upon a motionless butterfly that doesn't fly away as you come nearer and nearer. Look closely: It may still be in the grasp of a crab spider. Yep, it's a jungle out there!

Well, what about some white flowers? Yes, the tall fall flowers have some interesting white cousins, too. In your fall meanderings you may come across an array of tall stalks of tiny white flowers that are in the thoroughwort family. There are several species; one of the better-known ones is called boneset. While it is doubtful that it will make bones knit any better, it has been used for many years as a remedy for an assortment of maladies, including arthritis and rheumatism.

But a word of caution: You don't want to confuse your boneset with white snakeroot. Boneset tea might ease your rheumatism, but snakeroot tea could prove fatal. Snakeroot blooms in the fall, also, and likewise has many tiny white flowers. But white snakeroot is poisonous. Cows grazing on snakeroot give milk that when ingested causes an illness called "milk sickness." It was more prevalent back when the milk cows roamed more freely, and families often drank the milk of a single cow. Abraham Lincoln's mother is said to have died of milk sickness.

There are lots more fall flowers to discover and enjoy: the many varieties of asters, the big purple thistles, the blue chicory blooming up and down the roadsides. There are a good number of field guides available to help with identifications; some even specialize in fall flowers. Weeds or not, the tall fall flowers take the lush green background of late summer and throw a palette of bright waving colors across it, almost as if they are predicting the glorious fall colors soon to come. They're certainly growing where I want them to be.

LOOKING BACK—OR FORWARD?

Three of my favorite bird, wildflower, and general getting-outdoors places—Great Smoky Mountains National Park, Norris Dam Reservation area, and Blue Ridge Parkway—were either saved or created through some of the most difficult times this country has ever seen—between two world wars and in the midst of economic disaster.

The Stock Market crashed on October 24, 1929, and the Great Depression began. Herbert Hoover had taken office in early 1928, after 6 years of great prosperity under Calvin Coolidge. Hoover had promised "a chicken in every pot and a car in every garage" while on the campaign trail.

However, in less than 2 years, the American economy was brought to its knees. Stocks bottomed out, banks failed, and factories and businesses closed. The Great Depression lasted until 1940, when the economic stimulus of preparations for entering World War II caused it to fade quickly away. Anyone with a job, home, family, or any financial responsibility never forgot those days of economic hardship, and their financial decisions were affected by those memories for the rest of their lives.

Here in Appalachia, we were already living in one of the poorest areas of the nation. The average income of a hill-country farm family at that time was $86 ... *per year*. Roads were bad, electricity scarce, and unemployment high. But we East Tennesseans and our neighbors in western North Carolina reaped some surprising benefits from the Great Depression. Looking back from where we are now, we can see that a lot of good, lasting things came out of those really tough times, things that continue to enrich our lives up to the present time.

With apologies to Dr. James Tumblin, historian laureate of Fountain City here just north of Knoxville, I will proceed with a bit more history. Not up to Tumblin standards, but at least I promise not to make anything up. In 1932, the widespread poverty and dire financial straits across the country led to the decisive Presidential victory for Franklin D. Roosevelt and a change in government policy, ushering in the "New Deal." Incidentally, FDR's secretary of state was an outstanding Tennessean from rural Pickett County, Cordell Hull. Born and raised within 20 miles of his contemporary, war hero Alvin York, Hull served as the US secretary of state from 1933 to 1944.

But we digress. New Deal efforts to bring order out of chaos and stabilize the economic situation in 1933, in the depths of the Great Depression, produced a large number of new federal laws, agencies, and projects. One of those new agencies was the Tennessee Valley Authority (TVA).

The Tennessee River was potentially a great resource, but throughout the region's early history, there were two big problems associated with the river: floods and navigability. Floods had been devastating. There is a big panoramic photograph on the wall of the Tennessee Aquarium in Chattanooga, showing the city inundated by the Great Flood of 1917. There were many more floods, creating millions of dollars in losses. And as for navigation, if you needed a barge load of something shipped upriver from New Orleans or Memphis or Cincinnati to Chattanooga or Knoxville, you could proceed upstream only as far as the rocky shallows of Muscle Shoals, in northwest Alabama. Except for times of high water, the Shoals were the stopping point for navigation up and down the river.

Wilson Dam was begun by the federal government at Muscle Shoals in 1918 to allow barges to pass over the shallows and to supply electric power to two nitrate plants making explosives for the war effort. Finished in 1926, the dam stood idle while the politicians in Washington debated whether the government should produce electricity. Nothing sounds new there, does it?

The TVA was created and signed into law on May 18, 1933. Their nucleus was the old Wilson Dam, the two nitrate plants, and an even older dam below Chattanooga, Hales Bar. Their task was to build a series of dams for navigation and flood control on the main channel and a number of dams on the side streams for storage and power. Their first project was on the Clinch River some 25 miles north of Knoxville—Norris Dam.

They didn't just build a dam. They also built the Norris Freeway and the town of Norris. They set out demonstration tracts of different kinds of trees to be used in reforesting the denuded and eroded hillsides of East Tennessee. And they constructed a series of ponds for a fish hatchery below the dam to use for stocking the waters thereabouts.

The project started on October 1, 1933. My father was a young TVA personnel officer then, and his first job was to travel north to the wilds of Claiborne County, where they had set up an employment office above the post office in the town of Tazewell. In 1933 there was no problem in finding many hands eager for work. There, he hired men to come down and work on the big new project in Anderson County.

The gates of the new dam closed and began impounding the water of the Clinch River in May 1936. Apparently, the two major political parties were able to accomplish something together back then, because they named the dam for the Republican senator from Nebraska, George Norris, who was a prime force in the creation of TVA.

Today we can all enjoy the fruits of those labors. In addition to the expected water-related recreation on Norris Lake, there is great trout fishing in the tailwaters. On one side of the river below the dam is the Riverbluff Trail. It provides a spectacular spring wildflower show, with thousands of trout lilies across the forest floor and a couple dozen other species sprouting up before, during, and after the lilies. Across the river is Songbird Trail, winding through trees and shrubs full of spring migrants every April and May.

Meanwhile during those years, off to the southeast of us, the newly created Civilian Conservation Corps (1933), an army of thousands of young men supervised by military officers, architects, and engineers, were starting to build roads, bridges, buildings, and the 900 miles of trails for the newly created Great Smoky Mountains National Park (1934). The results of the vision and labor of those days continue to grace the park today.

And as Appalachia was becoming electrified by the TVA and preserved and beautified by the Great Smoky Mountains National Park, a third project with a whole new concept was under way in the highlands of Virginia and North Carolina. Called the Blue Ridge Parkway, it ultimately became a 469-mile scenic highway connecting the Shenandoah National Park with the Great Smoky Mountains National Park.

The parkway was approved in 1933, but it took 2 years of arguing about its name, its route, who was to pay for it, and who would be responsible for maintaining it, before work finally began in September 1935. Even the concept of what a parkway actually was had to be worked out!

It all turned out well, somehow. It was decided that the parkway would be a special kind of road, designed primarily for the pleasure of those who used it. It was to access as much remote scenery as possible along the route with the least possible disturbance. The concept of scenic easements was introduced, strictly limiting what could be done with any property visible from the road. The result? One guide book to the national parks describes the Blue Ridge Parkway as "almost too good to be true."

The parkway has limited access, no trucks, no billboards, and no roadside stands. There are 168 bridges, 16 recreational areas, 9 campgrounds, and 6 visitor's centers with museum-type displays. There are several viaducts where the roadway is built up on piers and goes around the shoulder of a mountain to avoid making road cuts into it. The most famous of these is the Linn Cove Viaduct around the shoulder of Grandfather Mountain. Completed in 1987, it was (at last) the final segment of the parkway to be finished.

Like the Great Smoky Mountains National Park, the Blue Ridge Parkway is another national treasure, there for all of us and for our grandchildren, coming out of tough times, serious decisions, and hard work. Eighty years later we can drive up the Norris Freeway to enjoy a morning at the lake or the park, or head out for a day of walking for miles in the mountains. We can find peace and quiet and mile after mile of beautiful high-country scenery, all very good stuff for the spirit! Next time you're out there, reflect for a minute on all the folks who were involved with creating those national treasures. I hope that 80 years from now, people will feel just as good about what we have left them.

ON THE MOVE AGAIN: ENJOYING FALL BIRDING

The birds are on the move again. And they aren't the only creatures stirring. Those people in the funny hats, carrying binoculars—the birders—are out and about, too. After 2 or 3 months of summer doldrums, big things are happening out there in the bird world.

Fall migration actually started back in the summer. Those earliest spring arrivals, the martins and the swallows, are also the first to head south in the fall. We saw a flock of thousands of purple martins gathering up in East Carolina for fall migration way back the first week of August. The second week of August, we found 200 tree swallows on the lines and swarming over our hayfield; 3 days later, none.

The last of the nighthawks, chimney swifts, and hummingbirds will be leaving any day now. But, many other species will be passing through in large numbers, through October and even into November, and now's the time to get out and see the fall show—birds passing through that we only get to glimpse for a few days each spring and fall.

Fall birding is full of challenges to confront the eager birder. A couple of major problems: familiar birds in unusual plumages, and lots of unusual birds, just passing through, from farther north. Migrating fall warblers, for example, are legendary in their difficulty. The Roger Tory Peterson field guides feature two whole pages entitled "Confusing Fall Warblers." So bright and colorful in the spring that they're called "the butterflies of the bird world," many of them molt this time of the year into drab—and sometimes quite different—plumages. And not just the warblers. Scarlet tanagers go from flaming red and jet black to yellow and olive, goldfinches go from

gold and black to drab shades of greenish yellow, and strikingly blue indigo buntings turn a motley gray or brown.

In addition, the gathering flocks are now being joined by equal or greater numbers of this year's hatchlings, full grown but still with mystifyingly different plumages from their parents. All this confusion, plus the possibilities of seeing unusual or even rare transient birds, make fall birding exciting and challenging, and bring about the annual fall reappearance of all those birders.

The Eagle Bend Fish Hatchery in Clinton, less than 20 minutes from my mailbox, is a small, but rewarding, local birding spot. The large open ponds and grassy fields pull in migrating birds like a magnet. You can check it out in less than an hour. Over the years, I've seen nearly 100 species of birds there, many for the first time. This fall, I saw such long-distance migrants as bobolinks there on September 14th and a spiffy American golden-plover there on September 26th. That's nice, you say; we don't usually have them around here. But why drive 20 miles and spend an hour trying to see them?

A big reason for all the excitement in finding these birds is that most birders understand the significance of where these birds are coming from and where they are going. Those range maps in the field guides that show where each species spends the summer, and then the winter? Look closely at them. They contain a ton of information and will tell you amazing stories of twice-yearly journeys of incredible distances, remarkable navigational skills, and especially the endurance displayed by all those small feathered creatures.

Take those bobolinks, for example. Sparrow-sized, seed-eating birds, the males are a striking black and white in spring, but in fall are a drab, streaked yellow-brown, blending in with the brown fall grasses where they feed. These little birds nest far to the north of us: the Great Lakes, upper Midwest, and on up into Canada. The ones at Eagle Bend were taking a rest and food break, less than halfway on their journey of thousands of miles to wintering grounds in southern South America.

The golden-plovers? They nest in the high Arctic tundra of northernmost North America. The one I saw at Eagle Bend was fueling up on East Tennessee bugs to continue its trip to southeastern South America, where, across the equator, it will find itself in early spring instead of early fall. When I saw it, it was only halfway on an 8,000-mile trip, which it will do the other way (north) in the spring. Every year. I consider it a true wonder of nature, and there I was, looking into its black beady eyes. You can't help but wish these birds good luck and safe travels!

There are lots of good local places to see fall birds 30 miles or less from Knoxville. We have Cove Lake State Park in Campbell County and the Norris Songbird Trail and the above-mentioned Eagle Bend Fish Hatchery in Anderson County. Knox County parks such as Tommy Schumpert, Victor Ashe, and Sharp's Ridge Memorial offer good birding close by. And the newest—and, in my opinion, one of the best—is Seven Islands State Birding Park, also in Knox County. It is home to over 400 well-managed, wildlife-friendly acres along the French Broad River. It sports weedy fields, wooded hills, and a pond, as well as the river frontage. Nice trails make it all accessible for good birding.

The park already boasts a bird list of more than 200 species, and well-guided bird walks occur frequently. I most recently visited there on a bright, clear Wednesday morning. Ten of us were treated to a cool, cloudless day and lots of fall birds. My list for the 3-hour, 3.5-mile walk that morning had 51 species of birds, including a bald eagle, various hawks, grosbeaks, tanagers, herons, ducks, and especially fun for me, 7 different species of those confusing fall warblers! It's even more fun when you have expert birders, like our two leaders that day, there to help a person sort them out. The spectacular view across the river valley on over to Chilhowee Mountain and Mount LeConte wasn't bad, either. East Tennessee fall birding at some of its best.

Fall birding may not be the rush that spring birding provides, but there are nevertheless a lot of interesting and challenging goings-on out there. And, a lot of great places nearby to enjoy the show.

As an autumn outdoor activity, it certainly ranks several notches higher than raking leaves.

SOME NUTTY STUFF

"Sometimes you feel like a nut, sometimes you don't." A famous line from the jingle for Mounds and Almond Joy candy bars, it actually sums up most of our human existence. But this isn't a philosophical treatise; it's a story about nuts.

Numerous species of trees offer up tasty and nutritious nuts that have been enjoyed by millions of people for centuries, and still are. We generally don't think of acorns as people food, but since ancient times oak trees all around the world have produced the main staple food for the large number of humans living with them. And those candy bar nuts in the jingle? They're almonds, a tropical species that is native to North Africa on up into Syria and raised commercially in California. Another tasty favorite, cashews, are native to the tropics as well.

Closer to home, the huge, stately American chestnut trees, most dependable and abundant of all the nut trees, fell victim—all 4 billion of them—to an imported fungus in the 1920s and 1930s. But today, it is hard to think of a nut tree that provides more of a connection between us and our forebears—and between us and some of the tasty delights of Mother Nature—than the handsome, soft-spoken American black walnut tree.

I have lived close to walnut trees most of my life. When I was young, my Dad, upon the advice of the county agent, planted hundreds of walnuts, reclaiming an old, worn-out cornfield, which was where we now live. I have enjoyed many pleasant hours in my shop, making some of that wonderful wood into boards and bowls. Working with the wood is wonderful, but the old tastebuds have to come into the discussion when you talk about a useful plant. I have fond memories of fresh-baked black walnut cookies, hot from my Granny Collier's old cooking range oven. The cool fall weather and the approaching holidays seem to bring those memories into sharper focus every year.

This year we've had an extraordinarily abundant walnut crop. There have been so many on the ground that a body could hardly get the riding mower steered through them, and the squirrels couldn't begin to keep up with them. And that abundance resulted in the sequence of events that led to this nutty column.

A friend of mine and I were comparing notes on walnut abundance, and he remarked that he knew someone who would love to have a few. That led a couple of weeks later to my encounter with a wise and talented, gray-haired, lady-in-perpetual-motion whom we shall refer to as Mamaw. I gathered and gathered nuts, and in the end, my new friend decided that eleven 5-gallon buckets would be about enough (picture a 55-gallon barrel of green walnuts). Upon delivery, she explained that she would get to them as soon as she finished planting the 300 tulip bulbs she already had waiting. And a very few days thereafter, I got a call saying that my empty buckets were ready to pick up and that a walnut pie was waiting for me.

Ambrosia! Food of the gods! It was a concoction of dates, coconut, egg whites, and walnuts, nestled in a flaky, homemade crust and topped with real, fresh-whipped whipping cream and big walnut nut meats. Neighbors, I would be willing to gather a really big lot of walnuts for another one of Mamaw's walnut pies.

The preparation of those walnuts for that pie involved a lot of hard, tedious work—easier if you know how but still a lot of work. Since there may be a few folks out there who are not fully aware of the many steps needed from tree to pie, we will describe some of the essentials to help them understand what a feat it really is (and remind those of us who already know).

The first thing to know is that you don't get out a ladder and go picking walnuts off the tree. The ones on the tree aren't ripe. They fall off when they're ready, and you pick them up off the ground, before the squirrels do. Next thing, you want to be efficient and only work on good walnuts. Insects can get to them and destroy the meats inside. To separate the good ones out, you toss them all in a tub of water. The good ones sink, and the bad ones float. You may have noticed that the squirrels take each nut and turn it over and over before going away with it. Squirrels can tell the good from the bad without the tub of water. They've been doing it for thousands of years.

Now you have a couple of problems to work through. Most tree nut fruits come securely packaged by Mother Nature, and black walnuts are some of the most secure. The tasty meats are down in there beneath, first, a hull (and black goopy stuff) and, second, a very hard shell. The greenish hull has to go first. A dozen clever methods have been devised to remove it, including hobnail boots, meat grinders, corn shellers, and automobile tires.

The black gooey stuff stains hands and clothes forever, so wear gloves. And it may be infested with little white walnut hull maggots. Not to worry, they don't harm the meats inside. That black gooey stuff is used for inks, dyes, and home remedies. I found a website that will sell you an 8 ounce jar of that black goop for $48.85 (with free shipping)! This could potentially be East Tennessee's answer to California's gold rush or Texas' oil wells!

But we digress. Once the walnuts are out of their hulls, the shells have to be allowed to dry a week or two. The shells of our walnuts are about the hardest of all the nut shells to crack, but once again, ingenuity comes to the rescue. Bricks and hammers, shop vices, commercial walnut crackers of various designs can be utilized for the heavy work. Then small sharp picks bring forth the nut meats, big pieces if you're a pro, little ones if not.

You get about 2 cups of nut meats from 5 pounds of cracked walnuts. Labor-intensive, tedious. But you get a unique, tasty, fat- and protein-rich reward that will keep for months in the fridge and almost indefinitely in the freezer. Recipes? They are numberless.

Besides Mamaw's walnut pie, you can make walnut cookies, cakes, fudge, and ice cream. You can make pickled walnuts, curried walnuts, and chocolate caramel walnuts. How about some orange walnut chicken, with a side of Hungarian walnut and poppy seed rolls?

I have been considering nominating the black walnut for Tennessee state nut, but wow, with so many other candidates out there, I doubt that a mere tree would have a chance.

A NEW WHISTLE PIG

Twice now in recent years I've had my old, faithful Ford Explorer, which has to sleep outside these days, off to my helpful car repair people because a small furry beast of some sort has chewed through a soft part of the fuel line. Gas out on the pavement. Yet other beasts have targeted my yard to the point that I've had to give up gardening. And now, one of my outbuildings is under attack by yet another furry beast—a wily groundhog, also known as the whistle pig.

Reflecting upon all this quiet but destructive mayhem, I remembered a book that I purchased while on a trip out West. It's by a fellow named Charlie Craighead, and it is entitled *Who Ate the Back Yard?* Now, it happens that Charlie lives in a place called Moose, Wyoming. This means that when Charlie talks about wildlife eating his back yard, he isn't talking just a bunch of mice, squirrels, and raccoons. He has encounters with the likes of porcupines, wolves, moose, and mountain lions.

In addition to a trove of biological information about all these critters, Mr. Craighead has a series of sidebars in his book listed as "True Encounters." They have such titles as "The Moose That Went Trick-or-Treating," and one that struck a nerve with me, "The Disappearing Garden." But you don't have to live in moose country to have your garden disappear.

Knoxville historian Jack Neely has addressed urban sprawl in several of his columns for local alternative papers and online. He reported that a recent nationwide poll by Smart Growth America lists Knoxville as 22nd out of the 25 worst places in America for urban sprawl. While that's a topic open to some serious debate, it's nevertheless true that just about everywhere, as more and more people move away from the city toward the countryside, there are more and more encounters with those who were there first—the critters.

With due respect to Mr. Craighead, I'm glad us folks around these parts don't have to worry about how to fence out bison and moose, or how to keep wolves and mountain lions from eating our livestock and pets. And us. That being said, we citizens of the Knoxville area still have to contend with wildlife that will, by golly, eat your shrubs and your garden, and your pet cat, and your front lawn, your hostas, and your birdseed.

All this hostile train of thought was set in motion by the arrival this year of the new furry beast under my shop porch. Welcome, neighbors, to the new boarder now living with us, in a cavernous hole under my shop . . . Mr. Whistle Pig. A formal announcement would include the notation that Mr. W now joins the resident deer who breakfast on the hostas and those long-time members of the community, Mr. and Mrs. Squirrel and their 400 children, who prefer black oil sunflower seeds but will settle for stealing tomatoes from the garden or harvesting black walnuts from a 5-gallon bucket if the opportunity should arise.

Everybody knows the groundhog story. If the groundhog wakes up and comes out and it's cloudy, we can joyfully prepare for an early spring. On the other hand, if the furry rascal wakes up on a sunny day and he sees his shadow, away he goes back to sleep and we have 6 more weeks of winter. The legend apparently has been around for ages. The ancient Germans had it, but theirs involved the ever-popular hedgehog. When the Germans came to settle what became known as Pennsylvania Dutch country, they didn't find hedgehogs, so they substituted groundhogs for the story.

Groundhog Day was first observed in the United States on February 2, 1886. It has always been a big deal in Punxsutawney, Pennsylvania, and now more than ever with the appearance of the 1993 movie "Groundhog Day," starring Bill Murray. The town apparently has crowds of 30,000–40,000 people on hand to watch the groundhog wake up since the movie came out. I guess any excuse for a big party will do.

Now, as for the drama about my hanging it up as a gardener. The last year that I gardened, I had trained a nice row of cucumbers to grow up a section of woven wire fencing. I could come out and select a tasty-looking cucumber at eye level from my fence; all was well. Then one morning, I came out and there sat a whistle pig with the last bite of cucumber foliage sticking out of its mouth, looking at me as if to say, "what?" And not only were the cucumbers gone, so were the vines and stems, down to a neat row of 2-inch-tall stumps. The last straw, as they say. I built a workshop on the site.

Since the average groundhog lives 3 years or so, I figure the new one under my shop porch is a great-great-grandchild of the one I caught eating my cucumbers. Right now, he's eating yard herbs and having a golden delicious apple for dessert, sitting up on his haunches and holding the apple in his forepaws. Spouse thinks he's cute. I'd think so too, if he was up in Cades Cove.

In spite of being cute, groundhogs famously wreak havoc around homes, farms, and gardens. They've been known to seriously undermine building foundations; their huge underground dens will collapse and gobble a big rear tractor tire up to the axle—try that with a baler hooked on the back. And, of course, they can often lead the disbelieving gardener to scratch his head and cry in anguish, in the manner of Charlie Craighead, "Who ate the garden?"

Well, I had planned to just accept the new arrival as another part of Mother Nature's fauna out at our place, and to be calm and content with my lot. But then as I drove out the other day, egads! A second, different, big, fat, waddley whistle pig ran across the driveway and disappeared into a new excavation beneath my neighbor's small horse barn. I sense that we're in for trouble ahead.

TENNESSEE'S SHORELINE

Lots of cities or regions vie for bragging rights to the best numbers and kinds of birds a person can expect to find there. Whether a town, city, or state, a state park or National Wildlife Refuge, birdiness is a big point of pride, and a big tourist draw. And it's like the real estate business; it really depends a lot upon location.

Different species of birds have distinct differences in the places they prefer to visit or live, so it stands to reason that the more different habitats a locality has, the greater the variety of birds you can find there. A state with mountains, valleys, deserts, and seacoast, like Oregon for example, has a big advantage on the number of bird species you'll see over a landlocked and rather featureless state like, say, Kansas. And in looking at these various geographic features, it seems that the one addition to a state that really makes a birding difference is water, and most of all, seacoast.

Just check out your favorite bird book and see what a large proportion of the species are associated with water: open ocean, coastlines, marshes, lakes, and rivers. There's no way bird lists from Iowa or Kansas can compete with those from California, Texas, or Florida. Even North and South Carolina and Georgia have ocean, shore, and marsh that make a birding trip to those states an exciting adventure.

So, what about landlocked Tennessee? Well, our official TWRA birding field card sports a list of 287 birds that a person might see in our state, in the right place at the right time. That's not a bad list considering we're several hundred miles from the ocean, and it includes lots of ducks, wading birds, and shorebirds.

And how can that be? Here are the facts: TVA's lakes in the Tennessee River Valley contain almost 1,000 square miles of lake surface area and are bordered by 7,000 miles of shoreline! Add to these all the lakes built by the US Army Corps of Engineers, Alcoa, and others, plus our western "coastline" of the Mississippi River, and you have all those square miles of water covering about 2.2% of Tennessee's total surface area, even though we're landlocked.

Open lake water brings ducks, coots, loons, grebes, and cormorants. Shorelines and shallows bring egrets and herons. Mudflats bring a variety of wading and sandpiper types. And most of them look like choice suppertime treats to a range of eagles, ospreys, falcons, hawks, and vultures.

Not all those birds live here; many are just passing through. And so, another important aspect of a state's location is where it is situated in the migratory flight path of those millions of traveling birds, and how inviting its geography is for them (read: how much stuff there is in an area to eat). Tennessee is visited by large flights of land birds, water birds, and shorebirds, heading north and south each year. It's happening right now.

Rankin Bottoms, up on Douglas Lake in Cocke County, has hosted just about every shorebird species in eastern North America at one time or another. It's a great place for birding because whenever the lake is drawn down by TVA, it exposes extensive shallows and mud flats, irresistible to those hungry migrating shorebirds as they look down for a place to rest and feed. Its array of birds has been sought out and well documented in excellent photographs by several dedicated, and often canoe-borne, birders.

Our big lakes rarely freeze over in the winter, so they make great wintering areas for the ducks, grebes, and loons that breed in the north and find refuge from the ice down here. During the winter of 2013–2014, we made many forays out into the cold to see far-north birds such as long-tailed ducks, red-necked grebes, and scoters, feeding and hanging out in the open waters of our lakes because their usual winter quarters, the Great Lakes, had frozen over.

A body really has to work at it to come up with that list of over 300 birds seen in Tennessee, and especially, to come up with some of the rarities that show up only occasionally or even only once in a lifetime. And those rarities that do show up are, more often than not, here because of one or another of Tennessee's water resources. For example, in fall 1987 we saw a pair of American white pelicans swimming in the Little Pigeon River in Sevierville. In July 1990 we watched two white ibis probing for worms in a marshy area of Union County.

And even rarer examples: In winter 1996, we drove out to Pickwick Dam in West Tennessee to see an ivory gull, a bird that is seldom seen south of Greenland, having a lunch of freshly caught minnows from the big lake there, near a flock of local gulls. Our latest water-related rarity was a stately pink bird, here from the Gulf coast and apparently blown in by a recent big weather system—none other than a roseate spoonbill. It was discovered hanging out with its new best friends, a pair of Canada geese, feeding in a farm pond out in Blount County, in full view of the Smoky Mountains.

But you don't have to find an occasional rarity to benefit birdingwise from our bountiful waters. There are innumerable swallows, kingfishers, ospreys and bald eagles, gulls and terns, ducks, geese, herons, and egrets out there—some in winter, some in the summer—finding places to nest and food to catch. Look at all those birds in that first third of your bird book, and be glad that you live here!

We don't have any oceanside resorts or big, long saltwater fishing piers, but our hundreds of square miles of lakes and rivers and thousands of miles of shorelines do bring us an abundance of interesting birds. Of course, ocean surf washing up on Tennessee shores somewhere would be nice, but we and the birds are doing well with what we have. And then also, mercifully, we don't have hurricanes.

FALL TREES

Trees. They are the backdrop for our daily lives here in East Tennessee, yet we tend to take them pretty much for granted. To quote the apt words of one gardening book, "Trees root us in place with their continuity; they assure us that what has been before us will be here long after. They mark the seasons of our year and are companions, lasting for lifetimes, generations, and millennia."

We're having considerable uneasiness about our trees in these parts, because in the collective lifetimes of those of us still here, whole species of these companions, presumed to be around forever, are now gone. Consider the billions of American chestnut trees, once the dominant trees in our forests, vanished, victims of an imported fungus. And the elms that lined many a city street, victims of another foreign invader, Dutch elm disease. The list goes frighteningly on: Fraser firs decimated by the balsam woolly adelgid; dogwoods, by the anthracnose fungus; and now hemlocks are being wiped out by another species of adelgid, the hemlock woolly adelgid.

The latest assault on our leafy backdrop has come from the imported emerald ash borer. We had far more stately ashes than I realized until I saw so many of them standing there dead. Many large old ash trees are now stark skeletons, and locally at least, they are facing extinction.

Thankfully, science fights back. Endless years have been spent in trying to produce a resistant chestnut tree. Already, there are resistant dogwood trees available, even though the fate of millions of wild dogwoods is in question. And biologists are unleashing hordes of tiny beetles in the Smokies to attack the hemlock woolly adelgid; we can only hope that they have a big appetite, and hopefully, only for the adelgids.

Even as these biological battles go on, our trees continue to provide us with shade, companionship, and beauty. With the wildflowers fading and the birds heading south, Mother Nature has one more spectacle in her show before we have to rake leaves and hunker down for winter.

The amazing phenomenon of autumn leaf colors is mostly an eastern one. From the Pacific coast, where the seasonal changes are modulated by the ocean winds, to the Rocky Mountains, where the fall colors are provided mainly by groves of golden aspens against a background of evergreens, across the grass-covered, treeless Great Plains, there is nothing that compares to our fall display of color.

The show begins in Maine, at the far northern end of the Appalachian Mountains, along about the middle of September. Autumn moves south at the rate of about 60 miles a day, and colors usually peak in the higher elevations of our Smoky Mountains about the first 2 weeks of October, and in the lower elevations from about October 15th.

Every fall is different, of course; some are early, some are late. Lots of factors figure in—some known, some unknown. Rain, drought, early frost, late frost. This year some trees were showing color in August. Some years, the leaves just dry up and fall off; occasionally we are treated to a year with a display of brilliant colors.

And what about those colors? Where do they come from? The green color in all the trees comes from chlorophyll. Chlorophyll is essential to the process of photosynthesis, in which green plants take water and carbon dioxide and use the energy of the sun to turn them into sugar. This not only provides food for the plant; it ultimately provides food for every living thing on Earth.

And it has an interesting byproduct, oxygen. The next time you take a deep breath, thank a tree. The next time you hear how many acres of rainforest are being permanently destroyed every day, take it seriously.

But we're digressing onto gloomy thoughts again. Back to that chlorophyll. As the days grow shorter and cooler, the trees stop making chlorophyll, and that present in the leaves begins to break down. But there are other materials in the leaves, too—chemicals called xanthophyll, carotene, and anthocyanin. These have different colors: yellow, orange, red. As the chlorophyll breaks down, these other colors can show through, and the different combinations of them in leaves are what give us our fall colors.

Different species of trees have different fall colors; some turn yellow, some red or orange. And some species, especially the maples, can have more than one color, even on the same tree, or even on the same leaf. In our neck of the woods, the colors come mainly from a few species: maples, black gums, beeches, poplars, oaks. Plus a number of smaller trees, such as the dogwoods and sumacs, and the shrubs and vines, to fill in the spaces.

In contrast to New England, we have relatively few evergreens to serve as a backdrop for the fall colors, but the pines, cedars, and hemlocks do a good job even in small numbers. You don't really have to sign up for one of those leaf color bus tours to New Hampshire; just get out and enjoy the spectacle we have around here!

MISSING MY NEIGHBOR

"No man is an island." Words written long ago, in 1624, by John Donne. He was saying that rather than separate little islands, we are all part of a single, big continent of humankind, and that we all lose a little bit of the whole when one of us is gone. And so, he concludes his poem with the famous line "Send not to know for whom the bell tolls, it tolls for thee."

My next-door neighbor passed away about a month ago. We didn't even hear the bell toll. We came home from church that Sunday, and I settled in to read the paper. Scanning the obituaries, I was shocked to find my neighbor's name. I reread it, checked the data, the names—yes, it was him. A year older than me, but totally active and busy, and now gone without our even knowing it had happened.

I thought back to the last time I'd seen him. It was a hot September day, and I was giving the grass around my mailbox its monthly punishment. He came over to chide me about waiting to work "in the heat of the day."

My neighbor and I didn't have much in common, except that he worked long hours, and I worked long hours. After a long day I would drive in, past his little horse barn, when he would be out after a long day, lights turned on, seeing about his horse. Just a beep of my car horn, a wave from him. After 30 years of that you become sort of accustomed to those small neighborly routines.

Not a whole lot in common. Though we both did like to get our yards taken care of, we had different interpretations of lawn care. My neighbor's yard was always neat and tidy, never a single blade of grass sticking up out of place. I tend to follow the live-and-let-live approach to landscaping. In fact, my neighbor once described the part of my yard adjacent to his as a "thicket." And his description was correct.

I guess we didn't have much in common, my neighbor and I, but we both seemed to have an affection for animals. My favorite beagle and adopted stray cat have died of old age now, one at 16 years and one at 17 years. They were very much a part of our family. My neighbor had a boxer years ago, a nice friendly dog that would come over and help me with my chores from time to time.

But my neighbor really liked his horse. Now, my idea of good transportation is something with a motor in it. But my neighbor loved horses, at least his horse. His horse barn was always absolutely spotlessly clean. He would tend to the horse, feed it, brush it, and talk to it at all hours of the day and night. He would have the farrier come for new horseshoes every so often, and he would ride the horse in our back field. The doors of the little horse barn would always be open in good weather and closed up tight in bad weather. Constant attention bestowed upon a beloved beast.

We didn't really have too much in common, my neighbor and I. On the rare occasions when we did stop and talk for a few minutes, neither of us had much of an idea what the other did at work, except that it took a lot of hours. So, we would usually talk about the weather. We usually agreed that it was too hot, or too cold, or too wet, or too dry. And we did agree that getting old could be a troublesome thing at times. He usually greeted me as "young man," which I thought was amusing because I was several years older than him, or so I thought. Turned out, he was actually a year older than me when he left us.

Well, life goes on, we say. But my neighbor's passing was more than just a notice in the paper. A little piece of our continent has washed away, and the bell tolled for us all. Maybe it's this melancholy time of year, with the flowers withering and the leaves falling. Maybe it's the 30 years of beeps and waves. After all, we didn't have much in common. Just work, and yard, and animals, and weather, and family, and living.

He was a good neighbor. We are missing him.

BLUE JAYS—EVERYONE'S FAVORITE?

What is it about the blue jay? You can be having a nice, pleasant conversation with folks about birds, and the subject of blue jays comes up, and all those bird lovers immediately start saying unkind things about the poor jays . . . about how loud and greedy and bothersome they are.

Well, come on now! They *are* family. They stay with us year round, giving noise and color and activity to bleak winter days. So, they rob a few nests and steal a few eggs, and they may wake you up squawking early on a Saturday morning, but we can blame some of their less-desirable traits on the fact that they are closely related to the crows.

In a recent article in *Living Bird Quarterly*, author Jack Conner discussed how important the blue jay is in the life cycle of oak trees, and how important oaks are to the blue jay. Acorns are a major part of a blue jay's diet, and in common with many birds that winter here, they have developed the behavior of storing away food for lean times. A single blue jay may store up as many as 5,000 acorns in a single season! And not just store them; the way they hide them away in the soil of the forest floor and leaf litter provides optimal conditions for the ones that don't get eaten to later sprout into new oak trees.

But you know who gets all the credit for planting oaks? Squirrels, but wrongfully so! Squirrels tend to bury their acorns so deeply that few have a chance to sprout. In addition, squirrels bury their acorns generally quite close to the original tree, whereas blue jays can carry acorns as far as 2½ miles from the mother tree and so spread them much farther and faster than squirrels.

Blue jays have excellent memories and supposedly can remember where they hide most of their acorns, but they inevitably miss a few, and so play a huge role in the movement of oak forests into areas that may be suitable for oaks but have only a scattering of them.

One big example of this that directly affected our part of East Tennessee came at the end of the last Ice Age, about 16,000 years ago. At that time, we didn't have glaciers here, but there was a 2-mile-thick mass of ice covering the land down to about 400 miles north of Knoxville. Arctic tundra covered the tops of the Smokies. According to UT scholar Hazel Delcourt's research, described in her recent book *Forests in Peril*, our area was covered with a great cold, moist northern forest of pines, spruces, and larches during the Ice Age. The mixed hardwood forest that we're accustomed to around here presently was pushed south into a narrow strip along the Gulf Coast.

So, when the climate warmed up and the glaciers retreated northward, and those northern forests died back—except for on top of the Smokies, where they are clinging on to this day—the old blue jays were there. They played a major role in the northward migration of that remnant of hardwood forest, moving acorns and planting them, until we have the woods around us that we see today.

And in recent times, when the American chestnut trees died out from their imported blight, the blue jays were there, getting the forests replenished with the food-producing oaks, getting them spread and established, at least partially replacing that great loss.

So, the blue jay has played a major role in making East Tennessee the way it is today. We can thank them for most of the oaks we see all around us. They may shriek you awake some morning or eat all the food in your birdfeeder, or act kind of loud and bossy, but don't be too harsh on them. C'mon, doesn't your brother-in-law act like that sometimes?

THE MIGHTY OAKS

The mighty oak trees are an important species in the woods of this part of the country. Biologists refer to them as a "keystone species," which means that without them, the habitat of which they're a part would fail or be drastically altered. In other words, acorns are a big deal out there in the wild.

This year has seen a fruitful fall. Acorns littered the ground as we hiked along the Cataloochee Divide Trail in the Smokies a couple of weeks ago, along with zillions of ripe wild black cherries. And, alongside the trail there were blackberries, blueberries, and wild grapes galore. The birds, deer, bears, and various other critters must be enjoying a season of great abundance, fattening themselves up and storing away extra for winter.

It may interest you to know that once upon a time, the human race may well have depended upon the generosity of the oak trees to provide them with their sustenance, and to do so in good measure.

I've been reading an interesting book lately called *Oak: The Frame of Civilization*, by William Bryant Logan. In it, he points out that when our ancient forebears emerged from the plains of Africa around 45,000 years ago and spread out into Asia, Europe, and later, North America, they settled almost exclusively in the areas where oak trees were abundant.

Archaeological studies of ancient dwellings, storage bins, and refuse dumps show that whole tribes based their basic food supply on the abundant acorns the oaks produced each fall. In fact, when the early Europeans came to the present state of California in the 1700s, they found scores of small Native American tribes that still depended on an annual harvest of acorns to get them comfortably through the winter.

Acorns are very nutritious food, high in protein and fat. Other beasts figured that out millions of years before people came on the scene. For example, take the jay family of birds. We've already discussed the relationships that our North American blue jays have developed with the oaks over the centuries. There are about 40 species of jays around the globe, and they live only in the same areas where oak trees are found. Jays depend on oaks for food, and oaks depend on jays to help them to keep spreading and thriving, all around the world.

But back to people: A large oak tree can produce 300–500 pounds of acorns in a season, and a small tribe of people could stake out a good grove of oaks, and in 3 weeks or so harvest and prepare enough acorns to last them all through the winter. There were lots fewer people around back then, and probably a lot more oak trees. But whatever the ratio, it appears that the oaks provided them an abundant if not luxurious diet.

But, the oak trees have provided much more than acorns to us human beings over the eons. There are 300–400 species of oaks, from the tropics to the edges of the great northern evergreen forests, and they have provided a great deal of the materials for the growth and development of human society through the ages.

Think about something as basic as staying warm in the winter. A cord of oak wood—a pile of 4 feet x 4 feet x 8 feet—contains 23 million BTUs of heat energy, equivalent to more than 100 gallons of heating oil.

And think of shelter, another basic need. Author Logan tells us that 95% of all the buildings constructed in the north of Europe between 300 and 1700 AD were made of oak. A surprising number of them are still standing. Some of them, notably the great cathedrals, have oaken roofs and soaring, vaulted ceilings, secured by complex mortises and tenons that are still sources of wonder to today's architects and engineers.

The oaks have provided lots of other basic needs: oaken buckets and barrels of every imaginable shape and size, oak casks for aging wine, and corks from the bark of the cork oaks to stopper the bottles, just to name a few. From oak bark came the tannins to tan hides for the leather in our boots and saddles. And ink? Both the Declaration of Independence and the US Constitution were written and signed with the finest ink available, made from oak galls. Water wheels to turn our mills and wagon wheels to haul our loads were made from oak.

And, there were the sailing vessels. With them, people explored and conquered the globe. Ships have been built for a long time; consider the Phoenicians, the Greeks and Romans, and the amazing Norsemen and Vikings. It turns out that more than half the wooden ships ever built were constructed in the period 1800–1875, and 95% of those vessels were made of oak. Oak wood is strong, heavy, and durable. It proved to be an ideal timber for ship construction, where those qualities were of major importance. As we will detail farther along, my favorite ship from that era would have to be the *USS Constitution*. Her nickname was "Old Ironsides." Launched in Boston in 1797, over 1,500 oak trees were used in her construction.

Although all our food comes from grocery stores now, and all our stuff is made of plastic from China, the mighty oaks endure. They can live for hundreds of years and grow over 100 feet tall. They give us beauty and shade and inspire awe and respect. Next time you're out, give your favorite oak tree a pat of appreciation.

VISITOR FROM THE NIGHT

Things that go bump in the night! There really are a lot of things going on out there in the dark. And they are often scary because they are so unknown. Hordes of creatures come out after dark, and hunt, catch, and eat things that are out there trying to hunt, catch, and eat other things. Most of us don't realize how much activity bursts forth when the sun goes down.

Think about moths, for example. There are way more night-flying moths than there are day-flying butterflies, about 11,000 species of moths in North America to about 600 species of butterflies. And most of us don't realize that there are so many more moths out there than a few of the more spectacular ones. Then there are the frogs, toads, salamanders and snakes—one reason why all those camping tents have floors sewn in them!

Many of our mammals do their best work at night, such as the ever-popular duo of skunks and possums, along with raccoons, coyotes, and foxes. And you wouldn't believe how many little rodents, such as rats, mice, and shrews, are out there scurrying around every night until you walk outside on a morning with fresh snowfall and see all those hundreds of tiny footprints going in every direction in field and woods.

All these creatures have learned to cope with the dark and use it to their advantage, both for cover for their hunting activities and for protection from what's hunting them. But the animals that, to me, seem to have mastered the dark and made it theirs are the owls.

Owls fly completely silently, yet have a voice that can carry for miles. They are seldom seen, but when they are, they have a unique and intense appearance. Owls have been objects of superstition and awe down through the ages, and they are considered omens of bad fortune, or omens of good fortune, and symbols of wisdom by all sorts of people.

Here in the environs of the Beaver Creek watershed, we have 4 species of owls out of the 12 that occur in eastern North America. Our largest is the fearsome great horned owl, powerful enough to subdue a skunk or a rabbit. The smallest is the little screech owl, very difficult to see, with its feathers a perfect tree-bark pattern of camouflage. The least common is the pale, ghostly barn owl, who in spite of its habit of nesting in old barns seems the least comfortable around humans.

And that leaves my favorite—the big, round, fluffy barred owl. It is the one by far the most likely to be seen during daylight hours. Instead of the fierce intense gaze of the big yellow eyes common to the other three, the dark brown eyes of the barred owl seem to look at you with a gentle and benign curiosity.

We used to have a barred owl that came and sat on a branch over the driveway and stared at the cat, and the cat would sit and stare back at the owl. I would try to imagine what each of them was thinking.

We hadn't seen one here in years, though I had been hearing an occasional "who cooks for you? who cooks for you-all" hoot owl call from the creek bottom this summer and fall. Then 2 weeks ago I got a rare treat. The current creek bottom resident owl paid a daytime visit to my yard!

About five o'clock one clear afternoon, I had just put up the mower and was enjoying the quiet, when I heard an unfamiliar but birdlike sound. I thought it might be a blue jay; they are good imitators and seem to enjoy making off-the-wall noises. As I closed in on the area of the noise, though, a big stocky silent bird flew right in front of me and glided smoothly up into a cedar tree. It perched, looked up, looked down, and then, satisfied that everything else was OK, settled down to stare at me . . . a barred owl!

After enjoying a great view of the seldom-seen bird, I eased into the house and got Spouse and the camera. The owl perched patiently and stared at us both with those big, dark eyes. It let me photograph it (from a respectable distance) and even shut its eyes for a mini-nap as we stood there and discussed what a cool bird it was.

Owls have a special feather design that enables them to fly with total silence. Their big eyes are designed to gather lots more dim light than human eyeballs, greatly improving their night vision. But unbelievably sharp hearing is really their thing. They can accurately pinpoint the sound of a mouse's footfalls in total darkness at a distance of 25 yards. Goodbye, mouse!

It turns out that the primary staple of the barred owl's diet is indeed rodents, particularly rats and mice. And at this time of the year, with all the field mice having meetings to discuss which parts of my house they plan to spend the winter in, I'm glad they are the owl's favorite meal.

Our owl was still sitting there quietly when we had had our fill and finally headed back into the house, but it was already gone by early the next morning, undoubtedly having spent the night terrorizing the local neighborhood mice and, hopefully, dining on several of them.

Welcome to our yard, owl.

SCENTS OF AUTUMN

Fall is really here. We've had three morning frosts. The leaves have peaked in color in the mountains and are showing up nicely, species by species, here on the ridges and in the valleys. The air is fresh and crisp, and those wonderful fall smells are in the air: wood smoke, dry crunchy leaves underfoot, and spicy goodies in the oven. The weather is great, and all those smells are wonderful.

Well, not all of them. Last month's bill from our local utility company included a flyer showing a picture of a little kid holding his nose and asking, "Does your nose know the smell of natural gas?" And, of course, it's important for everybody to know that smell, just in case there is ever a leak. But does your nose know the origin of that other sulphurous nighttime vapor, wafting in your bedroom window at three o'clock in the morning? That window that you left open to finally enjoy the cool nighttime air?

Clue: it's coming, not from the big yellow Knoxville Utilities Board pipes, but from something black and furry with white stripes and a bad attitude. Known to my Granny Collier as the henhouse-raiding, chicken-stealing polecat, our culprit is more properly known as the striped skunk. Skunks are on the list of creatures that we could stand a few less of around our yards and under our houses, along with raccoons, possums, and mosquitoes.

We don't see them all that often in proportion to how often we smell them, mainly because they're mostly out and about at night. This time of the year, they seem prone to getting into territorial disputes over who gets to dig up your yard, squalling and growling like cats, and often ending the fray by firing a shot of malodorous spray into the otherwise delightful night air.

Not that skunks are all bad. If captured and de-scented at a very young age, they are said to make a nice house pet, sort of like a cat. Up north, skunks are trapped and their pelts used to adorn coats and jackets. (One would presume that it would involve a good deal of know-how to make such an activity a tolerable source of employment.)

Besides in your henhouse, skunks do create some problems in your yard. They will eat almost anything, including your pet's food left outside and the seeds on the ground under your birdfeeder. They help to rid your lawn of various grubs and insect larvae, the only problem there being all those little tell-tale digging holes out across your carefully tended turf. (In my yard, this doesn't matter.)

The most serious social problem the skunk has, though, is its odor situation. Skunks have evolved a highly effective defense mechanism that makes them close to predator proof: the ability to shoot a spray of oily, sickeningly odorous liquid at any apparent threat, man or beast. And so, they waddle across lawns and parks with an obvious attitude of being absolutely untouchable. They're pretty much right.

The combination of chemicals in skunk spray makes an immediate and lasting impression on most would-be attackers, usually breaks off any current encounter, and generally prevents any future thoughts of a second attempt by the same would-be predator. Coyotes, wolves, and even mountain lions are known to avoid skunks. Only certain goofy, clueless breeds of dogs—we'll not mention names, you know who they are—will not only attack a skunk – they'll sometimes even come back again for another try.

So, what to do when old Shep indiscreetly gets a full dose of skunk spray? A soaking in tomato juice is the remedy you hear of most. It's a big, smelly job that uses a lot of juice, and besides that, it doesn't work. But never fear, it's science to the rescue! A chemist in Illinois named Paul Krebaum came up with a science-based, effective, and inexpensive way to salvage Poochie from being banned to the far backyard forever.

It seems that Mr. Krebaum developed, in the course of his work, an odorous product that his fellow workers found greatly annoying. He set about developing an effective antidote for said product, and since the product had chemicals in it similar to those in skunk spray, he figured out that his antidote would immediately neutralize skunk odor as well.

The recipe is free to the public, and described on any number of websites, along with detailed instructions and some precautions. You should check one out before using the recipe. It may be one of your most important holiday season recipes. Briefly, here it is:

1 quart fresh 3% hydrogen peroxide
¼ cup baking soda
2 teaspoons liquid soap
Soak dog thoroughly for 5 minutes, then bathe dog as usual.
Smell should be gone.

With all of that defense, is there nothing that will help us with the abundant skunk population other than nighttime automobile traffic? As a matter
of fact, there is, and it comes from an unexpected direction—the sky. One
of the professors at the UT College of Veterinary Medicine, in charge of
looking after large injured birds of prey, told us at Bird Club that any time
someone brings him an injured bird in a big box, and it smells like skunk,
he knows what's in there: a great horned owl.

Great horned owls apparently have a poor sense of smell, or a seriously
big appetite, and they are known to regularly take skunks. This would be
a natural and very handy meal for them, since both owl and skunk are out
and about at the same time of the night. So, yummy for the owls, and may
they enjoy many more such snacks. Just not in my yard.

JOYCE KILMER MEMORIAL FOREST

The old-growth forests in our area are unique and special places. Over in the Great Smoky Mountains National Park, we have around 125,000 acres of old-growth forest, but one 3,000-acre-plus grove of giant old-growth hemlocks and tulip poplars near us isn't even in the Smokies Park at all. Joyce Kilmer Memorial Forest is only an hour or so from Knoxville, by way of your choice of a couple of very pleasant drives.

One way to go is on US Route 129 out of Maryville, going towards Robbinsville, North Carolina. You drive past the scenic Chilhowee and Calderwood lakes, and then after going by the Cheoah Reservoir and below the old Cheoah Dam, you turn right onto Santeetlah Road, along the shore of yet another lovely lake (Santeetlah) and into the entrance to the Memorial Forest. You can also take the Cherohala Skyway out of Tellico Plains, Tennessee until it dead-ends over in North Carolina at Kilmer Road, turn left down into the valley, and there you are, from the other direction. Both routes have unbeatable high-country scenery with little traffic.

And once you're there at Kilmer, you will find a parking lot, a picnic area, and a towering forest of ancient trees. But not just trees. The Joyce Kilmer Memorial Forest is known far and wide for its incredible display of spring wildflowers. Trilliums by the thousands, and a carpet of all their early spring friends. And for those folks with good ears as well as eyes, and a good measure of patience, spring birding is great, too. There are singing Louisiana waterthrushes, winter wrens, black-throated green and black-throated blue warblers, and wood thrushes, to name a few.

You will find two 1-mile walking trails, each a loop, so that together they form a figure-eight through the grove of huge old trees. Sadly, all the magnificent hemlocks have been attacked and decimated in the last few years by the imported hemlock wooly adelgid, an aphid-like insect that is destroying thousands of our old-growth hemlocks. One tree found in the grove, a hemlock more than 400 years old and measuring 15 feet in circumference, was the North Carolina state champion for its species. And there were a lot more of similar size. Most of the remaining big trees are tulip poplars.

But how did these stately giants escape the lumberjacks' axes and saws, and why is it a memorial forest? Interesting stories, both of them. From the sequence of events, it would seem that the Joyce Kilmer Forest was just destined to be set aside and preserved.

A 3,800-acre piece of land in a remote mountain area known as the Little Santeetlah Creek Watershed, it had apparently barely missed being clear-cut by various loggers along the years. Then in 1935, it came to the attention of two brothers, Andrew and Nat Gennett, who ran Gennett Lumber Company and had been involved in cutting timber over much of western North Carolina. They were mightily impressed with the large stand of huge old trees.

Some folks contend that the Gennetts sold the tract to the US government because they were in financial trouble. But Andrew, in his autobiography *Sound Wormy* (named for the lumbermen's designation for a certain desirable class of cuttable timber) asserts that after seeing the wonderful grove in the Little Santeetlah Creek basin, he and especially his brother were so impressed that they wanted to see it preserved and consequently sold it to the US government.

After a couple of conversations with Andrew Gennett's son, now an elderly gentleman, I'm inclined to believe the Gennetts' story that they acted in the spirit of stewardship to save that remarkable tract of forest. Incidentally, Andrew's grandson still operates the Gennett Lumber business. No longer cruising and cutting timber, they have a lumber and specialty wood business in Asheville.

Joyce Kilmer was born in New Jersey in 1886 and wrote his famous poem "Trees" while a student at Rutgers University. He became a respected journalist, and while he was recognized for his endeavors in that field, "Trees" was his only poem to receive any acknowledgment. It was published in 1914, during the first year of World War I.

When the United States entered the war in 1917, Kilmer volunteered to serve. Given a desk job because of his journalism background, he turned it down and insisted on going into the fray in the front lines. He was killed by a German bullet, defending French soil in 1918, at the age of 31.

A New York chapter of the Veterans of Foreign Wars petitioned the US Forest Service to establish a fitting memorial for the fallen soldier-poet, and their search led to the Forest Service purchase of the Little Santeetlah tract from the Gennett Lumber Company in 1935 for $28 per acre, a good price at the time.

The dedication of the Joyce Kilmer Memorial Forest was held on the eighteenth anniversary of Joyce Kilmer's death on July 30, 1936. And so, the great trees, the rhododendron thickets, and Little Santeetlah Creek remain there today, pretty much as they were when the Gennett brothers sized it all up in 1935 and decided it was something that shouldn't be destroyed. It is all safely preserved, and it belongs to all of us. You ought to go see it.

CLEAN-UP CREW

Mother Nature doesn't like for anything to go to waste. She uses the building materials of life over and over and over. All those leaves that drop to the ground in the fall contain the leftovers of a year's work in accumulating sugars, cellulose, nitrogen, and hard-to-come-by trace minerals, which return to the soil to be reused by an unbelievable array of living things.

Think about how a really big old tree gradually breaks down after it dies, and how many organisms make use of it. Beetle grubs and wood-boring insects tunnel through it, fungi soften it up, and woodpeckers make nest cavities in it. Limbs fall off, the main trunk may crash down, and the whole thing gradually returns to the forest soil. A walk in the Smokies offers great examples of this process in every stage. You see whole gardens of new plants and trees growing up on the rotted remains of an ancient forest tree.

Now, the same processes hold true on the animal side of the ledger, but there, things tend to move along in a much more brisk and active fashion. There are a whole lot of animals out there, from insects to mice to possums and deer, and every one of them will die sooner or later and need to be recycled. Somebody has to clean up the mess.

There are a number of critters out there that don't mind eating up a dead morsel or two: Skunks, possums, coyotes, crows, gulls, and even eagles will all scavenge an easy dead meal when the opportunity arises. But we also have a crew that works full time at clearing the fields and woods and roadsides of carcasses—the vultures. There are several members of this family of birds in the New World, the largest being the great condors of the Andes and of the American Southwest. They have wingspans of over 9 feet and can fly over 100 miles in a single day's foraging.

We have two species of vulture in East Tennessee: the familiar turkey vulture and its relative, the black vulture. Both are frequently referred to around here as "buzzards." The British call any large hawk a buzzard, and the early settlers continued to use the word when they arrived here, but it is not a specific, scientific word for any one bird in particular.

Turkey vultures have a lot of interesting habits. With an average body weight of only 4 pounds and with big wide wings spanning nearly 6 feet, these skilled flyers can ride the wind currents and rising columns of warm air, the thermals, all day and never flap a wing. They hold their wings in a slight "V" and seem to teeter and totter as they adjust to the currents and glide along. The fingerlike feathers at the ends of their wings break up the turbulence of the air at the wingtips, allowing them to fly and maneuver well at unusually low air speeds.

Turkey vultures are dark in color, but with silvery undersides of the flight feathers, which gives the wings a two-toned look when seen from below. Like most vultures, they are often seen at roost sites sitting out in the sun with their wings spread—catching some rays, warming up, and drying the dew off, before the day's flight.

Turkey vultures live in the Southeast year round and spread out over most of North America in the spring to breed and nest. I use the word "nest" very loosely; they don't actually *build* a nest. They just scrape off a bare place in some remote spot, such as a cave or a deep crevice on the face of a bluff or in the top of an old dead tree snag.

Turkey vultures mate for life. They may use the same nest spot year after year, and they may live 20–30 years. They usually lay two eggs. Now friends, these aren't chickadees, which sit on their eggs for a couple of weeks and feed the young birds for a couple of weeks, and they're up and gone. With turkey vultures, they incubate their eggs for nearly 6 weeks and then feed the hatchlings for close to 3 months before they're ready to fly. The young birds remain dependent on their parents for months, following them to feeding sites and then being fed by them.

The parents feed the young birds regurgitated, partially digested carrion. How's that for a great lunch? Why don't they get sick from eating all that rotten and decaying stuff? It so happens that their digestive systems are so powerful, they can destroy whatever bacteria and toxins they encounter, even serious disease-producing organisms. This is a major benefit they provide to us humans in cleaning up the environment.

Turkey vultures are unusual among birds in having an acute sense of smell. They can locate a dead mouse under a woodpile from a considerable distance and altitude. In contrast, their cousins the black vultures hunt by sight, often watching for turkey vultures that have found a suitable meal and then following them to it.

Black vultures, our other kind of buzzard here in the South, are often seen flying with turkey vultures, but unless you know that you're looking at another species of vulture, they're easy to mistake for just another turkey vulture.

Black vultures are blacker and have silvery wing tips rather than the two-tone coloring all along the wing as do the turkey vultures. Black vultures don't soar like turkey vultures either; they tend to take several short, choppy wingbeats and then glide. They can be differentiated high in the sky by their shape. Black vultures have short, square tails that barely stick out past the bird's body, and they hold their wings nearly flat, rather than in a "V." And on the ground, turkey vultures have red, featherless (some would say ugly) heads, while the black vultures have black heads.

In spite of their unsavory but very useful eating habits, vultures are not bad guys. They are actually shy, sensitive, and intelligent. (Does that sound like somebody's recommendation for a blind date?) A director at a raptor rehabilitation center in South Carolina once told me that the turkey vultures learn the routines faster than the other birds, and learn how to steal scraps, open latches, and do other problem-solving tasks.

Rather creepy and ghoulish while going about their tasks on the ground, when the vultures take to the air their seemingly effortless gliding flight quietly shows the other birds what being the masters of the skies is all about. The vultures are important members of our family of fellow creatures.

WATER WARS

Hooray, October is here! It's always been my opinion that the month of October is, just by itself, reason enough to live in East Tennessee. It usually has a near-perfect combination of cool temperatures, blue skies, and low humidity. And it seemed to be starting off that way this year.

However, we'd had an above average amount of rain for the year. All those flooded roads and overflowing streams had me thinking about our water supply, and how it's sometimes plentiful, sometimes scarce.

Remember 2007? That year of drought, our farmers were buying hay from Texas and Louisiana, or selling off their cattle. Wells were going dry, and some nearby communities were on water rationing. Atlanta's Lake Lanier was the lowest it had ever been, and they were trying to scheme a way of tapping into our Tennessee River to fill swimming pools and water lawns down in Georgia.

Everywhere, the need for water—lots of water—is growing steadily, and the supply is shrinking. People have been fighting water wars out West nearly forever. Everything's fine as long as the people upstream from you don't take out a noticeable amount from your creek or river. But what happens if they build a dam up there and your water supply turns into a trickle? Just whose water is it, anyway? And who decides who gets how much?

California is often a good predictor for what is going to happen to the rest of us. And the city of Los Angeles is a scary example of what a big city with a lot of political connections can do. As the city grew to a metropolis of millions of people, it developed a huge appetite for water. So, through decades of politicking and dealing, arrangements were made to supply Los Angeles' insatiable thirst with a series of aqueducts, those wonders of engineering siphoning water over mountains and through deserts, past towns and farms, away from the local users and down to the city.

One of its aqueduct systems reaches as far north as the mountains east of San Francisco. Another goes 338 miles up the eastern side of the Sierra Nevada Mountains, nearly to the Nevada border. It has drained so much water from the streams feeding two of the salt lakes in the area that one of them, Owens Lake, has gone completely dry. It is now a salt flat blowing alkali dust storms over nearby farms and ranches.

The other one, Mono Lake, is famous for being a major feeding stopover for hundreds of thousands of migrating birds, especially in the fall. They would stop and refuel on the trillions of brine shrimp and alkali fly larvae that grow in the lake. The Los Angeles aqueduct had drawn off almost the entire inflow to the lake, causing its water level to drop some 60 feet since it tapped in. This drastically decreased the food supply for the migrating birds, and exposed many nesting sites to predators such as coyotes (the 60,000 gulls formerly found there have left). The situation set off a series of lawsuits that have gone on for decades and reached the California Supreme Court, ultimately resulting in a landmark 1994 decision seting forth principles about whose water it is.

For good measure, Los Angeles also siphons off a percentage of what little water remains in the once-mighty Colorado River. That river has been sucked dry—it no longer empties into the sea because it runs out of water before it gets there.

So, what has Los Angeles got to do with us? Well, we are sitting 200 miles north of a very thirsty city of millions of people—Atlanta. Chattanooga, on the Tennessee-Georgia state line, is only about 100 miles north of Atlanta. And the Georgia legislature has been talking about moving the Tennessee–Georgia border north, so they can tap into the Tennessee River. We chuckled at first, but after the drought of 2007 it doesn't seem so funny anymore.

We're getting a lot thirstier here in the South as well. A report in the latest *National Wildlife* magazine relates that over the last 40 years, water usage from rivers and reservoirs has increased by 149% in Tennessee, by 249% in Georgia, by 349% in North Carolina, and by an astonishing 947% in South Carolina!

The state of South Carolina filed a lawsuit against the North Carolina towns of Concord and Kannapolis that has gone all the way to the US Supreme Court; the two towns petitioned to withdraw 36 million gallons of water a day from the Catawba River. Now, the Catawba River already has 14 dams and 2 nuclear and 3 coal-fired power plants and provides drinking water to nearly 2 million people.

The real beef here, though, is the fact that Concord and Kannapolis are in a completely different watershed from the Catawba River. The water they withdraw and use would never be returned to that river, to continue on for the multiple reuses downstream. Think about Atlanta. Interbasin transfer of water wasn't even legal until steps were taken in 2008 to weaken the US Clean Water Act. Whose water is it, anyway?

Los Angeles, Atlanta, us—we're all, one by one, learning the truth—that water supplies are really, actually, no longer unlimited, and that we will, sooner or later, have to learn to do with less, to conserve, and to use the water for the really essential stuff. Stay tuned; more water wars are in our future.

TRACES FROM THE PAST

The third weekend in October has come and gone. We know where at least 106,000 of our neighbors were on the third Saturday of the month: at the UT–Alabama game, making a very large amount of noise. Another event took place in Knoxville on that same weekend. It was on a slightly smaller scale, and definitely quieter. And it has a tradition going back only 15 years, instead of decades.

The Knoxville Gem and Mineral Society's fifteenth annual Show and Sale was held at the Kerbela Temple downtown but across the river from the football game. The show is organized and attended by a bunch of folks with all the enthusiasm and expertise of UT Vol fans but without the screaming. There were aisles bordered by tables, cabinets, and cases of glittering crystals, polished gems and jewelry, interesting mineral specimens, and fascinating fossils.

All of this served as a reminder that there is a lot more to this old world than just what we see around us every day. No matter how much we enjoy the sky, the trees and flowers, and all the various critters, it's also interesting to contemplate all the stuff beneath our feet.

Geology was one of the earliest sciences to get its act together as a more or less modern-day discipline. A recent book by Simon Winchester, called *The Map That Changed the World*, tells the story of William Smith, who published a geological map of Scotland on August 1, 1815. It looked pretty much like the geological maps of today, with all the different ages and types of rocks accurately depicted in their proper locations and sequences, each kind represented by its own assigned color. The author says that this was the first true geological map depicting any location in the world. Smith's map was widely studied, accepted, and imitated. His methods were embraced, and modern geology was on its way.

Today's geologists have a dazzling array of tools to study the processes at work in the Earth's crust: electron microscopes, spectrophotometers, methods for dating things by measuring radioactive decay of various elements. But the old guys, on foot or by horseback, and armed mostly with pick and shovel, managed to come up with most of the important principles accepted today. These include the facts that the Earth is very, very old and that the processes that we see going on around us now have been going on since the Earth was born.

Geologists have to be great detectives. They take the evidence they find, figure out what the clues mean, and piece together the history of what has happened to this old Earth. Early on, they realized that the relative ages of different layers of rock could be determined. If the layers remained undisturbed as formed, then the oldest layers were on the bottom, and as you went up in the layers, each one was younger than the one below it.

I like to think of the layers of sedimentary rocks as a big apple stack cake. It's not a very good example, but it sure is fun to think about. Anyway, the early geologists found that all those layers had their own peculiar traces of the ancient life that was stirring when the rocks were laid down as sediment. And wherever that age of rock was found—across the road, across the ocean—its group of fossils served as a reliable marker for its age and sequence in the layer cake.

Fossils are the remains of ancient plants and animals preserved in rock, mostly. There are, however, some notable exceptions. Everyone knows about those DNA-bearing mosquitoes perfectly preserved in amber; we met some in the "Jurassic Park" movies. Excellent skeletons of a variety of beasts, dating back some 40,000 years and including the famous saber-toothed tiger, are preserved in the gooey asphalt of the LaBrea Tar Pits, in what is now downtown Los Angeles.

Woolly mammoths have been found frozen in the arctic ice, so well preserved that some of the explorers who found them cooked and ate the meat. These creatures could probably be cloned with today's technology, but then what would you do with a woolly mammoth?

Mostly, though, fossils mean rock. They formed as the remains of snail, clam, fish, or dinosaur were entombed in sand, silt, or mud, which then over the eons of time and vast tons of pressure, became rocks. Sometimes the cells were replaced by solutions of minerals percolating through the ground, forming very hard and tough, and very colorful, replicas of the original.

Then, as the ages passed, the surrounding rocks eroded away, leaving the fossil exposed, to be discovered by some eager rockhound. Excellent examples of that process can be seen in such places as Petrified Forest National Park in Arizona, with huge trees now replaced by spectacularly colorful agate lying around on the surface.

Other fossils are found still firmly in place in the rock, requiring huge amounts of tedious work to extricate them. A good example of this is the Dinosaur Beds National Monument in Utah. There, enclosed in a big, weatherproof building, is a cliff face full of dinosaur skeletons, many species jumbled together. Scientists work on various areas as you watch, slowly releasing the great lizards from the rocks.

Sometimes fossils are just signs of something having been there. There are fossilized worm and clam burrows. You can see fossilized ripple marks, formed by the gentle lapping of ancient sea water on a sandy ocean bottom. And, some of my favorites, there are fossilized tracks—footprints of ancient lizards, dinosaurs, even people—squashed into the prehistoric ooze that later hardened, was covered over, and turned to stone. Seeing a set of those tracks really brings the ancient world to life.

And what about our part of the world? Well, sir, we're no slouch when it comes to fossils! The state of Tennessee is home to hundreds of species of fossils. Most of eastern North America was covered from time to time with warm, shallow seas, and many of our local fossils formed during those eras. Some areas of shore on Dale Hollow Lake are littered with fossils called crinoids, stacks of disclike structures that were the trunks of plantlike sea animals, sometimes called sea-lilies. Closer to home, road cuts and creek banks here in the Beaver Creek Valley yield dozens of seashells called brachiopods and colonies of coral-like branching structures called bryozoans.

As time went on, our area was covered with warm, wet swamps filled with large tree ferns that through time formed the layers of organic rock that we call coal. Coal forms when peat, the layers of dead plants hundreds of feet thick, are mashed under massive pressures to form seams. Where the mashing is less severe, imprints of the ancient plants, and sometimes even the carbonized plants themselves, are preserved. Up on Windrock Mountain above Oliver Springs, and on Cross Mountain above Lake City, fossils of the trunks, roots, and leaves of the tree ferns whose cousins went on to form our coal can still be found.

Of more recent origin, a site in west Tennessee has long been famous for its well-preserved turtle and crab fossils, and the Gray fossil site near Johnson City has yielded a wealth of peccaries, sloths, and other prehistoric animals since its discovery in 2000.

To learn more and see some dandy fossils and some dioramas show-ing what things looked like way back when, spend an hour or so over at the McClung Museum on the UT Knoxville campus. It has all manner of beautifully-presented, interesting displays of the ancient life that once lived in our area of the world. Admission is free. If you haven't been there, you should take advantage of this local treasure!

OUR STATE BIRD

One of my earliest bird song remembrances involves one of my first and least favorite job opportunities. Along about age 12 I had the privilege of being a "carrier-salesman" for the *Knoxville Journal*. This involved getting up long before any lights were on in my neighborhood and staggering out into the dark, hoping they didn't bring the papers that day; they always did.

But, dark and lonely as it was out there, there was always a faithful, cheerful, determined mockingbird to sing for me along the route. He made sure to always throw something different into his song, as if to remind me of his skill and talent—a masterful, improvising musician.

Mockingbird was voted in as our state bird in 1944, just barely beating out the steadfast robin. He is also the state bird of Texas, Florida, Arkansas, and Mississippi. As you can surmise from this list, the mockingbird is traditionally a bird of the South, often associated with magnolias and Spanish moss. In spite of that image, they are gradually spreading northward, even some into southern Canada.

The mockingbird is one of those trusting species that seems at home around human activity, farms, homes, and neighborhoods. Although not a flashy dresser, with gray and white coloration and the noticeable trademark white wing patches so obvious with wings outstretched, the mockingbird makes up for whatever they lack in appearance with what they do in behavior.

Their most recognizable behavior is their song. Mockingbirds are in a group of birds known as the "mimic thrushes," which also includes the gray catbird and the brown thrasher. The mockingbird has a distinctive song even among that group. He repeats each melodious phrase several times, then switches to another. He may throw in an exact imitation of another species, such as a cardinal, phoebe, or warbler.

Author Robin Doughty, in his interesting little monograph *The Mockingbird*, says that the mockingbird can imitate more than 30 bird songs—I would say probably more than that—and can do the red-winged blackbird so well that the blackbird can't distinguish between a mockingbird and one of his own species. They also do crickets, frogs, chickens, and machines. At least one mocker that lived in a large Knoxville mall parking lot was alleged to accurately reproduce the ringing of a cell phone. Apparently, the bird loved to do that one and then watch all the humans reach in their pockets and purses!

There was a huge fad of keeping caged birds, and even whole aviaries of caged birds, starting back in the late 1800s and lasting up until laws were passed in the early 1900s to prevent the capture and sale of song birds. Mockingbirds were very popular as caged song birds. Thousands were caught here and sold in Europe, where they were prized by British and German bird enthusiasts.

Although it's hard now to imagine loads of caged mockingbirds being sent to Europe as pets, at that time it was big business. Some European enthusiasts took great pride in being able to breed and raise the somewhat difficult and independent mockingbird in captivity, and there was a great controversy as to whether the American mockingbird or the European nightingale was the better singer.

Safe from that sort of foolishness now, the mockingbird holds forth in our yards. He sings to guard his nesting territory, attracting a female partner and then building a nest and helping to feed and raise the young. He defends his territory against all comers— snakes, cats, and sometimes even human beings.

Once family duties are completed, mockingbirds establish a different fall and winter territory, depending upon available food supplies. This is often centered on a holly or dogwood tree full of berries. They defend these territories as far into the winter as possible, usually successfully, unless outnumbered and overwhelmed by a flock of 50–100 cedar waxwings that swoop in and clean them out.

Our mockingbirds are with us all year round. With the blue jays, robins, wrens, and chickadees, they hang in there as our support group through the dreary winter days. And they fill spring and summer days, and nights, with music that no other bird can match.

CRITTERS WHITE AS SNOW

From time to time, we get reports of folks seeing birds with patches of white where there shouldn't be any, and sometimes even an all-white bird that is supposed to be some other color. Two or three friends in the north Knoxville area have told me about seeing a mockingbird or a robin in their yards, "white as snow," that they had been watching off and on for various periods of time. In typical fashion, the mockingbird had "run everybody else off" and had claimed a section of the yard as its inviolable territory. And the white robins were likewise behaving in typical fashion, harvesting earthworms from the lawns in their methodical way.

Albino birds and animals are very rare in nature, considering the vast majority that turn out with normal coloration. Because of their lack of protective coloration, all-white birds and animals generally have short lives. Perhaps the fierce mockingbird, being typically aggressive and take-charge, will fare better.

Not all white animals are albinos, of course. Look at those big, tall, all-white great egrets, whose range is expanding slowly up the TVA river system. Then there are the smaller snowy egrets and cattle egrets, and down south, we have huge American white pelicans soaring over the Everglades.

To the north, the polar bears and snowy owls use their all-white color as camouflage against their snowy winter surroundings. But even more interesting in the north country are those animals that turn white only as winter approaches. In summer, they are the various grays, browns, and blacks that one would expect of them all year round in more southern localities. But up there, as winter approaches, they molt and shed and become white, enabling them to blend perfectly with the white of their winter world.

Good examples of this phenomenon are the brown-and-gray speckled ptarmigans, chickenlike birds in the grouse family, as well as gray arctic foxes and brown snowshoe hares, all changing to snowy white as wintertime approaches. Except for a black tail-tip or beak, these animals disappear against a background of snow.

The ones that more southerly folks would most likely recognize in their winter fur are the long-tailed and short-tailed weasels. Brown in summer, they turn white in winter, with only a black tip on their tail. Adorning kingly robes and ladies' coats, they are known in the fur-trading business as ermines.

Back to the albinos, though. They're not just white animals. They have no black wingtips or tail-tips, or yellow legs, or any colored parts. They have a total absence of pigment cells, even in their eyes, and their startling pink eyes are a tell-tale sign of an albino. Albinism is a genetic condition, caused by getting one recessive gene from each parent, though both parents may appear normal.

Birds are a little different, in that they can exhibit what is called partial albinism. This means they may have a few white feathers here or there, usually wing or tail feathers. We have all probably noticed a bird with a distinctive white spot that helped us tell it from others of its kind and recognize it when it came around again. These birds are partial albinos.

Human albinos can face serious challenges because of their sensitivity to sunlight, since a lack of pigment cells in the skin and eyes provides no shielding from ultraviolet radiation. Those living near the equator are especially vulnerable. In third-world countries, where resources and medical care are often nonexistent, albinos often end up blind or dying of extensive skin cancers from the ravages of ultraviolet radiation, things which could be largely prevented by such simple measures as wearing a broadbrimmed hat and sunglasses.

In the animal world, serious problems come from lack of protective coloration, and all-white robins, sparrows, and squirrels are sitting ducks, if you will, for cats, hawks, and other predators. It's like having a target painted on your back, except it's all over. Often all-white members of a normally colored species fail to attract a mate, since their courtship depends so heavily on the right coloration, especially in the males.

Years ago, we visited a pavilion at the Cincinnati Zoo, dedicated entirely to albino animals. There under one roof were all-white possums, raccoons, squirrels, birds, and turtles. The middle of the building had been transformed into a swamplike habitat, and there swam a couple of huge, toothy, menacing, but all-white alligators! I have occasionally pictured myself on a moonlit night in the bayou, sitting in my flat-bottomed boat amidst the big black cypress trunks, and seeing a 12-foot white alligator gliding silently toward me. Literally scared to death? You bet!

NATURE STRIKES BACK

It is fall, and although so far not a very colorful one, we do notice in rambling around outdoors that some trees and plants have for some time now been fairly bright with autumn foliage. The dogwoods and sumacs are two of the best examples. Both of these smallish trees have turned a nice deep red; both also have lots of berries on them.

Botanists have coined a term for plants that seem to turn to their fall colors early, perhaps a programmed adaptation to advertise their fruits to birds that will eat the trees' fruits and then spread the seeds. The scientists call this phenomenon "fall foliar flagging," an unusually catchy phrase to be coming from the halls of science. Anyhow, whether or not it really works out the way they hypothesize, we can look around us and see it going on. Certain wildflowers in particular seem to be using brightly-colored foliage and stems to advertise the availability of their fruits.

Another plant that should certainly be included in this category is probably one of our least favorite vines, poison ivy. All up through the trees, you can follow its path of nice red leaves. And on the bigger ones with big hairy stems sometimes 2 inches or more in diameter, you can see the hanging clusters of waxy whitish berries.

Poison ivy spreads two ways. It spreads widely with underground runners that zoom along and come up with more plants as they go. And it also spreads by the seeds of those white berries, which the birds eat and then fly away and deposit at some more distant spot, starting a new colony of the pesky vine.

Poison ivy is a significant winter food source for numerous birds. The berries seem to be a special favorite of the yellow-rumped warbler. The berries resemble those of the wax myrtle, another favorite food for that species and from which they got their older name "myrtle warbler." I've observed downy woodpeckers, even huge pileated woodpeckers, feeding on poison ivy berries in the winter.

Poison ivy and poison oak are recognized by their three leaves. The ivy climbs as a vine; the oak is an upright plant or small shrub, more commonly found out West. A cousin of theirs, poison sumac, has multiple leaflets like the other sumacs, and grows as a small tree. It grows in wet swampy areas and thankfully does not occur in East Tennessee. There are several other vines that are sometimes confused with poison ivy. The widespread Virginia creeper vine has less hairy stems and five leaflets. Trumpet vine has big orange flowers, beanlike fruits, and many leaves.

Poison ivy makes us itch because it produces an oil, 3-pentadecylcatechol—the longest word you're likely ever to read in this column—commonly known as urushiol. The oil is produced by most every part of the plant except the flowers; this includes dry branches, trunk, and roots. It is spread by contact with the plant, and also by contact with garden tools with the oil on them, and you can definitely get a big dose of it by contact with pets who have been in contact with the plants. Even sneakier than that, people can be severely affected by having rain water drip off the vines onto them and by being exposed to smoke when the vines are burned. Inhaling smoke from burning poison ivy can even lead to life-threatening reactions in the throat and lungs.

The rash, blisters, and bad itching come from the urushiol bonding to the skin and eliciting an allergic reaction. The oil is not soluble in water and can be spread around the skin by inadequate washing. Once the rash forms, the oil has changed, and the poison cannot be spread further by scratching, in spite of what your mama told you.

Through the years, numerous folk remedies have been said to cure the rash and itching, but in truth most of them were either worse than the original problem, or just something to do while you waited for time to take care of the problem on its own. One old remedy that apparently does work, though scientists have been unable to explain how, is applying the juice of the jewelweed or "touch-me-not" plant to the rash. This same remedy also works well to ease the sting of the stinging nettle. Often, you'll find jewelweed and nettle growing together: irritant and cure, side by side.

For this time of year, the main message is that you can get a bad case of poison ivy even after the leaves are gone, cleaning out the hedgerow or a brushy corner, burning, or grubbing out roots. Interestingly, the roots of poison ivy are one of the richest sources of the sap. They are juicy, and the sap can easily get on gloves, shirt sleeves, and skin. The sap turns black upon contact with the air, and the early folk used it as a good source of black dye for dyeing clothes, baskets, and the like. I would presume that the dyeing process destroyed the allergenic properties of the oil; otherwise, I imagine that it would have given a lot more justification to their children's complaints about their itchy black sweaters!

A DIFFERENT KIND OF NUT

It's nut season in East Tennessee. Now, this piece is not about the nuts out on our roadways, looking at the phone in their laps as they drive toward me with half their car in my lane. Not the nuts, either, who will soon be coming to blows with one another, in the spirit of Christmas, over the unbelievable bargains surrounding them during the holiday shopping season. We're thinking nature here, not human nature.

And for nature and its critters, it's a time of abundance. A carpet of small nuts sits under my shagbark hickory trees, and we can't walk around the place for the walnuts on the ground—ankle turners for sure—buckets and buckets of them. They should be a sign of walnut pie in my future, helping tune up the taste buds for Thanksgiving.

For the animals, though, this is a critically important time of year to either stock up on supplies or fatten up their bodies for the winter ahead. One exception is the morbidly obese groundhog that lives under my workshop and does nothing but eat and sleep all year long, and who appears to me to always be ready for hibernation . . . just in case of a severe cold snap in July. The rest of nature's creatures depend on the big fall food crop to get them ready for several cold months of slim pickings.

Acorns, walnuts, and hickory nuts provide a source of rich, fattening food for millions of mice, chipmunks, squirrels, turkeys, and deer . . . and 350-pound bears. The size of the mast crop is what often tells the tale on surviving the winter and early spring, and even how many cubs, if any at all, those mama bears will produce during hibernation.

We've previously mentioned how, through the centuries, humans have benefitted from the nut harvest as well. Historically, whole communities of people in numerous parts of the world have learned to survive and thrive on abundant and dependable crops of chestnuts or from huge oak trees full of acorns. And in more recent times, autumn was the time for heading out into the woods especially for those big chestnuts, full of protein and fat, but even after their demise in the 1930s, still foraging for walnuts and hickory nuts. And then there were the seldom-seen others: beech nuts and their close cousins the chinkapins and the cousins of the walnuts, the butternuts.

But then, there are exceptions to every rule. Think of a big, shiny, brown, abundant and tasty-looking nut that isn't . . . isn't edible, I mean. That would be our common buckeye. Many country folks, and probably some of us older suburban types, too, carry a buckeye in our pocket for good luck or to relieve rheumatism. Maybe both. I suppose if your rheumatism gets better, that's good luck.

Either way, buckeyes are an interesting member of the nut family, one that city folks are often unfamiliar with, unless you're an Ohio State sports fan. Of our two large native buckeye trees here in the United States, the Ohio buckeye has the widest distribution, growing in a wide swath west and north of us from Texas, on up through Missouri and Ohio, and slipping down to grow in middle Tennessee. Its fruits have spiny husks and usually only one small nut.

Our buckeye trees here, called the yellow buckeye or sweet buckeye, have a smaller distribution, mostly in East Tennessee, Kentucky, and West Virginia. They can grow to be very old and large. They have fruits that, in contrast to the Ohio buckeyes, have thick, smooth husks that break open to yield from one to three large, shiny nuts. The brown nuts each have a large pale spot that make them resemble the eye of a deer, hence their name.

The problem here lies in the fact that those lovely brown nuts are poisonous, at least to humans. The toxins they contain do not affect squirrels or deer, proven by the fact that the buckeyes that fall in abundance around our place tend to disappear somewhere at a rapid pace. One piece of folklore has it that buckeyes are poisonous only on one side, and the squirrels are able to tell which side is safe to eat. And one of my dependable rural life consultants swears that he remembers classmates bringing one of his school teachers buckeyes, and he remembers her sitting at her desk and munching them.

Perhaps more factual are accounts of Native Americans who used powder made from buckeye pulp to put into a stream to paralyze fish for easy capture. And as most experienced farmers know, just as wilted black cherry leaves from a fallen tree in the pasture can poison cattle (the leaves develop cyanide compounds), buckeyes are definitely toxic to cattle. Eating buckeyes can cause staggering, paralysis, and even death if the animals eat enough of them.

As for people and poisons, most plants used for their medicinal properties are poisonous if used incorrectly or in excess. Buckeyes are listed in texts of medicinal plants as having been used for a number of disorders, and even as food, after having been boiled, blanched, pounded, baked, and so forth. These uses are not currently recommended.

There are well-documented incidents of human poisoning and even deaths, especially in children, that make my physician antennae go up at times such as Halloween. In some locales, a popular treat is made from peanut butter, dipped in chocolate and leaving a bare spot so the inside yummy brown stuff shows, to closely resemble a buckeye. Not too surprisingly, they are called buckeyes. And are probably scrumptious. Maybe all the little kids in those locations are taught the difference between the good Halloween buckeyes and those poisonous ones that they come upon outdoors. Nonetheless, I worry. Kids will be kids, of course.

But hey, my rheumatism has been feeling a lot better lately, since I've been carrying my new buckeye in my pocket. I'm sure that wouldn't have anything to do with this nice dry fall weather, would it? And I'm looking forward to the good luck part of the magic kicking in any day now. You'd better find yourself a buckeye, if the squirrels and deer haven't already polished them off!

PUMPKIN SEASON

This is pumpkin season. A recent news item confirmed this has been a bumper crop year for pumpkins in Tennessee. We're seeing folks with pickup trucks and flatbed trailers loaded with the big orange vegetables up and down the roads and byways, offering a selection of this year's big crop.

There was a blurb on the evening news a couple of weeks back about a fellow who had won a big blue ribbon at his state fair for growing a 2,040-pound pumpkin. They showed the prize-winning behemoth being carried around with big straps, dangling from a front-end loader.

Just imagine how many people you could feed with a couple of acres of those babies! By my careful and exacting calculations, a 1-ton pumpkin should be sufficient to produce about 800 pumpkin pies, or about 6,400 good-sized servings. That should take care of most any family gathering, including all the cousins and in-laws, plus any strangers that happened to show up.

Pumpkins are in the same family as the other winter squash, of which there are many. They're not just to carve into jack o' lanterns for Halloween; they're good food. They are native to the New World, and the early colonists here discovered them being grown by the Native Americans. Our newly immigrated European ancestors quickly adopted them as a major food source. We are told that pumpkins saved many an early settler from winter starvation.

The early New Englanders initially prepared a pumpkin for eating by cutting out the top, jack o' lantern style, removing the pulp and seeds, and then pouring in cream, honey, and spices. The "lid" was put back on, and

the whole thing roasted in the coals on the hearth. When it was done, they ate the resulting "pudding" right out of the pumpkin.

That sounds to me like a pretty satisfactory way to fend off starvation. But the settlers did go on to develop pumpkin pie, more or less as we do it today. Sugar was unavailable as a sweetener, hence the honey in the pumpkin pudding. They also used molasses as a sweetener, and one account tells of a group of Connecticut pioneers with a molasses shortage postponing Thanksgiving until they could produce enough molasses to make their pumpkin pies.

This time of year, with cool, frosty air and falling leaves, we instinctively turn to foods that seem appropriate to the season. We've gone from fresh greens, new potatoes, and green onions, through okra and tomatoes, and now to autumn foods. Dessertwise, November doesn't feel exactly right for the likes of Key lime pie. I have a personal theory that we've been given pumpkin pie to help our systems transition from the lighter summer desserts to the glorious pecan pie and eggnog of the high winter holidays. I like to use all parts of the theory, in their proper sequence, of course.

Pumpkins yield some other goodies, too. Pumpkin seeds are a tasty treat, especially when roasted and salted. South of the border they are known as *pepitas*. And pumpkin seed oil, a thick greenish cooking oil, is usually mixed in with other oils to give a distinctive flavor to cooking oils and salad dressings.

But back to that pumpkin pie; don't forget the spices. Remember the spices in the Pilgrims' pumpkin pudding recipe? One of our fast food establishments had its milkshake flavor of the month for October advertised as "pumpkin spice," a popular, if considerably overused, flavor down through the years. The spices usually used in pumpkin pie recipes combine with the flavor of the pumpkin itself to give us that distinctive yummy flavor. Consultation with my go-to encyclopedia of culinary information, Rombauer and Becker's *Joy of Cooking,* and a conversation with my knowledgeable chef daughter tell me the proper spices for a pecan pie are cinnamon, ginger, nutmeg, and cloves or allspice.

Amazingly enough, those spices had been known to European cooks for centuries before settlers came to North America, even though they originated in the tropical climates of such places as the West Indies, Southeast Asia, and India. Even in the snowy wilderness of colonial New England, those folks would have had those spices available to them. Most likely, each housewife would have insisted upon bringing some of each of those rare and precious cooking treasures with her into her new home in the New World, and then, using her cooking skills, applying those exotic spices to that wonderful new vegetable, the pumpkin.

Perhaps thinking back on those determined, snowbound folks hammering out an existence in wintry New England, and their pausing long enough to enjoy a spicy piece of pumpkin pie created from a newfound local food product, will add just a little more pleasure to your piece of Thanksgiving pumpkin pie. A dollop of whipped cream won't hurt either.

THE BOREAL FOREST:
SOURCE OF SONGBIRDS

We've all heard about the destruction of the tropical rainforest in South America. It's home to thousands of species of plants, trees, and animals, many of which are probably yet to be discovered. Lots of North American migratory birds winter there, or pass through on their way to and from sites farther to the south.

The rainforest is a critical part of their life cycle, and indeed is a critical part of ours, too. The vast miles of greenery regulate global temperature, suck up tons of carbon dioxide, and give off tons of oxygen for us earthlings to breathe.

But wouldn't you know, just when we become sort of accustomed to being worried about the rainforest so that we can get a little sleep, up pops something else to worry about.

There is another forest—a really big one—that stretches from Alaska, across all of Canada, to Newfoundland. It is the great North American boreal forest, the North Woods. Named for Boreas, the Greek god of the North, this great wilderness contains 1.4 billion acres, enough to contain 14 Californias! It contains countless uninhabited miles of pine, spruce, larch, aspen, and poplar forest.

A fascinating report by Paul Tolme in the current issue of *National Wildlife* provides interesting facts about the boreal forest. Besides its sheer enormity, an astronomical number of birds make their home up there each summer. According to the article, the great boreal forest is summer home to at least 298 bird species. As many as 3 *billion* birds migrate up into the northern forest each spring, from as far away as southern South America, and raise enough young so that there are an estimated 5 billion birds to migrate back south each fall!

Some 40 of these species have more than half of their entire global population located in the boreal forest. Up to 1 billion sparrows and 2 billion warblers hatch there annually. Many birds that we here in Tennessee see only in migration come from there, including Tennessee, Connecticut, palm, and Cape May warblers; Blackburnian warblers; and Baltimore orioles. Four out of every 10 species of North American waterfowl breed in the region's bogs and wetlands. American white pelicans, seen in Florida in winter, nest on the lakes of the boreal region in the summer. Dark-eyed juncos and whitethroated sparrows, common North American winter feeder birds, also breed in the northern forest.

So, what's to worry about? Several things. Timber companies have been munching away at the boreal forest to the tune of 2.5 million acres per year. About 80% of the wood products harvested go to the United States. What's really troubling is the fact that about two-thirds of that harvest is pulped to make newspapers and catalogs. And 17 billion catalogs—59 for every US citizen—are mailed out across this country annually. Mostly made from virgin timber, most go in the trash. There's something really wrong with that.

Additionally, I think it is important to note that Canada, not Saudi Arabia, is the United States' largest supplier of fossil fuels. Oil and gas, as well as the timber harvest, are beginning to cut large swaths, fragmenting the once-unbroken forest.

A long and depressing list of bird species from the area shows a steady decline in their numbers, many of them at levels 50% or less than their numbers of just 40 years ago. Rusty blackbirds are dropping by 11% per year. Ask the old-timer birders watching for the once-abundant spring migrants on Sharp's Ridge overlooking Knoxville, and they'll tell you the warblers are disappearing at a frightening rate.

On the positive side, a lot of work is in progress to protect large areas of the northern forest, and to ensure forest harvest is wisely managed and sustainable. But there is a long way to go, and very many dollars of potential profit are involved.

Like the tropical rainforest, the boreal forest plays a role in regulating the Earth's climate. On the forest floor is a layer of plant material sometimes 10 feet thick. It acts as a carbon sink, and a layer only 1 centimeter thick can contain 2.5 tons of carbon per acre! When the forest is cut or dies off, this layer warms up rapidly and gives off huge plumes of carbon dioxide into the atmosphere, contributing to global warming.

As it gets warmer, predators such as bark beetles invade northward, killing more of the forest. As you can see, everything that goes on out there in the world is part of a living web, all linked together, and we're one of the links, for better or for worse.

GOBBLERS

It used to be hard to find a turkey. Back 25 years or so ago, a birder who wanted to add a wild turkey to his viewing list had to be very diligent and get up really early and go somewhere like Cades Cove in hopes of seeing one. Although there were an estimated 10 million turkeys in North America when the first white settlers arrived, they were steadily eaten up and run off through the years, so that by 1952, a survey showed that turkeys were present in only 18 of the 95 counties in Tennessee.

The first wild turkey I ever saw was in the Tennessee National Wildlife Refuge, out along the Tennessee River where it runs north in West Tennessee. It was in the early 70's, and my wildlife biologist brother Ries had me out in his Volkswagen Beetle driving through the high weeds. There they were: two or three big birds, standing nearly 4 feet tall, staring down at us in that Beetle.

Up close, the wild turkey is an impressive creature. It sports a large, red and blue featherless head adorned with warty appendages. They have dark, bronze-brown body feathers with black barring and a large tail they fan out in display. The males have a bristly beard hanging off their chest. They court the hens with an elaborate display, calling, fanning out their large tails, spreading their 4-foot wings so the tips drag the ground, and strutting from side to side.

Fred Alsop's excellent Smithsonian book *Birds of North America*, published in 2001, contains this statement about turkeys: "Wild birds unlikely in areas of human habitation, though widely domesticated. Increasing." Well, things are definitely changing, because most everyone who looks around these days will see a turkey, or a dozen of them. A couple of friends of ours who live out on Beaver Ridge, a lovely wooded area maybe a quarter-mile from the bustling activity of Brickey Elementary School, are regularly entertained by a flock—anywhere from 25 to 50 of them—checking things out under the birdfeeders. And another couple we know, who live 3 miles from downtown Halls, has a flock of 25 standing in their front yard when they come home from work, waiting for a handout of corn.

So how come we're replete with turkeys? Needing wildlife information, I put in a call to the TWRA in Nashville and got a call back from staff person Doug Scott over there. He generously shared a bunch of turkey facts with me, reinforcing and adding to the info I had partially remembered from a great turkey lecture at the Pigeon Forge Wilderness Wildlife Week last winter.

It turns out that the TWRA got really serious about turkey restoration in the 1970s. From the low point in the 1950s, the turkey population grew to where, by around 2000 when they declared the restoration project complete, there were an estimated 160,000 to 180,000 turkeys in Tennessee. There are so many turkeys in Tennessee now that there are hunting seasons in all 95 counties, and about a third of the counties allow a second season in the spring.

Why the amazing success story? Well, for one thing, the wily old turkeys have adapted themselves better to being around people. They formerly liked to live in big, open, mature forests, but now are found in second-growth woods, fields, edges, thickets . . . and yards.

But equally important, the TWRA did a tremendous job of catching and relocating the turkeys. It was discovered that pen-raised turkeys, when released in the wild, were never able to successfully establish a new local breeding population. But wild-raised birds, trapped with cannon nets and released in areas low in turkeys, did a great job of establishing themselves. So, the TWRA folks spent a lot of time in the field, working to outsmart a very suspicious, capture-resistant bunch of critters and get them moved, and we enjoy the results today.

Our domestic turkey, according to John K. Terres' *Encyclopedia of North American Birds*, was developed from a subspecies of our wild turkey from southern Mexico. It was taken to southern Europe as early as the 1500s. And because they finally found their way into northern Europe and England by way of the Turkish Empire, they were called "turkeys."

Mama turkeys scrape out a nesting place on the ground and lay 10–12 eggs, which hatch in about 28 days. After a couple of days, the young follow their mother off the nest and out into the world. They can fly to low perches after about 2 weeks, which certainly improves their chances for survival.

Turkeys like to eat nuts, acorns, insects, and other hard stuff, which they grind up in an extra-muscular gizzard aided by ingested gravel, and which can grind things up with pressures above 300 pounds per square inch. They roost in trees at night, flying up into their tree one at a time, making all sorts of flapping and thrashing noises until they finally get settled in.

Fine-looking, large, and impressive birds, the wild turkey missed out by just one vote when Congress officially adopted the bald eagle as our national bird on June 20, 1782. There were a lot of pros and cons to that argument. I'd sure rather be sitting down to a Thanksgiving dinner of turkey and dressing than eagle. But on the other hand, I can't imagine getting that lump in my throat when the UT band accompanies Lee Greenwood in a patriotic song at halftime, if a trained turkey were to come swooping down out of the stands.

Always have a great Thanksgiving holiday and enjoy your bird.

AT HOME UP NORTH

Thanksgiving in Vermont. This column comes to you from New England, not so very far from where Thanksgiving first began. Spouse and I have family way up here, 60 miles from Canada. More often than not it snows for us on this, our traditional visiting week, but not this year. So far, only a few scattered flakes have sprinkled down, falling as we were looking at loons and gulls on a cold windy day along the edge of huge Lake Champlain, which separates the states of Vermont and New York.

Of course, being with much-loved and hospitable family who are providing lots of wonderful eats and catching up on the past year's news makes for a warm and comfortable time. Also of interest to someone who is aware of their outdoor environs, such as an elderly birdwatcher, is the comfortable feeling of being in an area where the outdoors is familiar and welcoming, too.

Northern New England has a good feel about it—Maine, New Hampshire, Vermont, a thousand road miles from East Tennessee—and it makes you glad that you're there. An experience some years ago helped explain to me why it feels that way. We were looking for seabirds at a park along the rocky shore of New Hampshire. As I scanned along with my binoculars, a tree appeared in my field of view; it had compound leaves red with fall color, a big crop of red berries all over it.

Where had I seen that striking shrub before? It was a mountain ash, and the last one I had seen before that was at the top of Mount LeConte, in the good old Smokies, at an elevation of 6,594 feet above sea level. That tree, which we had always considered to be one of our rewards for climbing up

well over a mile in elevation into the high country of East Tennessee, was growing beside the ocean, 1 foot above sea level, in New Hampshire!

I had always read in the Great Smoky Mountains National Park literature that driving from Knoxville to the top of Clingman's Dome is equivalent to driving from Knoxville to Maine, as far as the natural scene of plants and animals was concerned. That mountain ash growing by the sea confirmed it.

If you're a tree or a salamander, how high you are above sea level is about as important to your life as how far north you live. Your genes are adapted to let you thrive in a certain niche, decided largely by latitude above the equator and elevation above sea level. So, if you're a northern species, but want to live in the South, you'll have to live in a place where it's cool, damp, and shady, somewhere up high.

Our East Tennessee and western North Carolina mountains are high. Mount Mitchell in North Carolina, in fact, is the highest point east of the

Mississippi River, measuring 6,684 feet above sea level. Haywood County, North Carolina, is the highest county in the eastern United States, with 20 peaks over 6,000 feet. In the Great Smoky Mountains National Park, Clingman's Dome is the highest point at 6,644 feet. Mt. Guyot is second at 6,621 feet, and Tennessee's own Mount LeConte checks in at 6,594 feet.

At around 3,500 feet in elevation, climate and life begin to change, and things *really* change at about the 5,000-foot line, a vague and variable boundary between "down here" and "up there." At those highest elevations, the damp, dark, cool New England feel takes over, and that is where there dwell all the organisms whose ancestors moved south ahead of the ancient glaciers and then who were left behind when the last great glacier retreated from the Ohio Valley 10,000 years ago.

Some plants and animals are more particular than others about where they live. You'll find the laid-back robins, for example, or the crows, hopping around in Halls and Powell, and you'll find them a mile higher at Newfound Gap. But a lot of others are very picky and specific about such matters. They obey the urging of their northern genes and insist upon living up in the 5,000- to 6,700-foot zone, or else on up farther north, as far as southern Canada. Living down lower in the valleys is not an option for them. Good examples of these include the Clinton's lily with its porcelain-blue berries, the mountain ash we mentioned earlier, the mountain maple, and the firs and spruces.

Birdwise, Tennessee is home to a nice batch of high-elevation birds found elsewhere only farther on north up into Ontario and Quebec. These include the common raven, brown creeper, winter wren, and such wood warblers as black-throated blue, black-throated green, Blackburnian, and Canada.

Lots of other things, great and small, live up there, too, such as the scarce northern flying squirrel and the endangered, tiny, spruce-fir moss spider. Needless to say, birders and other nature lovers enjoy seeing their favorite birds, flowers, and other foci of study in the Smokies rather than traveling 1,000 miles north to find them. At least this nature lover does!

So, when I walk along a Vermont road amongst the big dark spruce and fir trees, it's only natural to feel the same comfort as I do when I leave the traffic, crowds, and malls behind and ascend the mountains to stroll in our Great Smoky Mountains north woods. Our East Tennessee outdoor types know what a real treasure we have here in the high country of East Tennessee and western North Carolina. We have New England, 50 miles from home.

TWO TENNESSEE FIRSTS

In recent years the birders of East Tennessee have been the happy observers of two remarkably rare birds; one, the first of its kind ever recorded in Tennessee, and the second, the first for all of North America.

You may recall that we mentioned how the technology of geolocators had crowned the champions of long-distance songbird migration, the northern wheatears, at 18,640 miles per annual round trip from Alaska to central Africa and back.

A truly remarkable story about a species of bird that, although filed in my interesting facts department, I would never, ever expect to see. So, imagine the electricity in the birding community when the call went out on a mid-November day that an intrepid member of the Knoxville Bird Club had discovered a northern wheatear at a farm in Loudon County!

We were there at half past eight the next morning, the fog so thick you couldn't see 50 yards ahead, not to mention the smoke from the drought-induced, widespread wildfires. The location was Windy Hill Farm & Preserve, a lovely 500-acre working cattle farm fronting on the Tennessee River. The owners, in spite of trying to run their farm, graciously admitted all of us rarity-crazed birders. By ten o'clock in the morning, the fog had lifted, and there were some 20 carloads of people from as far away as Chattanooga and Nashville with binoculars, spotting scopes, and cameras lining the fence along the farm road.

And there it was, the fabled wheatear, creating joy and excitement akin to a Tennessee football victory over Alabama. The little 1 ounce feathered world traveler was just doing its thing, sitting on a fencepost, flying down to the ground to nab an insect, freezing beside a stone for several minutes when a menacing Cooper's hawk flew across the field.

The wheatear was in its winter plumage, as would be expected at this time of year. It could have been mistaken for a female bluebird at a casual glance, but with no blue anywhere. It was about the same size, though, but it stood a bit taller, on longer legs. Its back was gray, and its chest a pale rufous (robin's breast) color, with a beady black eye and a white eyebrow. Its tell-tale identification feature was easily seen as it flew—a bright white rump and upper tail, bordered by a sharp inverted "T" at the end.

A very cooperative little bird, it had probably seen very few human beings in its life, considering where it has lived. I imagine that it just presumed that we, like the cattle, were just some strange, large, nonthreatening non-bird-eating form of wildlife. Everyone got good close looks and excellent photographs, and it was a couple of hours of marvelous birding enjoyment for those of us fortunate enough to have been there. A rare bird? As noted, it was the first time ever that a wheatear had been recorded in Tennessee!

Well, then, not to be outdone by a mere wheatear, another world traveler dropped in on the state in a December event. That story unfolded like this: On December 3rd, a couple of knowledgeable ladies from the Crane Foundation stopped by the Hiwassee Wildlife Refuge, located on the Tennessee River north of Chattanooga, to admire the 10,000 sandhill cranes arriving there for the winter. And among the crowd of huge, tall gray birds they spotted someone different. Hanging out with all the other cranes was one a bit shorter, with a slaty-gray body; black wings, tail, and legs; and a striking white head and neck. The ladies called their headquarters in Wisconsin for backup, and the stranger was quickly confirmed to be a very rare bird from Asia, a hooded crane. Just like gossip in a neighborhood, the word spread through the birding community with the speed of an iPod. People began showing up from all over the country to see the bird.

Spouse and I thought we'd give it a try on the way home from Christmas at our son's house in north Alabama. Thanks to immobile traffic on Interstate 26 south of Chattanooga, we didn't arrive at the Hiwassee Refuge till a quarter past four the afternoon of the 26th. There stood 20 or 30 eager birders with scopes and cameras, including birder and author Stephen Lyn Bales from Ijams Nature Center and birders from Maine, Oregon, and Florida. A lady from St. Louis had driven all night to be there for a glimpse of the exotic traveler.

There were innumerable sandhill cranes, but no sign of the hooded crane we'd all come to see. After a while, a bald eagle flew across the scene and stirred things up a bit, sending hundreds of cranes scattering in the air. And as all those cranes settled down again, the lady from Missouri, eye glued to her scope, announced, "There's our bird!" Out it walked, a black-and-white figure in a sea of gray. And we all stood and stared at this creature that had flown over the bogs of Siberia to stand in a field in Tennessee. It's the kind of happening that birders love to sit back and recount for months and years afterward.

Hooded cranes nest in a remote area of Russia north of Mongolia, in a cool, wet world of peat bogs and stunted larch trees. The species was first described in 1834, but because they breed in such a remote area, the first hooded crane nest wasn't discovered until 1974 . . . 140 years later! They are best known in their usual wintering grounds, where some 3,000 of them stay on the Japanese island of Kyushu, feeding in harvested grain fields and rice paddies. It was hanging out at the Hiwassee Refuge because it felt safer with that big bunch of related birds, those wintering sandhill cranes. As the first hooded crane ever recorded in North America, it was a very rare, and very exciting, sight for the birders of East Tennessee.

When Spouse and I first started birding back in 1985, we found out about rare birds by using a chain of telephone calls; that would be your wired-in home telephone— remember those? Each person notified would then call two to four others, and so on. That was how we came to see, back in February of 1996, the previously-mentioned very-rare-for-Tennessee resident of the far north, an ivory gull, out at Pickwick Dam in West Tennessee. Thanks to our then very effective Telephone Rare-bird Alert System, other rare birds followed.

That was then; this is now. Nowadays such news, including photographs and GPS locations, goes out instantly to anyone, anywhere, who has the appropriate app on their information device. More birders are out there now, attuned to the notion of finding more and more rarities, and everyone seems eager to share the information. Nice people and great technology meet Mother Nature. How good is all that?

WINTER

ENTERTAINMENT AT ABRAMS FALLS

You can generally depend on having a nice time in the Smokies on a clear, cool day in late November. Most of the leaves have fallen, and most of the tourists have retreated back up north or gone on to Florida.

Bird life has narrowed back down to the species that stay all year round, with the addition of a few new visitors from farther north that come to winter here with us, such as the white-throated sparrows, yellow-bellied sapsuckers, sometimes the pine siskins, and rarely, these days, the evening grosbeaks.

Things can be interesting outdoors as fall yields to winter. All those missing leaves open up contours of hills and vistas of mountains that you don't see in the summer. The bare trees reveal all sorts of gnarly and intriguing structures. There are lots of tall dried grass and weed stems with an assortment of seed heads and seedpods, the leafless persimmon trees and wild grapevines loaded with fruit. It is a landscape colored with an artist's palette of tans, browns, and grays.

A group of six of us headed for Cades Cove on a recent Friday. The weather was pleasant, the traffic fairly sparse, and the company, great. After fortifying ourselves at one of our favorite Cove overlook turnoffs with ham and cheese sandwiches and homemade chocolate chip cookies, we pressed resolutely on to the Abrams Creek trailhead for the 2.5-mile hike to Abrams Falls.

Abrams Creek, incidentally, derives its name from a warlike Cherokee chief, Old Abraham of Chilhowee. (Indeed, Cades Cove itself is named for a little-known Cherokee, Chief Kade.)

Abrams Falls Trail is a very popular one; there was a tour bus full of kids from Illinois enjoying the trail the day we visited. The trail is a long-time standard for a 5-mile Boy Scout hike, and a present-day favorite for us more senior hikers because it is wide and gentle and follows along Abrams Creek for almost the whole way.

Abrams Creek, low on water in this drought year and with a lot of exposed rocks, drains from Cades Cove, out of the park and into Chilhowee Lake. It is large enough to attract an interesting variety of wildlife. At the beginning of the hike, right there at the bridge, some enterprising beavers have engineered a tidy, level, and efficient dam across the creek. A little farther down, we encountered a belted kingfisher flying back and forth along the creek, giving its rattly call. And we even flushed out a great blue heron, a bird that you don't see every day in the Smokies. But the real surprise came at our destination, in the big pool below the actual falls. There we encountered a very active furry entertainer, doing its thing and hamming it up for the crowd.

In the seven decades since the Great Smoky Mountains National Park came into existence, a lot of different wildlife species have come and gone, both along and in Abrams Creek. Ideas about what was "natural" and "wild," and how they should be managed, have varied widely through the years. A recent book called *The Wild East: A Biography of the Great Smoky Mountains* by Margaret Lynn Brown, explores these notions.

Take trout, for example. The only native trout in the Smokies were the brook trout. But early on in the life of the park, it was considered important to provide visitors with a "wilderness" experience, including trout fishing á la the Wild West. In the Wild West, you trout fish for rainbow trout. Rainbows, a western species, are larger and a little less picky about their environs than the native brookies and, thus, outcompete them when introduced into brook trout waters. And so, the National Park Service planted hundreds of thousands of western rainbow trout into Smoky Mountain streams year after year. And wouldn't you know, before long some of the anglers were asking why nobody was catching brook trout anymore.

Then, concerned about "rough" fish from Chilhowee Lake competing with the introduced, nonnative rainbow trout, the federal government, in June 1957, approved the poisoning of a 14.6-mile stretch of Abrams Creek with rotenone, attempting to kill every living fish in the stream. And they did: They killed 47 species in all, including the spotfin chub and the Smoky Mountain madtom, both of which went on to become endangered species. They also polished off the rare yellowfin madtom and the duskytail darter.

But along the way, conservation and wildlife lessons have been learned; some progress has been made, and some victories won. The peregrine falcons that once nested on Peregrine Ridge below Alum Cave Bluff had been rendered extinct east of the Mississippi by the 1950s and 1960s by the widespread agricultural use of DDT. (Many readers of this book have residual DDT in their bodies—just so you know.) Once DDT was banned, a captive breeding program was started, and young peregrine falcons were released from Greenbrier Pinnacle beginning in 1984. And then, in 1997, a pair of peregrines successfully fledged a family of three youngsters, most remarkably from a nest site located on Peregrine Ridge, last used by the species some 50 years before.

And those obscure little fishes poisoned out of Abrams Creek? Small remnant populations of them were discovered living in a stream in the Cherokee National Forest in the early 1980s! Eggs were gathered, then hatched and raised in an aquarium at UT. They are now back, hopefully able to sustain themselves in the now-friendlier waters of Abrams Creek.

But the source of our delight in the big pool below Abrams Falls on that Friday afternoon in November? A river otter! Interesting fact: The Indian name for Cades Cove was apparently Tsiyahi, or "place of the otter." But hunting, trapping, and habitat destruction had pretty well wiped out our river otters by the early years of the 1900s. Since they were known to have lived in Abrams Creek in fairly recent times, it was a logical place to attempt a reintroduction of the little beasties. The first ones were added to Abrams Creek in 1986, and by 1994 well over 100 otters had been introduced onto the park.

The Chattanooga Aquarium has a great river otter exhibit, where you can watch them hanging out on the rocks and then see them below the surface, swimming around like little furry torpedoes.

Out there in the wild, our specimen was behaving just like its Chattanooga cousins. It caught a crawfish (their favorite food); took it up on shore, ripped it up, and ate it; and to complete the demonstration for us, carefully washed paws and face. Then ZOOM! Under the water, out into the big pool, and up to the surface again to watch the tourists—apparently totally comfortable with all of us hikers standing on the rocks watching him.

A species that can, given a fair chance, fit back into a restored and improved habitat, with adequate cover and food, is a wonderful thing to see. We've had the excitement of putting our spotting scope on fluffy white peregrine falcon chicks in their nest on Peregrine Ridge. And now we've seen a river otter catch and eat a crawfish and frolic in the cold water of Abrams Creek!

Behind both of these remarkable outdoor experiences, there are years of research and countless hours and days in the field by a whole array of dedicated people. It gives one cause to hope for the continued success with the whooping cranes, the California condors, the Florida panthers, and all the less famous species out there, clinging to existence. Them and us—we're really all in this thing together.

SAD? YOU'RE NOT THE ONLY ONE!

SAD—short for Seasonal Affective Disorder. The acronym pretty well describes the symptoms. Moodiness, lack of energy, loss of interest, and depression—sadness. The disorder is caused by a response to the decreasing of daylight hours as fall progresses into winter. We come by the problem honestly; it's a response we share with just about every other living thing on the planet.

You may have noticed that winter begins on December 21st. And although winter is upon us on that date, the days began getting longer the very next day.

Now think back to those nice balmy days like June 21st, the first day of last summer. Although we rejoiced that summer had come at last, the joy was tempered a bit by the realization that it was also the time when those wonderful long days began to get shorter again.

As time went by, and each day got a minute or two shorter than the one before it, a certain critical point was reached. Along about mid-August into early September, the shorter days and longer nights triggered an ancient chain of events that made all life here in the Northern Temperate Zone—trees, frogs, birds, bears—begin to prepare for winter. It's sort of like going to the mall to buy a bathing suit in September; all you can find is winter stuff, even though it's 90 degrees and sunny outside. The merchants, like the critters, are planning ahead. These astronomical changes affect us human beings, too, and not just in our shopping plans. More about that in a moment.

The trees, and many other deciduous plants, prepare for winter by beginning to move sugars and other goods from their leaves down into storage in the roots, and preparing all those millions of leaves to shut down production, and eventually, to fall.

The birds respond by molting, changing their showy spring feathers for more drab fall ones. The new fall feathers amount to up to 50% more plumage, due to the addition of after-feathers, which are little, extra, fluffy feathers with good insulating qualities to withstand the chills to come.

Birds also adjust their body chemistries in complex ways that allow them to burn their fat reserves more efficiently and become several times more cold tolerant than they are in the spring and summer months. The migrators instinctively become voracious eaters, like high school football players, sometimes doubling their weight in the fall. And they become restless, nervous, fidgety, making short little flights in the direction of their Big Trip before finally, one clear evening, launching away, heading for some place they know they're supposed to be going, but where most of them have never been.

The furry beasts respond to the ancient astronomical signs, too. They eat and put on extra layers of fat. They grow an additional coat of short, soft, thick fur that increases their tolerance to cold, some by as much as 40 degrees. The animals that hibernate, such as the groundhogs, bats, and bears, undergo metabolic changes that enable them to slow their heart rate and their breathing, and to use their stored-up energy very efficiently. Bears neither eat nor drink for months at a time, yet emerge in the spring ready to hunt, forage, and get on with life!

Animals that are active most of the winter, such as rabbits, squirrels, and deer, also grow thicker coats and fatten up on the fall bounty of nuts and seeds. But even some of those species, such the squirrels and jays, spend the fall in a frenzy of storing up food supplies for winter, sometimes gathering up an amount that would equal two, three, or more winters' worth of food and squirreling it away, so to speak.

All that eating and fattening, and storing and sleeping: It's all in place now in January, all around us. But it was all set in motion back in the months of August and September in response to a change in the light. Those quickly shortening days caused special photoreceptor cells in the skin, brain, and eyes of all those critters to stimulate a small organ in their brains, called the pineal gland, to secrete a hormone known as melatonin. As in so much of our existence, hormones are what make things happen. And melatonin is at the bottom of all these peculiar fall–winter goings-on.

And—you guessed it—people have pineal glands, too. Although we consider ourselves to be highly advanced and sophisticated, and we light our world with electricity regardless of the time or the season, our brains still reach back to an earlier time and still respond to those same ancient cycles.

Melatonin has been studied for years, in hopes that some of its many functions in the body could be put to use as medicine. It is available in health food stores and drug stores as a remedy for sleep disorders and as a treatment for Seasonal Affective Disorder. But since the source of the trouble is lack of sunlight, someone figured out that a good remedy is to provide more sunlight, or light similar to sunlight. Some workplaces and hospitals now use special overhead lights that simulate sunlight, and they find an improvement in everyone's attitude and sense of well-being. You can get similar lights for your home.

So, during these long gloomy days of winter, if you're feeling sad, grumpy, sleepy, or hungry, don't be alarmed. All the bears and groundhogs feel the same way. But they just go with it; they get fat and go to sleep. When all is said and done, it comes down to the fact that we are all just another one of Earth's creatures, and we function like the rest of them—mushrooms or maple trees or eagles. You may feel SAD, but it's OK. You're certainly not alone!

WINTER BIRDING

January and February can be gloomy, cold, and damp. Up in Vermont they call this time of year stick season. Aptly named . . . just look at the hillsides of bare limbs and twigs. All you see are sticks.

This is prime season for watching our familiar yardbird friends come and go at our birdfeeders, especially if we've planned ahead and can see the feeder from the comfort of a living room chair or the kitchen table.

So why in the world would someone even consider going out on a cold, damp morning into a world of sticks and stems to look at birds, especially since there's nothing out there but a few cardinals, chickadees, and a bunch of little brown sparrows that all look alike and are nearly impossible to see anyway?

Well, now, that's a good question! It has some good answers, or I wouldn't have asked it in the first place. For one thing, just getting outside in the winter, birds or no birds, is something everyone should try. Not so very long ago, it was a necessity to be out in the winter, to bring in the firewood and feed the stock, or go squirrel hunting for meat for the table. Nowadays, we can generally get by simply going from warm house to warm car and back, then hunkering down and waiting for spring.

But once you've been out and about in the winter and found that you can survive, and even be comfortable, it tends to grow on you. You will discover that all those trees and bushes and grassy fields that were there in the summer are still out there; they just look different. Even though they're bare and brown, they are full of bird food. All those weeds and flowers have produced zillions of seeds, and the sumacs and grapes and poison ivy vines

still have dried fruits and berries. And on most days throughout the winter, lots of tiny, tasty insects are out and about on all that vegetation.

This adds up to a lot of food for the scores of bird species that choose to winter here with us. They're all busy making a living, foraging all through the short winter days, often too busy to pay much attention to a nearby, nosy birdwatcher. They're generally easier to locate and observe without all those millions of pesky leaves all over the trees and bushes, and you can often have time to really watch some of the harder-to-spot ones, like the sparrows, and get to know them a lot better.

We know there are a lot of them out there. Christmas counts around here can identify 80 or more species on a single day. Once you're in a good place, you'll be amazed at the numbers of species and individual birds that you can enjoy seeing.

We have no end of good winter birding opportunities in these parts. Close at hand, we have numerous city, county, and local community parks. With no baseball or soccer at this time of the year, these parks are usually peaceful, quiet, birdy places. Having nearby streams, good open fields, and brushy and forest-edge bird habitats—plus nice walking terrain and even paved walking paths—they make winter birding easy and fun. We spent a couple of hours at Schumpert Park in North Knoxville one morning in December and spotted 25 species of birds, including 4 species of sparrows and a surprise flyover by 3 sandhill cranes. Nice, easy, pleasant birding.

In the winter, any place with water seems to offer a higher concentration of bird life. Even as small an area as the duck pond in Fountain City often offers a surprise wild duck or gull. Places a little farther out, such as Eagle Bend Fish Hatchery on the Clinch River in Clinton, the Songbird Trail along the river below Norris Dam and the Norris State Park above the dam, Cove Lake State Park at Caryville, and Fort Loudon Dam and the lake above it up through Knoxville, all offer the promise of the usual—as well as unexpected— water and shorebirds all winter.

With a little more time, some of the more dedicated (compulsive? weird?) of us birders enjoy trying for winter wonders a bit farther afield, looking for birds that wouldn't ordinarily be expected to be here. For example, word recently got around that a couple of short-eared owls had been seen hunting for prey over the tallgrass meadows of Cades Cove. Short-eared owls nest in northern Canada and the Northwest, and winter down through the middle of the United States and even into West Tennessee, so it would be a real treat for us East Tennesseans to see some.

And so, in the midst of a remarkable warm spell, three of us set out for Cades Cove. The hills and fields were lovely and traffic nearly nonexistent. We set up our birding scopes on a grassy elevation along Hyatt Lane. Sure enough, as dusk approached, there they were, flying like big feathered moths back and forth over the fields. One was even kind enough to perch in a handy leafless tree some distance out and pose for us for over 30 minutes.

As a bonus, the owls were accompanied by three owl-like hawks called northern harriers, which like to hunt over the same marshy fields favored by the owls. Together, they put on a great bird show. Also easy to see in the sparse winter landscape were lots of wild turkeys and numerous deer. And then, as if the park were trying to compete with some nature program, across the road came a fat, shiny mama bear with three cubs! With a backdrop of the winter hills and fields of Cades Cove, it was a scene that will stay with us for a long time.

Winter outings are a great alternative to the couch or the mall. It can be a spur-of-the-moment zip over to the nearest pond, field, or woodlot, or an all-day trip to a lake or park. Stick season may be here, but the fields, woods, and ponds are there, full of activity waiting for you to discover. And they're free of mosquitos, ticks, and snakes now, so take advantage of those extra perks and head on out!

RED HEAD, RED BELLY

Would you believe that there are 22 species of woodpeckers in North America? (I know, it's not something you sit around and ponder.) Anyway, at least 17 of these species have red on their heads, at least the males, so there is a bit of confusion about what a "redheaded woodpecker" is. Let's see if we can clear that up, so you readers can stand around talking after church, or at the grocery store, and smugly know what kinds of woodpeckers we have out there.

Around these parts there are five species that occur regularly all year round: downy, hairy, red-bellied, and pileated, and the northern flicker. In addition, we have a species that seems to like to spend our mild winters with us after living up north and raising a family in the summer. This is the yellow-bellied sapsucker, who should win a prize for the coolest name, if nothing else. And finally, we occasionally see the locally scarce, true redheaded woodpecker, a handsome bird with solid areas of bold, black and white coloration, and with a solid red head.

Woodpeckers, being around here during the winter when all the leaves gone, are both interesting and entertaining, and they play an important role in nature's complex, interrelated scheme of things. In fact, they are sort of feathered real estate developers.

Some 84 species of birds in North America are listed as cavity-nesting birds. They nest in hollowed-out holes in trees, dead limbs, and snags. With few exceptions, only the woodpeckers are able to actually excavate their own cavity in a tree. All the others rely on Mother Nature rotting out a hole here and there, or on the industrious woodpeckers doing the work.

It turns out that some woodpeckers prefer to make a new nest hole every year, including our own very common downies and the big pileateds. This provides a lot of new real estate, so to speak, available for next year's cavity nesters. So, the woodpeckers have a key role in the health and welfare of many of our other bird populations, such as the bluebirds, tree swallows, chickadees, and titmice. The pileated woodpeckers excavate a nest cavity large enough for a family of squirrels, and as time and decay enlarge those spaces, they can eventually be used as home by owls, raccoons, and possums.

But let's get back to this business of red-headedness. One species of woodpecker in particular, is assertive, handsome, and lives with us all year, and it is often mistakenly called a red-headed woodpecker, because it has a lot of red on its head. This is the red-bellied woodpecker.

The red-bellied is one that will frequent your winter birdfeeder. It's a take-charge kind of bird, one that even the starlings will step aside for. It will take one black oil sunflower seed at a time, then fly away, wedge it into a crevice in some bark, and peck it open and eat the meat, and then return for another. It also really likes high-energy suet, because these birds are all meat eaters by nature, normally living on insects and grubs they search out under tree bark and in rotting wood.

Both male and female red-bellieds have crosswise black-and-white barring on their entire back and a mostly white belly. Their name comes from a small reddish area on the lower belly, really hard to see unless conditions are just right. The female has red on her head, but it is limited to a bright red patch on the back of her head and the nape of her neck. But here is the problem. The male has brilliant red coloration from the base of the bill, over the forehead and crown, and down the neck to the shoulders, almost as if he has on a red hood. This is why so many folks mistake it for the red-headed woodpecker. Actually, the real red-headed woodpecker has a solid red head, throat, neck and all, as if someone held him upside down and dipped his head in a can of red paint.

For reasons not clear to the experts, the real red-headed woodpeckers have become very scarce here in East Tennessee, even though the other species seem to be doing alright. One possible explanation is the huge numbers of very aggressive, cavity-nesting—and cavity-stealing—European starlings that plague us by the millions. Red-headed woodpeckers seem to be doing better out in West Tennessee.

At any rate, that handsome black-and-white striped guy with the red crown and nape at your feeder, although he has a red head, is not a red-headed woodpecker. I'll leave it up to you to explain all this to your friends, now that you have the facts.

FELLOW TRAVELERS

There are countless ways that a humble, well-meaning husband can get into trouble with Home Management. I certainly won't list any of those here, except for the one that is our subject for today. This particular shortcoming has a specific name, which I first saw in print years ago in the "Last Page" column of an issue of *Wildlife in North Carolina*.

The author called this sin "tracking in," and he blamed it on his faithful old work boots. He even scolded them, saying "bad boots!," and put them out on the back porch. Well, maybe that worked for him, but it sure wouldn't fly around my house.

Now, miscellaneous leaves, shop shavings, and grass cuttings can possibly be stopped outside the back door, especially if those errant boots happen to be in a cooperative mood that day. But then, as is so often true in life, there are problems out there that prove more difficult. Some things just won't stop at the door.

We used to tell third and fourth graders on Ijams Nature Center walks that we call this group of troublemakers "fellow travelers." Fellow travelers are those pernicious little weed seeds that have managed to work out, over 150 million years or so, ingenious ways of getting themselves spread all over the place, often far away from their original Mother Weed.

Just think about such botanical friends as beggar's lice, Spanish needles, and the delightful cockleburs. They use a variety of clever devices to latch on to us. Cockleburs are so effective they became the basis for the idea behind Velcro, invented by a Swiss engineer in 1948. They have the hooks; we are the loops.

Humans weren't around when all these devices first showed up on the scene, but there were plenty of furry creatures around, on which they could hone their latching-on skills. If you think Skippy the golden retriever is a mess after a romp in the cockleburs, just imagine what a woolly mammoth or a giant ground sloth would have tracked in!

Through the eons, most every plant has developed a strategy for getting its seeds spread around as widely as possible, to sprout and grow in as many places as possible. Early on, back in the Coal Age, clubmosses and ferns, which often grew to be tree sized, used microscopic spores, so small they floated away on the air currents, to seek out new territories.

Then plants figured out flowers and produced a wide variety of fruits, such as blackberries, grapes, cherries, and apples, which were good food. This enticed the birds and animals to eat the fruits and so disperse the seeds abroad. Using a different method, the touch-me-nots have developed seed pods that, when ripe, and then touched, snap open with such force that it tosses the seeds some distance from the plant.

Plants use some sneaky strategies, too. Take the trilliums, for example. Trilliums produce a fat-rich food body called an elaisome, attached to the outside of the seeds. These food bodies attract ants, which then nab the seeds and carry them off to their nest. There, the fat body is eaten and the seed tossed into the refuse heap, hopefully to sprout and grow far away from the original trillium plant.

And some of the more interesting flower seeds, much like fern spores, depend on the air and the wind to disperse them far and wide; think of those tiny seeds with fluffy parachutes. Who hasn't puffed away a cloud of dandelion seeds from their round seed head to watch them drift away? And others, such as thistles, milkweeds, and clematis vines use variations on that same theme.

But back to our fellow travelers. These guys get themselves spread around by using us. And getting us outdoor types in trouble at home. They don't just drop off harmlessly on the mudroom floor. They cling tenaciously to shoe laces, socks, and pant legs until they find an even better destination, such as carpets, couches, and bedspreads, and then, other clothes in the dryer.

Some fellow travelers are worse than others. Spanish needles can be plucked off fairly easily. The little round sticky seedballs from bedstraw aren't too hard to remove. But those tiny adherent triangles of beggar's lice, known in some places as tick-trefoil, can be a chore to dislodge when they attach to clothing by the dozens. And they seem to keep on turning up for days.

Cockleburs are among the champions of fellow travelers. The plants can grow to 5 feet tall and produce over 5,000 sticky burrs covered with hooked spines, each containing 2 seeds, or a total of over 10,000 seeds per plant. And when you try to remove the attached burs, unlike the more benign beggar's lice, the cockleburs bite back with their prickly spines.

Well, I suppose all those plants with clinging seeds are just trying to make a living, too. But l sure wish they would figure out a different way to disperse their young, or at least cling to something besides me. It's tough being in trouble all the time.

A HOLIDAY BIRDING TREAT

Our 520-plus National Wildlife Refuges, covering 93 million acres, offer great opportunities for folks to get out and enjoy nature. Their endless variety of rivers, lakes, swamps, fields, and mountains are home to myriad varieties of trees and flowers, bushes and grasses. That means they are also home to innumerable creatures that people like to watch—big animals, butterflies, and in the case of birders, birds!

Over 200 of our NWRs were set aside specifically to protect, manage, and restore habitat for migratory birds, and one result of that effort has been to yield a list of over 700 species of birds that have been seen in America's refuges. And the good people who manage those refuges have made many of them very birder friendly, with wildlife drives meandering through all their different natural features, plus nature trails, photo blinds, and observation towers.

Through the years, Spouse and I have accumulated many fond memories, and some large bird lists, from such places as Santa Ana NWR in southern Texas; Savannah NWR in coastal South Carolina; and Malheur NWR, the recently hooligan-occupied but still wild and beautiful refuge located in eastern Oregon.

And through those years, one of our favorites has been the reasonably nearby 34,500-acre Wheeler NWR, only a 4-hour drive away in north Alabama, spread out along TVA's big Wheeler Lake. Its headquarters are located just east of Decatur, Alabama. It was established in 1938 as a wintering area for ducks, geese, and other migratory birds and consists of woods, water, and hundreds of acres of agricultural fields managed primarily as a source for bird food.

It also happens to be a convenient 12-minute drive from our son's home, where we usually find ourselves at Christmastime, the high season for the hordes of waterbirds that congregate at the refuge in December, January, and February. The late December weather there in north Alabama can be dicey for birding: We've had inches of snow one year, all-day monsoons of rain another. But this particular year was calm, dry, and a balmy 72 degrees by midday—a great Christmas present from Mother Nature! And a marvelous 2-hour birding trip to Wheeler NWR in shirt sleeves on Christmas Eve was a perfect addition to our holiday festivities.

The best plan for enjoying Wheeler NWR is to start at the visitor's center, where friendly and knowledgeable volunteers tell you what's going on out there and where you are likely to find an unusual bird or two. You'll also find interesting displays of wildlife, maps, and other information. The major attraction, though, is the observation building, 200 yards from the visitor's center down a wooded gravel pathway. Sitting right on the edge of the water, the observation building is there for one purpose: observation. You walk into the back of the building, and there before you are two walls, front and side, facing out over the big embayment of calm, bird-filled water, one-way glass from floor to ceiling. Most first-timers walk in and can be heard to say "wow!"

Across the water from the building is a huge farm field managed to produce bird food, lying fallow at this time of the year; beyond that, woods and more water. The numbers of waterbirds peak in January; when we were there the refuge personnel estimated that the big farm field held around 11,000 sandhill cranes; it looked like a million to us! This time of year, the sandhills are joined by tens of thousands of ducks, innumerable geese, white pelicans, gulls, and herons, with smaller numbers of less commonly seen species just waiting to be discovered.

The sandhill cranes set the scene and the mood for the bird drama. Thousands of the big, gray, 5-foot-tall birds stand around in the field and along the shore, making a constant din of background noise with their strange, bugling crane calls. And more of them are overhead, coming and going in V-formations of 3 to 30 or more, flying high and low. That overall picture in and of itself makes the visit worthwhile, a scene right out of a nature documentary!

But against that backdrop there were more wonders to be seen. One noted authority on cranes was quoted as saying that Wheeler NWR is one of the best places in the world to see whooping cranes. And sure enough, in the far back of the big field there were 15 white blobs, which, with the aid of binoculars, became 15 big whooping cranes! Ironically, back in 1941, at their lowest point, there were only 14 or 15 whooping cranes left in the wild, but here we were, seeing 15 of the approximately 600 whooping cranes in the world today, all in a single bunch! And we didn't have to charter a boat or plane trip to go somewhere to see them.

And, as if to make things even better for us, one of the big whooping cranes decided to come over close to the observation building to hang out with a dozen or so of its new best friends, the sandhill cranes. It flew in, sipped some lake water, worked on its feathers for a bit, and sat down for a nap, all within a couple hundred feet of those of us watching behind the glass, in awe of seeing, up close, one of the rarest birds in the world!

Once one has had a full dose of crane watching, one turns to the ducks. And there they were, probably more than a thousand of them, in the water and on the shore just outside the windows. We identified eight species, loafing, swimming, eating, and occasionally chasing one another, constantly in motion. And in addition to large numbers and good close looks, the ducks provided us with one more rare-bird treat for the day.

Among all those ducks, we saw the two most numerous duck species, the gadwalls and American wigeons. Both are totally familiar to our duck-hunting friends; both species were there in the hundreds. But then there is another wigeon, called the Eurasian wigeon, that breeds in Europe and Asia. It is known to winter along both coasts of North America, though only rarely at inland locations like the TVA lakes. Not an especially rare bird, but rarely seen where we are. The refuge staff had told us that there was a Eurasian wigeon around; one fellow at the observation building had driven down from Nashville just to see it. And after 2 hours of looking at all those ducks, there it was, close enough to see well and to photograph! Icing on the birding cake!

A brief scan for small landbirds at the headquarters feeders and nearby woods, and we were back in our car and POOF! Back to the world of cars and gas stations, fast food places, and last-minute shoppers. But we were happy to have had that time outdoors, seeing a tiny corner of the Earth as it was intended to be, and knowing that those refuges are there, all across the country, saving those treasures for everyone. So, a Happy New Year to you all; get out somewhere and enjoy your natural surroundings!

PORKERS—THE GOOD,
THE BAD, AND THE UGLY

Having all just endured the rhetoric of another year's midterm elections, I'm sure we've all been reminded that there are at least two opinions about almost everything. Today's subject, the pig, is no exception. For example, the ancient Hebrews declared pigs unclean and therefore not to be eaten, some 3,000–4,000 years ago, and their Near Eastern neighbors, the Muslims, followed suit a little later.

In contrast, the savages to the north, who most of us descended from, thought pigs were delicious. They caught the mean and rangy wild boar, the original pig, and domesticated him into the docile, fat, tender delicacy that we enjoy today. Picture the big Christmas feast in the English castle of old, with madrigal singers and the roast pig, on a platter surrounded with vegetables, and with an apple in its mouth.

Pigs went forth with the British navy to conquer the world, in the form of big barrels of salt pork, which the sailors subsisted on with dry biscuits and a daily ration of rum. (With that food, I'm sure they needed the rum.)

Fast-forwarding now to more recent times, we have a somewhat similar difference of opinion about pigs—the wild ones, at least—in East Tennessee today. But first, some essential pig historical facts and family history. For one thing, there were no native North American pigs; they're all imports from Europe. The first ones supposedly arrived here with Hernando de Soto and his band of Spaniards in 1539, and many other subsequent groups of explorers and settlers brought pigs and other livestock with them from the old country.

Often, back then, the pigs were allowed to roam free in the woods to fatten up on chestnuts, acorns, and whatever else they could find. When the time came to round them back up, there were occasional escapees, which became wild again, or as the biologists call them, feral. Now, as feral pigs breed in the wild, they gradually lose some of their domestic pig characteristics and tend to look more like their ancestors, the European wild boars.

In our neck of the woods, some hunting enthusiasts contributed another whole set of ferocious genes to the feral pig situation. In 1912 a small group of Russian wild boars was brought to a game preserve on Hooper Bald near Murphy, North Carolina, for breeding stock to build a herd for hunting. Sure enough, they multiplied, and in 1920 some 100 of them escaped from the preserve. They spread out, and some worked their way to the Smokies. They had crossed the state line and were digging up Gregory Bald by 1958. These wild boars interbred with the feral pigs already running around up there, so that most of the wild hogs now are a mixture of boar and feral domestic pig. And they are all ugly.

Anyhow, here is where we get into today's differences of opinion about wild pigs. Wild boars can weigh over 300 pounds; have four big, sharp tusks; and can tear a hunting dog to shreds. And they can be good to eat.

All that adds up to an ideal big game animal roaming about in our forests and mountains, and they are a big favorite. The village of Tellico Plains has been the unofficial center of boar hunting for decades, and the national forests and other lands continue to yield up a yearly harvest of the hairy tuskers.

The Great Smoky Mountains National Park is another story. There, the mission is to protect and preserve the land as close to its natural state as possible. The wild hogs are a nonnative, introduced species with almost no predators, like kudzu. They are omnivorous, which means they will eat anything. They compete with the bears, deer, turkeys, and squirrels for the mast crop—all the fruits and nuts that grow out there.

Another of their favorite foods is wildflower bulbs. They root up these bulbs by the acre, rolling up large areas of turf as effectively as a rototiller. Thousands of wildflowers such as spring beauties, lilies, orchids, and trilliums are destroyed. These heavily damaged areas are easy to see in more open sites, such as grassy roadsides or on the balds.

Hogs also eat bird's eggs, snakes, frogs, and salamanders. The red-cheeked salamander, sort of a poster animal for the Great Smoky Mountain Park, is found mainly on the upper slopes of Mount LeConte and nowhere else in the world outside the park. And, wouldn't you know, the most common salamander found in the stomachs of wild hogs taken at higher elevations has been the red-cheeked salamander! A wild hog could eat a whole stomach-full of a rare, local creature in one evening.

Trapping hogs began in the park in August 1959. The success rates depended directly upon the amount of funds that could be allocated for hog control, and that has been very slim of late; federal funding for national parks has been woefully inadequate. In spite of the many difficulties, the park ranger in charge of hog control reported several years ago that they had caught their 10,000th wild hog since 1959! He estimated the park's hog population at around 500 and stable.

The farming community has concerns about wild pigs, too, because they carry two serious diseases that are of significant economic concern. One is swine brucellosis. If it gets transmitted to domestic swine herds, it causes miscarriages and infertility; cattle and humans also can be infected.

The other worrisome wild hog disease is called pseudorabies. It can weaken domestic pigs and lead to miscarriages and stillbirths; it can kill cattle, sheep, goats, dogs, and cats. Wild pigs in 10 states have been found to carry swine brucellosis; in 11 states, they have been found to carry pseudorabies. Fortunately, so far, neither disease has been found in Tennessee or North Carolina.

Recently, the hog problem had grown so bad that they were causing millions of dollars in crop damages, particularly in West Tennessee. It appears that for now, these agricultural losses have trumped the sporting value of the beasts, and they have been declared a nongame animal, with no season or limitations on harvesting them – a huge victory for the farmers and for our environment!

So, there you have it. Most everybody agrees that the domestic pig is a fine addition to any dining table. But the wild ones? It depends upon whether you're a park ranger trying to save a national park, a farmer trying to make a living, or a hunter after your favorite game animal. I believe I'll fry up some sausage and go sit down and think about it.

MINNESOTA IN THE WINTER

Odds are, very few people in our part of the country have ever heard of the Sax-Zim Bog. Neither had we, until Spouse and I looked into a trip called Minnesota in Winter, offered by our favorite birding tour company. It was one of those things you see and initially chuckle at, and then think about it for a while, and then, do it.

Minnesota is cold—really cold—in the winter. But the key point here is that it's 1,000 miles south of places that are really, really cold, as well as mostly dark, all winter long. Food supplies can be iffy in the far north, abundance and plenty running in cycles with years of scarcity and hunger. Some years have flocks of interesting and seldom-seen birds coming down to the relatively balmy environs of northern Minnesota, searching for a winter of dependable food sources. And that gives us warm-climate types a great opportunity to get out and watch them.

So, Spouse and I set out on in late January driving north, just ahead of a big ice storm in Kentucky, and arrived in sunny (and 6-degrees-above-zero) Minneapolis 2 days later. We joined our group, seven birders and a skilled leader and guide, and headed even farther north to Duluth. There, we spent 4 bitter cold nights in a warm, cozy motel and 4 really splendid days driving in a heated van and walking the snowy back roads of northern Minnesota.

That's where the Sax-Zim Bog comes in. Probably the best-known birding area in Minnesota, it's a vaguely defined area northwest of Duluth, maybe 10 miles on a side each way. It's named for two tiny villages, Sax and Zim, which are hardly findable. It's a mixture of big evergreen woods, low boggy wetlands, and scattered farms with large mowed hayfields and cornfields. And the bog is famous for its huge collection of winter birds.

The temperatures ranged from –8 degrees to a high of 14 degrees while we were there. And the snow was deep, up to the house windows in Ely, Minnesota, and over 2 feet deep in the woods. We quickly learned not to step off the hardpacked trails.

So, what do you get for spending a day outdoors in northern Minnesota in January, bundled up like the little brother in "The Christmas Story"? You get a lot of wonderful close observations of an assortment of birds remarkably adapted to survival in the depths of winter. We saw a total of 46 species of birds up there, busily going about their life as usual, just like the schoolkids in Minneapolis.

There were the familiar crows and blue jays, starlings, and a few robins. But mostly, we saw birds that never make it down to where we live here in the South. The ones of primary interest, the ones we really hoped to see, were the owls, the northern woodpeckers, and a batch of boreal forest birds that show up only sporadically: the redpolls and pine and evening grosbeaks.

We saw lots of regular far-north birds. There were flocks of snow buntings and common redpolls. There were gray jays, called whiskey-jacks, so bold that even the wild birds will take a peanut out of your hand. There were red and white-winged crossbills. These colorful little parrotlike birds use their unique crossed bills to pry seeds from spruce cones. We had seen the red ones on Mount LeConte but had never seen the white-winged ones; we were delighted to be able to stand on the snowy road and watch them work the spruce cones at a distance of 20 feet!

We had mixed results with the owls. Our largest North American owl, the great gray—one that everybody wants to see—didn't make an appearance. (They probably had plenty of mice to eat up in Canada.) And our only snowy owl was a mile out on the ice in Duluth harbor; we could have gotten closer to the one hanging out last month at the Saturn plant in middle Tennessee. But that's the way birding goes.

We really scored on two other owls that trip. One of our prime finds was the fierce, daytime-hunting northern hawk-owl. Described in the books as "fearless and aggressive," they are usually seen perched on the tops of trees and snags. Hawklike as well as owl-like, they prey on both birds and rodents, and seem to enjoy the warmth of the 6-degree Minnesota winter. We saw a total of five of them, including one hawk-owl hunting over an open field.

The other unusual owl we found was the little, far-north-dwelling boreal owl. They are slightly larger than our screech owls and eat mice for a living.

Ours was perched against the trunk of an evergreen tree, casually preening its feathers and looking back at us as if it was wondering what everybody was staring at.

But probably the most memorable sights from the trip were the two scarce, seldom-seen species of northern woodpeckers. While most woodpeckers have four toes on each foot, two pointing forward and two pointing back, these two have only three toes and so are together called "the three-toed woodpeckers." They both live in the great northern forests and spend their days gleaning grubs from under the bark of dying spruce trees.

The first one, called the American three-toed woodpecker, we had never seen. In fact, it was the only remaining North American woodpecker species (there are 22) that we hadn't seen. So, you can imagine our delight in standing under a spruce tree in the SaxZim Bog and watching an American three-toed woodpecker, apparently unfazed by the below-zero weather, calmly foraging for grubs just over our heads. And 2 days later, we stood in the snow in an area with several dead spruce trees and watched, at eye level and 10 feet away, the other three-toed species, called the black-backed woodpecker. It was flaking off the bark from one of the dead trees and eating grub after grub. It was a picture not to be forgotten, one of many we brought back from the frozen wilds of the Minnesota winter.

MR. BENTLEY AND THE SNOWFLAKES

Citizens, take heart! February 3rd marks the midpoint of winter: 45 days gone, 45 days to go! We've all been enjoying the Alberta clippers, usually with 2 or 3 days of continuous below-freezing temperatures, some in single digits, and with some snowflakes thrown in. Nevertheless, things here are not as bad as they could be. Folks in Minnesota and Wisconsin have been experiencing blizzards and double-digit below-zero temperatures, and some communities up there have already used up their whole winter's supply of road salt.

And it's certainly not as bad here as it has been in times past. Knoxville experienced its coldest day on record on January 21, 1985. We hit 24 degrees below zero, colder than Anchorage, Alaska, that day. How cold was it? It was so cold that morning that, when I went out to belatedly check the antifreeze in my old truck with a little squeeze-bulb thing with floating balls in it, by the time I got the hood up and the radiator cap off, the squeeze bulb was so frozen that it shattered into a dozen pieces when I squeezed it.

And snow? Those of us who were here remember the thunder–snow storm we had during the blizzard of 1993—big drifts of snow, all roads down, power out, a storm worthy of Buffalo or Green Bay. But the record in Knoxville for the most snow in 1 day, according to National Oceanic and Atmospheric Administration's national report, was 17.5 inches on Saturday, February 13, 1960. I remember that one, too.

Back then, UT seldom closed down due to weather, under the logic, I suppose, that most students lived on campus and could get to class no matter

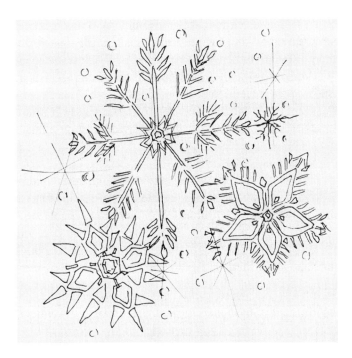

what, leaving us student commuters to deal with the elements as best we could. And, being college students, we of course accepted the challenge. It had snowed at least once a week that February, but that one on the 13th was a zinger. The following Monday, three of my friends and I set out for school in my 1950 Plymouth, snow up to the running boards. The Interstate was not done through Sharp's Gap, and the trip over Sharp's Ridge to the west of the Gap was the stuff of which legends are made. Those were the days!

But even that would have been just another regular snow shower for the folks up in New England. Their snow starts at Thanksgiving. I know this because we have it there every year for Thanksgiving when we visit our daughter and her family. And it melts in April.

Vermont is where Wilson A. Bentley lived, on a farm in the village of Jericho, about 50 miles south of the Canadian border. Bentley was born in 1865, and while he was still a teenager he set about building an apparatus with a microscope and an old-time bellows view camera using glass photographic plates, to take very-up-close photomicrographs of individual snowflakes. Generally, when you're surrounded by a landscape filled with piles, mountains, drifts, fields of snow for several bitter-cold months every year, you don't tend to think a lot about the millions of tiny individual pieces that go into creating all those white expanses.

But Bentley sensed that there was more to snow than just big piles of white stuff. He worked out a system to capture, select, and photograph individual snow crystals, in their fresh, pristine, unmelted state. And he developed a way to have them come out crisp and clear on a black background. He took his first successful photomicrograph of an individual snow crystal on January 15, 1885. The Jericho Historical Society says he was the first person to photograph individual snow crystals.

Bentley's snowflakes opened a whole new world of magical natural beauty to a lot of folks. Through his career he took some 5,000 images. Articles showing his snowflakes were published in *National Geographic* in 1902 and again in 1923, as well as in *Nature*, *Scientific American*, and others. And then after 45 years of work, all the time at the same farmhouse where he was born and lived there in Jericho, he was asked to collaborate with W. J. Humphreys, the chief physicist for the US Weather Bureau, to publish a book of his photos, called *Snow Crystals*. It came out in 1931 and contained 2,400 of his amazing images of those intricate six-sided ice crystals that make up our snowflakes, never any two alike.

Today, Bentley's work is preserved and displayed at the Jericho Historical Society, housed in a typical picturesque Vermont mill in Jericho, beside a typical picturesque Vermont river and adjoining park. There you can read all about "Snowflake" Bentley, as he came to be affectionately called, and see some of the originals of his famous photographs. They even issue yearly, dated, pewter ornaments copied from Bentley's photos, so you can adorn your Christmas tree with a Vermont snowflake.

Intrigued by the work of people like Bentley, scientists around the world have been studying snow for many years. They study such things as how and why the ice crystals form, why they assume the many shapes they do, and why they are always six-sided. They grow them in labs, on rabbit hairs and little needles of ice and delve into their molecular and crystallographic makeup.

But for us mere mortals, the message is that all of that not-always-welcome snow is actually made up of millions of amazingly intricate six-sided crystals. And each one lasts only for moments, and they're gone. It might help one's attitude a little bit to quit grumbling and go out there and let some crystals fall on a dark coat sleeve, and take a peek at them with an eyeball or a hand lens. It will make the snow a lot more tolerable.

Like all of nature, the more you look into things, the more amazing you discover they are. And there are always way more questions than answers; that should serve to keep us always looking.

BUGS IN THE WINTER

We're smack-dab in the dead of winter, bare trees and brown grass all around. We've had a morning or two of temperatures in the teens, a flake or two of snow, and one icy morning. And yet, we don't really even think about what winter can be like up where it *really* gets cold, in the high mountains or up in the Arctic, unless we're studying Eskimo culture or planning a ski trip somewhere.

The Eskimos of Alaska, now properly called the Inuit people, have 15 or so different names for snow, depending on its texture, depth, and other characteristics. Winter is really serious business for those northern folks, and snow is with them for much of the year. They may have complete snow cover for months. It certainly defines how they live. Their ingenious, snug igloos, made of hard-frozen snow, are comfortable because, at around 32 degrees, they are still 40 to 60 degrees warmer inside than it is outside.

Well, you say, at least they don't have to contend with all of our bugs! Surely no self-respecting bug would choose to live in such conditions. Guess again. We visited Churchill, Manitoba, on the shore of Hudson Bay one April, to see the Northern Lights. We rode a dogsled, made an igloo, and on Easter weekend, experienced wind chills of 45 degrees below zero. The cold aggressively seeped into every crack and cranny, as it seemed to be searching us out to lay a hold on us.

And yet, when we were in that same area in late June for bird watching, any time the temperature got above 40 degrees, vast swarms of blood-thirsty mosquitoes appeared out of nowhere to cover us up. Six months of deep freeze didn't seem to have slowed them down at all. And, as we know, millions of birds migrate to the far north every spring, just to take advantage of the hordes of insects that are available to feed their fast-growing nestlings.

So, how do all those bugs make it through those bitter winters that make ours here in East Tennessee look like balmy springtime? There is a lot more to the bugs-and-winter business than you might imagine. James Halfpenny, an author and teacher in the field of cold-climate research, is quite correct when he says that a study of insects in winter provides a "fascinating glimpse into a little-known world." His area of expertise is in alpine and arctic research, but that observation also applies to what goes on in Maine, or West Virginia, or East Tennessee.

Insects have a different set of problems in tolerating winter cold than do either plants or mammals. They are small, and so tend to lose heat easily to their cooler surroundings. They are poorly insulated, being covered as they are with a hard, thin shell-like exoskeleton. Halfpenny remarks that insects are essentially a "liquid-filled box." Within their hard exoskeleton, their organs float in a watery hemolymph—insect blood—seemingly an easy target for being frozen.

Insects have many ways of ensuring that they make it through the winter, or at least that their offspring do. They overwinter in different stages of their life cycle—adult, egg, larva, nymph, pupa. Some adult insects solve the problem by just leaving town; they migrate. Perhaps the most famous migrating insects are monarch butterflies. Others, like the little orange Asian ladybugs and those delightful imported stinkbugs, simply migrate into our houses.

Some adults just stay where they are up north. Honeybees, burning their stores of honey for fuel, can keep the interiors of their colonies at a near-steady 97 degrees even when it's below zero outside. Other colony-dwelling insects, such as wasps, hornets, and bumblebees, solve the problem by having only the already-fertilized queens survive the winter; the rest of the colony dies. The mourning cloak butterfly hides in crevices in tree bark in the North Woods of Maine, flying about any time the temperature gets above freezing. But the really remarkable ones are those that overwinter in the seemingly tender stages of egg or caterpillar.

Dr. Berndt Heinrich, a biologist at the University of Vermont, spends a lot of time in the woods of Maine. He has made some astute and original observations during his time of trekking about in the subzero snow. And he became curious about how the golden-crowned kinglets were able to survive North Woods Maine winters. They are tiny birds, with a high rate of metabolism like hummingbirds. They have a normal body temperature of 110 degrees, and must eat two to three times their weight each and every day to survive. Well, sir, after tromping around in the frigid Maine woods for days on end and being very cold himself, Heinrich discovered their food source—caterpillars!

Heinrich found that a prime food source for the kinglets was a steady supply of frozen caterpillars of a certain species of moth. Frozen, yes; dead, no. And then lots more study revealed that, while many caterpillars in the South may be freeze resistant, these guys were actually freeze *tolerant*. That is, they could freeze solid, then thaw out and carry on life as usual. (They are trying that on people, for a big price, but I wouldn't recommend signing up just yet.) So, it turned out, the kinglets weren't eating a bunch of desiccated, dead, frozen worms. The food was frozen, but alive, and presumably as full of calories and nutrients as fresh meat!

There is one species of caterpillar that lives on barren rock, within 100 miles of the North Pole, frozen most of each year. It thaws just long enough each year to grow and molt. After 13 or 14 years, it finally pupates into an adult, mates, lays eggs, and dies in a few days. Are insects amazing, or what?

Everybody's favorite caterpillar, the woolly bear, can supposedly help us predict what kind of winter we're going to have by the colors they sport as cold weather settles in. Sadly for that legend, they all start out black and get redder with age. It doesn't matter, because I can never remember which color means cold weather and which one means warm anyway.

Nevertheless, they overwinter in the caterpillar stage. Here in the South, they curl up in a crevice or some leaf litter and snooze away until spring. Up north, however, the woolly bears can freeze solid! Anyhow, possibly with those Arctic caterpillars (another woolly species) in mind, Dr. Heinrich took some specimens of the northern brand of the familiar woolly bear caterpillars, froze them in his freezer to –10 degrees, so hard that he could rap on his table with them, thawed them out, and they were fine. And, he could do it over and over. The kinglets' caterpillars weren't just an isolated finding; other species were doing it!

These and other, more sophisticated studies have revealed, in part at least, how they do it. It was found that after cooling for a couple of hours, the caterpillars produced high levels of glycerol in their bodies: antifreeze. Insect eggs contain lots of glycerol, making them freeze resistant, too. Insects' bodies produce other antifreeze-type substances, and they use other fancy chemical tricks as well, like allowing the tissues around their cells to freeze to protect the cells themselves. The more insects are studied, the more unimaginable things they reveal! Lots of molecules are involved, enzymes, that sort of thing. Never underestimate the ability of the insects to adapt to most any adverse situation that Mother Nature hurls at them.

I had a wise old country friend who, every fall, would say, "What we need is a good cold winter to kill off all these bugs!" We probably should not wish for a winter cold enough to kill off all the bugs; it would likely not be a pretty sight for us humans, either.

SOME SWEET THOUGHTS

Roses are red
Violets are blue
Sugar is sweet
And so are you.

Valentine's Day. Time to send those greeting cards that say all those sweet things that we couldn't think of ourselves. Maybe even send flowers or a box of sweets to that special person. Sweethearts, they're often called. So where does all this sweet talk come from? Why is being sweet so special? It comes from one of our main concerns in life: food and eating. In our dim and distant past, diets were drab and dull, and sweet things were rare and special treats that stood out from the ordinary.

A long, cold winter could mean three meals a day of potatoes and turnips. The Irish had a humorous saying, half true, about a supper of "potato and point," which meant they took a potato and pointed it at a piece of salt pork hanging over the table, and ate the potato. Imagine what a spoonful of fruit jelly or a blob of honey would have meant to them!

About the time I was thinking about a column on sweet stuff, a very sweet gesture helped to focus my thoughts about the subject. A very kind neighbor named Irene Hayes brought me a recipe, handwritten in pencil, for molasses cookies. And what was so special about it was that it was written in my Granny Collier's own hand! Granny had given it to Irene's mother, Helen McElroy, I would say over 50 years ago. The lost recipe for the molasses cookies of my childhood! How sweet was that?

It turns out that Irene's late father James McElroy made molasses for my grandmother. Only last year, they sold his sorghum mill to someone who wanted to continue on with making molasses.

But more about that in a minute. Let's get on with the story of sweets. . . . Mankind has craved sweets apparently from the beginning. They discovered, hunted, and gathered sweet stuff from as far back as we know. At first it was high-sugar fruits and berries. In the warm, arid cradle of civilization, the Near East, figs were the sweetest fruit. Figs and fig syrup have been used for sweetening foods in that region for untold centuries.

The first ready-to-eat sweetener was honey; people have robbed bee's nests since time immemorial. In the tropics, many species of bees make their nests out in the open, often high up on cliff faces, protected only by a blanket of bees, many bees thick. There are a number of prehistoric cave paintings in Europe, Asia, Africa, and Australia depicting honey-hunting expeditions. The depictions usually feature the honey hunters climbing up impossibly high, flimsy ladders to do battle with a swarm of stinging bees. Some of the paintings show an unfortunate hunter dropping, head down, to his doom. Those people really wanted that honey!

Domesticated beekeeping was known in India around 4,000 years ago. The Egyptians from about the same time had figured out how to make lightweight beehives and move them around to different farm fields to promote better pollination. It's always amazing to run across one more thing the Egyptians had carefully worked out, 3,000–4,000 years before it was rediscovered in Europe. The Egyptians used honey as a delicacy for sweetening their meals, for various rituals such as embalming, and in their medicines.

Sugar is the most commonly used sweetener, of course. Most of it came from sugar cane until the 1900s. A lot of our sugar now comes from sugar beets, which tolerate cooler and dryer growing conditions, but cane still is grown for sugar all around the world. Sugar cane was first domesticated in New Guinea around 8000 BC and was later carried by traders and travelers to the Philippines, Indonesia, and India. For centuries, people chewed cane stalks and sucked out the juice. Market production of crystallized sugar from the cane didn't come along until the Christian era, around 500 AD . . . still a long time ago. At first, it was a rare and expensive luxury, used by the very wealthy, but by the 1700s it had become a household commodity to have in your tea or your dessert.

Sugar cane was first brought to the New World in 1493, by Christopher Columbus, on his second voyage—he became a regular commuter—and sugar was first exported back to Spain in 1516. Soon the Spanish were making much more profit from sugar than from Inca gold! Not to be outdone, the British, French, and Dutch got into the act. The story of sugar became one of colonialism, sea power, slavery, politics, money, and war. Things have settled down now with mechanization of production and harvesting and ample worldwide supplies. Our biggest concern today is the more than 100 pounds of sugar per person annually consumed in the United States and all the unpleasant health consequences of it: "the Revenge of the Sugar Cane"!

But back to the key ingredient of those wonderful cookies: molasses. Worried about the colonies trading with other sovereign nations, the British Crown passed the Molasses Act in 1733, placing a hefty tax on all non-British imports of sugar and molasses. By then, folks were taking their sweets very seriously, and molasses was the sweetener of choice, right up into the 1800s. The tax really riled people up, about as much as the infamous tax the British imposed on tea. So, molasses helped to fan the flames of revolution. Then, we fought for sweets; now, for oil. It doesn't appear to me that we're making much progress.

You can buy several types of molasses at your local store. There are light, dark, and blackstrap types, for example. These are all byproducts of the making of crystallized sugar from cane or beets. They are all used in various ways in cooking. But the really good stuff doesn't come from sugar cane at all; it's from one of its distant cousins, sorghum. Sorghum is a cereal plant, with a stalk a little like corn, and a head with lots of little seeds like millet. It was especially popular throughout the South in the 1800s and is still especially popular with me.

My early recollections of the sorghum business come from my Granny Collier's farm on Beaver Creek, and I now suspect that James McElroy was a key figure in sorghum production in our area. The family grew a stand of sorghum down in the creek bottom—a few acres, I suppose. When the time was right, they cut the cane and ran it through a mule-powered mill to squeeze out the juice. The mule walked round and round, connected to the mill by a long pole. That turned two big, vertical metal cylinders that squashed the cane stalks.

The juice was collected, put in a big, long, flat pan with baffles in it, and then slowly cooked using a carefully-managed wood fire located beneath the pan. The expert in charge would move the syrup along through the baffles, skimming the impurities off from time to time, and at last, at the end of the pan, out would come molasses! People, mill, mule, fire, smoke, and steam . . . great and memorable sights and smells! Imagine how an 8- or 10-year-old boy could stand there spellbound. Especially after a taste or two of the final product.

You can still see all this for yourself (and for the kids). Molasses is still made at the Cable Mill visitor's center in Cades Cove in the fall. You can also see molasses making in Townsend, with a little bit shorter drive from Knoxville. They usually have some of the delicious condiment to sell, and sorghum molasses produced elsewhere around our region can be found in stores.

Molasses makes delicious barbeque sauce, and is scrumptious on a hot biscuit, preferably heavily buttered. But I'm really waiting anxiously for the rebirth of my Granny's molasses cookies! Many thanks for the recipe, Mrs. Hayes!

PENCIL TREES

Cedars are high on my list of favorite trees. Maybe it's because they've been such a nice dry refuge in the times when I've been caught out in a sudden shower. You catch your breath, look around, and everything's getting wet, but there under your cedar tree, it's all still nice and dry. Early on, my family's Christmas trees were always cedars, selected and cut after a great deal of discussion, at my Granny Collier's place, and brought home to fill the living room with that wonderful, memorable cedar smell.

Now, the fact that our local birds—cardinals, chickadees, titmice, sparrows—can manage to survive the rigors of wintertime seems nothing short of miraculous to me. So, when my latest issue of *National Wildlife* magazine showed up with an article entitled "Helping Birds Cope with the Cold," I was on it. And to my surprise, the article discussed how cedar trees are an ideal wintertime environment for birds. The author quotes a Clemson biology professor saying that cedars are among the top 10 plants for wildlife!

Those familiar, widespread evergreens that we call cedars are properly called Eastern red cedars. They aren't really cedars (like the Cedars of Lebanon) but are actually in the juniper family; their scientific name is *Juniperus virginiana*. And just so that you know, the Eastern red cedar was adopted as the official Tennessee state evergreen tree by our state legislature in 2012, so I would presume that somebody besides just me thinks they're praiseworthy.

Cedars are widespread, not just in Tennessee but all across the eastern half of the country, from the Atlantic coast to the Great Plains, and they are native to 37 states. In our area they can grow to 100 feet tall and live to be 300 years old. They can grow in most any type of soil other than in a veritable swamp and can thrive in any environment except for shade. They are early and abundant invaders of abandoned fields and pastures, a fact known to many a farmer trying to keep his pastures clear of unwanted vegetation.

As for their value to our birds and other wildlife, they provide both shelter and food. Their very dense foliage makes a natural haven for nesting, used by many species of birds in the spring, as well as for concealment and nightly roosting. They are favorites for owls to hide in by day; hawks, by night. And they provide many an East Tennessee cow or horse with winter shelter good enough for them to be referred to as "outdoor barns."

Cedars are dioecious, which means there are separate male cedar trees and female cedar trees. Only the female trees produce fruit, small blue berries borne abundantly every 2 or 3 years. They are a favorite food for their namesake bird, the cedar waxwing, as well as for bluebirds, turkeys, grouse, and numerous other species, "helping pull wildlife through tough times," as the Clemson professor puts it. There is even a specific butterfly seen in warmer weather called the juniper hairstreak that depends exclusively upon cedars for egg laying and caterpillar feeding; I've observed them in my cedar-filled back field.

One down side to Eastern red cedars is that they harbor a fungus that spreads to nearby orchards, infecting apple trees with an economically serious disease called cedar apple rust. After the apple trees are infected, the spores of the fungus spread back to the cedar trees, to start the cycle over again. This phenomenon led to a major conflict in the early 1900s in the apple-growing region of the Shenandoah Valley of Virginia. With the slogan "cedars or cider," the apple people got a state law passed that permitted orchard owners, with the consent of any 10 neighbors, to cut down the cedars in the vicinity of an apple orchard, even against the will of the cedar trees' owner. It reminds me of the range wars out west between the cattle people and the sheep people. I doubt that such a law would have worked out well here in East Tennessee.

The aromatic wood of the red cedar has been known for its striking color and good wood-working qualities since the first Europeans landed on the coast of Virginia. Cedar was used to make countless fenceposts, buildings, linings for clothes closets, and pieces of furniture. But our Tennessee cedars reached national prominence because of quite another use discovered for them. The 2012 Senate bill that made the cedars our state evergreen tree states that "one of the earliest forest industries in the state of Tennessee was the cedar pencil industry." Check the tree books and you'll find that an alternate name for the red cedar is "pencil tree"!

Lead pencils have always been important in our everyday lives; even today, more pencils are sold around the world than ballpoint pens. And when the British quit importing pencils to the young United States during the War of 1812, Yankee ingenuity kicked in, machines were invented, and by 1861 the first US pencil factory was open in New York City.

Lead pencils required wood that was lightweight and dense, yet soft enough to be easily sharpened but not splinter, affordable, and easy to mill. It turned out that the knot-free heartwood of Eastern red cedars filled the bill. It became the pencil wood of choice, and the big cedars of Tennessee and Kentucky were the best. So much so that by 1912, over 1 billion pencils per year were being made from cedar wood from the two states, and by 1920 Tennessee red cedars were nearly wiped out. Timber cruisers were haggling for cedar windbreaks and old cedar buildings, even offering to swap farmers new woven wire fencing for their old cedar fencerows.

Annual pencil production in the United States exceeds 2.5 billion units. Fortunately for our cedar trees, manufacturers have found satisfactory alternatives to old-growth cedar. They now use a number of western species of juniper and even plainer woods like basswood, dying it and giving it a scent similar to the classic cedar perfume.

There is still a healthy cedar timber industry here in Tennessee, but fortunately the supply exceeds the demand. Our cedars are hanging in there, abundant and green in the winter and useful in lots of ways year round. And I'm glad they thrive here. Each for our own personal reasons, the cedar waxwings and I really enjoy having them around.

HIBERNATION

The birds have flown away south, and the trees have dropped their leaves. Most of the butterflies and the other insects are spending the winter as eggs or larvae, the adults dead and gone. Here in our Northern Temperate Zone, all the outdoor living things have to cope somehow with the transition from the warm abundance of summer to the cold, Spartan existence of winter. And, they have developed some remarkable adaptations for doing it.

This is not to say that everybody just closes up shop. One sunny, crisp January day, Spouse and I hiked a portion of the Cataloochie Divide Trail, running at or near the 5000-feet elevation line in the southeast corner of the Great Smoky Mountain National Park. It had snowed the night before, and we were amazed to see the stories of the previous night's activities, written in hundreds of tiny footprints in the snow, apparently left by a whole lot of little mouse types, any number of the dozen-and-a-half species known to live in the Park. The tracks went here, there, everywhere, often heading into the open end of a hollow log or a small hole dug into the trailside earth.

Also of note were a set of big bear tracks, documenting where the grumpy beast, apparently having some sort of insomnia problem, had trudged up one side of the ridge, over the rail fence on the Park boundary, and away down the other side.

So, lots of activity out there in the winter, furry beasts out looking for food, eating, and some, undoubtedly, being eaten. You could think of all those mice as potential fast food; the owls, foxes, bobcats, and weasels as the drive-in customers.

Out there in the critter world, many of the obsessive types spend their summer and fall laying up stores of food in their dens and nests, to snack on at times when they awaken during the winter. Others approach the situation by shopping around outside, gathering and then hiding or burying morsels of sustenance to be recovered later in the season, using their amazing memories, as weather and hunger dictate. Nevertheless, as we mentioned earlier in the discussion about Seasonal Affective Disorder, some creatures just go with the flow, fatten up in the late summer and fall, and then sleep through the winter.

Frogs, snakes, salamanders, even some butterflies hibernate also, but when we talk hibernation, most of us generally picture the likes of black bears, bats, chipmunks, and groundhogs. Those animals have all developed a system that involves becoming immobile for long periods of time, then conserving precious energy by significantly lowering their heart rate, their breathing rate, and their body temperature.

Some of these animals, such as the bats and chipmunks, go into true hibernation, involving a long, deep state of sleep and slowing of all bodily functions. In the bats, for example, the heart rate slows from their usual incredible 300–400 beats per minute to around 10 beats per minute. They may take only one breath per hour. And their body temperature drops to close to their ambient temperature, which in a big cave could be in the '40s or '50s.

Those bats are living on the edge. Even a moderate amount of disturbance during hibernation can cause them to burn enough energy stores so that they run out too early, before the air-borne insects, their only food source, are out and about. The white-nose syndrome is a prime example of how closely-tuned all this system is; an irritating and not necessarily fatal fungus causes death by starvation.

Groundhogs? What can I say? Mr. Whistle Pig always looks prepared for hibernation to me, waddling around my yard and garden. He definitely keeps all his saved-up calories on board, rather than cluttering up his cavernous den under my shop with dried goods. What a life, what an animal.

Our black bears are a special case. They do not enter a true state of hibernation; they go into a state called torpor. This is also a deep sleep, with slowing of pulse and respirations, immobility for long periods, and cessation of bladder and bowel functions. But unlike the deep sleep described for the bats, bears can wake up more quickly and easily.

Dr. Michael Pelton, professor emeritus of wildlife science at the University of Tennessee, having led fifty years of continuous study of the black bears in the Smokies and our local yet world-recognized expert on things bear, relates that this state of affairs is of considerable concern to those intrepid biologists (and especially to their poor graduate students) who climb into dens and hollow trees to check on the status of our wintering bears. They follow their vital signs, how many cubs have arrived (cubs are born during hibernation), and various other health matters. I would really not want to wake Momma Bear up, taking her temperature or pulse rate.

This way of coping with winter allows the bears to respond more quickly in the event of some danger, or to be out and about when conditions are good for foraging. It also explains why we saw those bear prints in the January snow, and how we came to observe the momma bear and her three cubs frisking out and about on the winter day in Cades Cove (Winter Birding).

Dr. Pelton tells us that bears don't always find a nice big hollow tree to winter in. With a population of about two bears to every square mile in the Park, bear real estate is somewhat limited. Many have to settle for curling up under an overhanging rock shelter or big fallen tree, maybe less than ideal conditions in bad weather. They seem to do fine, though, with lots of bear fat for insulation and a thick layer of winter fur for warmth.

In contrast to the bears and the little mice, you aren't going to see bats, chipmunks, or whistle pigs out frolicking in the snow. They *really* hibernate. Once into it, they stay put until things become reasonable again in the spring, and food begins to reappear outside their dens.

When you really look into it, or especially go out into it, winter has a lot of goings-on that can rival a spring or summer day. We've found that it's even that way in frozen Minnesota. But then, they have all those snowmobiles to get you there.

WHAT'S IN A NAME?

It was half past nine o'clock on a wet, chilly winter Saturday morning. A group of interested observers was standing around in the parking lot by the McWherter Technology Building at Pellissippi State Community College in the Hardin Valley section of Knoxville. We were there to see the maiden voyage of Dr. Paul Baxter's Techno-Van, a rolling Geographic Information Systems (GIS) laboratory he had developed as a teaching and research tool. He hopes to use it at our local high schools to entice promising young computer wizards to become students of the GIS trade, hopefully turning their video gaming skills into useful, paying careers.

I was there representing the Beaver Creek Watershed Association, to suggest ways the Techno-Van's capabilities could help us in our task of inventorying our openspace resources in the Beaver Creek Valley. Our goal is to identify and prioritize some of these areas while they still exist, for preservation or rehabilitation, and maybe get Beaver Creek off the federal 303(d) list of impaired streams.

At any rate, as is often the case with birdwatchers, I found myself with one eye and ear on the project, and the other eye and ear tempted away by interesting sounds and sights in the trees. The trees in this case were a monoculture forest of Bradford pears, bare of leaves now with official winter fast approaching. The sound? A cat's persistent meew, meew, meew. But it was coming from a pair of birds busily flitting from tree to tree, clinging to the tree trunks and checking each one with careful scrutiny. So, what looks like a woodpecker and meows like a kitten?

Why, a yellow-bellied sapsucker, that's what! The bird with one of the neatest names in all of birddom. Ranks right up there with the bristle-thighed curlew and the double-striped thick-knee. (Those are honestly both real birds.) We name ball teams Blue Jays and Cardinals and Ravens and so on, but imagine a team named the Yellow-bellied Sapsuckers! They would have to be really big guys to have jerseys large enough to put their name on. And, of course, they'd have to be able to stand up for themselves when somebody heard the name of the team.

In addition to a really fine name, the yellow-bellied sapsuckers have a number of other unique woodpecker traits. For one, though rather common here at this time of the year, they live in our area only in the winter. They generally show up around here about the third week of September, stay until about the third week of April, and then head back to the Great Northern Forest of the northern United States and Canada to mate and raise a single brood of young. A possible exception—they are suspected of rarely nesting in the high elevations of the Smokies.

Another interesting trait is their characteristic drumming. All woodpeckers use drumming instead of singing to establish their territories and attract mates. Mostly, this consists of a loud Brrrrrrrrrrrrt! tapped out on a nice resonant hollow limb (or on your gutter downspout) and is clearly a form of communication and not the methodical pecking involved with seeking food. But not the yellow-bellied sapsucker. He produces the beat of a different drummer!

His drumming starts out fast, then at the end slows down progressively, becomes individual pairs, then single beats, and then stops, as if he has run out of energy. So, the yellow-bellied sapsucker is the one woodpecker that you could confidently identify just by hearing its drumming.

And another difference from your run-of-the-mill woodpecker is the way the yellowbellied sapsuckers harvest their food. Rather than lifting up layers of bark in search for insects, or chiseling out chunks of wood to get at boring grubs, sapsuckers drill the neat horizontal rows of holes that we see in the trunks of trees. These create little wells of sap, a sugar-charged high-energy food. The sapsucker then makes daily rounds of their sap trees, using their specialized, brush-tipped tongue to lap up the juice. When the temperatures are warm enough, lots of insects are attracted to the sap wells, and the sapsucker eats them, too, for a little extra protein.

And those rows of holes producing that sugar-rich sap? In early spring up north, when the hummingbirds show up a bit early or encounter a cold snap . . . sapsucker holes to the rescue! Hummers have been documented using those little sources of sugar as lifesaving emergency sources of food.

Folks do get concerned when they find one of their favorite yard or orchard trees with rows of holes across its trunk. But unless the tree is already sick or stressed from other causes, say the experts, the sapsucker holes are unlikely to cause the tree any serious harm.

Yellow-bellied sapsuckers are medium-sized woodpeckers, between the downies and the redbellieds in size. They have a neat black-and-white striped pattern over their face and a noticeable white wing patch high up in the shoulder area. Their belly is indeed a pale mottled yellow color. They have a red forehead, and the males have a red throat.

So, when you're out and about in the park or the woods this time of year, keep your eyes and ears open for the yellow-bellied sapsuckers, a winter woodpecker with an interesting catlike call, interesting habits, and a really great name!

UNDEFEATED!

Undefeated—that is the title of a book I recently bought in a small museum at Boston Harbor. It was written by a distinguished US Naval officer and historian, Commander Tyrone G. Martin, and unfolds the amazing history of our most famous warship. The *USS Constitution*, nicknamed *Old Ironsides* after a British cannonball was seen to bounce off its side into the sea early in the War of 1812, is still moored at the ship's berth in Boston, fully maintained, fully rigged, seaworthy, over 200 years after the end of its remarkable career.

Spouse and I were in Boston at Thanksgiving to gather up our second oldest grandson from college and see the sights. One sight I really wanted to see, besides all the beautifully preserved historic buildings and Boston's wonderful Museum of Science, was *Old Ironsides*. The great ship is kept in the harbor where it was built in three years, from 1794 to 1797, launched in October 1797, and put to sea in July 1798. *Old Ironside's* glorious fighting days long over, it's still a fully commissioned ship of the US Navy, under the constant watchful care of an attentive crew of active-duty US Naval personnel.

I have always been fascinated by the *USS Constitution*, not only because of its amazing career on the high seas, but by how it was built. Back then, there were no big machines or any power tools, and ships were built essentially of wood, tons and tons of it, and pieced together by hand and ingenuity. Being a tree and wood person, I find it remarkable that all that wood—of several important varieties and from many different parts of this new country and elsewhere—got assembled into the best fighting ship on the seas.

A bit of historical background is necessary here to explain why the *USS Constitution*, its two sister ships, and three smaller warships, were needed and came to be built. After we won our War for Independence from the British in 1781 (more officially with the Treaty of Paris in 1783), the United States of America, tired of war, penniless, and just trying to figure out what they really were, apparently breathed a sigh of relief and did away with their navy. The last units of the Continental Navy were sold off in August 1785.

Within a week of the disbanding of the Continental Navy, writes Commander Martin, the notorious Barbary pirates of North Africa seized two American ships and held their crews for ransom. Previously under the protection of the powerful Royal Navy, the now-vulnerable, unarmed American merchant vessels could be picked off by the pirates at will.

And so it continued. The last 3 months of 1793 saw 11 American merchant ships taken by the pirates and over 100 crewmen held for ransom, a situation that finally roused the US Congress to create a new navy. A select committee was appointed, which recommended construction of four 44-gun warships and two smaller 20-gun ships. But then, as now, politics dominated the scene.

Arguments went back and forth, with some politicians even suggesting that a strong navy could lead to the overthrow of our fledgling government. There was a lot of parsimonious wrangling and name calling. But at last, reason prevailed, and appropriations were agreed upon. Designs for the big warships were drawn up, engineering ahead of anything then on the seas. Preparations were begun to build one of the three big ships at a shipyard in Boston Harbor, and work began in 1794.

Now, it takes a lot of material to build a big warship. Fifty-four cast iron cannons, 32 of them weighing in at 5,600 pounds each, were forged in foundries in Maryland, New Jersey, and Rhode Island. The ship's three anchors weighed over 5,000 pounds apiece. Paul Revere's foundries supplied 4,200 feet of one-and-one-eighth to one-and-a-half inch copper bolts to hold the parts together. Over 4,000 sheets of copper, ironically from British mills, were tacked over the bottom with 40 copper tacks per sheet. And finally, the acres and acres of sail were made from more than 10,000 yards of 20-inch-wide flaxen canvas.

And what about all that wood? More than 1,500 huge oak trees, weighing over 1,200 tons in all, were harvested from at least six states. Shipbuilders used white oak planking from New Jersey and live oak from the islands and swamps of Georgia for the massive structural pieces. Towering white pines for masts, cut in Maine, were floated to Boston by sea. There were cedar logs for interior frames and planks and yellow heart pine for flooring. Over 50,000 "tree-nails" of black locust, 18–30 inches long, were used to nail the frame together; these came from England, almost all produced in the small village of Owlesbury.

The structural strength of the great ship came from the oak. Oak is very strong and very heavy, and the framing pieces for the ship were massive. A cube of white oak only 12 inches on a side weighs 42 pounds! The largest piece for the keel was 80 feet long and was 18 x 24 inches across. That adds up to 4½ tons, and it had to be accurately shaped by hand and laid in place with no power equipment. The huge oak ribs, in some places 12 x 21 inches across, were laid less than 2 inches apart. Covered with oak planking, some of it 40 feet long and 7 inches thick, Old Ironsides' wooden sides were an incredible 21 inches thick!

The *USS Constitution* put to sea in July 1798 and had already distinguished itself against the varying enemies of the time, whether British, French, or the Barbary pirates, when the United States again declared war on the British on June 18, 1812. At that time, America had the second-largest fleet of merchant vessels in the world, but the smallest navy of any major power. Our entire navy totaled 17 ships; the British Royal Navy, about 900.

During the War of 1812, with unsurpassed design, construction, and seamanship, the *USS Constitution* pulled off three narrow escapes from vastly superior British naval forces and decisively won three major engagements, the last against two Royal Navy warships at the same time.

Commander Martin concludes that in helping to win the Second War for Independence, the *USS Constitution* and its sister ships uplifted American morale at the time spectacularly, ended the myth that the Royal Navy was invincible, and proved that American ingenuity and engineering were equals to any other nation in the world. Isn't it wonderful what a bit of genius, a few oak trees, and a lot of hard work and sacrifice can accomplish?

A MOST IMPORTANT BIRD

Years ago, when you went to Granny Collier's house for Sunday dinner, you didn't find a skillet full of chicken breasts or chicken thighs. You found a whole chicken, cut up into the usual pieces, of course, but only the pieces that came with that one chicken. And you saw pieces that you may not see that often anymore. I remember my Mom and Dad sharing carefully divided halves of the heart, liver, and gizzard, while my brother and I would pretend to cover our eyes and not even look at those delicacies.

Then there was a certain pecking order, so to speak, that determined just who got which part; it was definitely not a random event. The visiting preacher or other company always got first choice, which was usually a big piece of the white meat. And if not them, then Grandpa or big brother. Those unfortunates lower down on the totem pole had to wait on the better stuff until somehow, they worked their way up; or else they had to wait for the next church potluck for an opportunity to grab a choice piece (or two) from the bountiful table.

That's all changed now. We go to the store and buy only the pieces we want, almost never a whole chicken. One of the wonders of the chicken, in contrast to other farm animals, is how quickly they mature and how rapidly varieties can be bred for any number of desirable characteristics—for meat, for eggs, for suitability to thrive in different climates, and so on. Meat chickens, for example, can be ready for market in only 6 or 7 weeks and can be bred to make more white meat or dark to suit the trends of the market.

A 2014 article in the journal *Science* concerning the search for the ancestral wild chicken quotes a biologist from Georgia Southern University as saying that the chicken is "the most important bird in the world." They've been domesticated for thousands of years and are a major food source for literally billions of people all around the globe.

In the United States we're producing something like 90 billion eggs per year, and some 40 billion pounds of chicken meat per year. Now that's a lot of chicken! We export around 7 billion pounds, or about 18% of the total. And as for that whole chicken versus many parts thing, almost all chickens are sold as parts these days, rather than as whole birds. People are eating everything from buffalo wings to chicken-foot soup, from breasts to thighs to nuggets.

An October issue of *National Geographic* magazine had an informative two-page spread about the destination of all our chicken parts. It turns out that we Americans prefer blander food than other folks, and so we export very few breast quarters. But we sell hundreds of thousands to millions of tons of the other parts overseas—wings and feet (yes, feet) to China, legs to Russia, feathers to Indonesia, and innards (for pet food and fertilizer) to South Africa. Good eats here at home, making some money trading abroad.

Did you ever wonder where chickens originally came from? They weren't always just here, scratching around in the side yard. It's a complex story that the scientists haven't fully nailed down as of yet, but the general story is that our domestic chickens were derived from an original wild species called the "red jungle fowl," from Southeast Asia. They range from 5,000 feet in the Himalayas down through Malaysia into Indonesia and are believed to have been domesticated somewhere between 4,000 and 8,000 years ago.

Red jungle fowl look and act a lot like present-day fighting chickens. They are smallish, fast, wily, and aggressive. They have reddish bodies, golden-red neck feathers, and shiny black tail feathers. There are few pure-blooded red jungle fowl left in the world, due mainly to all that domestication and interbreeding by many civilizations over the centuries, and that has the biologists worried that the original species will soon be lost forever.

Some attempts were made back in the 1960s to collect Asian red jungle fowl and propagate them in the United States, and as a result, there are some purebred birds scattered around in aviaries and labs in this country. And there are still some hiding out there in various places in the wild. In Vietnam, for example, it is illegal to trap them, but the practice continues because they bring premium prices as fighting chickens.

In the unlikely event that you're suddenly seized with the desire to actually see a wild, free-range red jungle fowl not too far from here, let me tell you about Fitzgerald, Georgia. It seems that in the 1960s, the Georgia Department of Natural Resources released some 10,000 jungle fowl all over the state of Georgia, to be used as game birds, hunted like quail or pheasants. The project failed spectacularly, but there was one batch of birds released down along the Ocmulgee River that faced their situation with more determination. They didn't care for their riverside site, so they moved along west for a few miles to the inviting town of Fitzgerald, a peaceful place founded in 1895. There they took up residence, with the eventual acceptance and support of most of the humans dwelling there. And today, there are several hundred of them, scratching in gardens, eating grasshoppers in churchyards, and ambling across streets.

They used to have an annual rattlesnake roundup in Fitzgerald, but the jungle fowl got to be such a phenomenon the town now has an annual Fitzgerald Wild Chicken Festival every March. Its motto: "We're strutting our stuff." There is the big Friday night street dance, followed the next day by the 5K run, the pinewood derby race, and the ever-popular chicken-crowing contest. The festival is scheduled for the latter part of March, and Fitzgerald is a quick run down Interstate 75, a couple of hours south of Atlanta. You may want to make your reservations early. Or, you could just stay around home and go out to your favorite place for some wings or nuggets.

Fighting chickens, tourism, major food source.... Chickens are important birds, to all of us.

THE POSSUMWOOD TREE

In my travels over the holidays this year, I learned another way to predict what sort of weather the upcoming winter holds for us. The method was disclosed to me by a wise old outdoorsman in north Alabama. That's a part of the world where, like in the hills of East Tennessee, people still seem to be in touch with their natural surroundings.

Anyhow, the prognostication involves knives, forks, and spoons, and the common persimmon tree, *Diospyros virginiana*. More details in a moment; first, a bit more about the persimmon tree.

The persimmon or possumwood tree, as it is known in some places, grows only in the southeastern quadrant of the United States; a similar version grows in Texas. Almost everyone is familiar with the pulpy, orange-to-purple persimmons that fiercely pucker up your mouth if you chomp into them before they're ripe.

What you may not know is that persimmon trees are very close relatives of the ebony trees of Africa and Southeast Asia. Those trees are noted for their very hard, dense, black wood. Because the best wood comes from small trees, and because the wood tends to split while drying, ebony is generally available only in smaller pieces rather than big boards. It is highly prized for carving, and for inlay and accent pieces in wood-turning and cabinet-making. Ebony is listed in the book of Ezekiel as being on par with ivory as a valuable item of trade, and as you might imagine, is still quite expensive today.

Ebony's East Tennessee cousin, our common persimmon, also has very dense, closegrained wood. It ranks right up there with dogwood (used for World War I airplane propellers) and ironwood as the hardest of our native woods. Rather than black, its wood occurs in varying shades of light gray, with some interesting grain patterns.

Because of its hardness, density, and weight, persimmon heartwood was once used exclusively for making golf club heads. Perhaps a senior golfer out there may remember them, or even still have one. And before plastic and such, the sapwood, somewhat lighter in color, was used to manufacture shuttles for the weaving industry. A good persimmon shuttle could be expected to last more than a thousand hours before needing replacement.

But the persimmon is probably best known for its unique fruits, the persimmons themselves. The Latin genus name for the possumwood is *Diospyros*, which means "fruit of the gods." There could be some debate as to whether persimmons deserve that designation, but they are definitely edible by man and beast. Some folks find them delicious, and possums certainly do!

Persimmons are very astringent, or sour, in the mouth before they are fully ripe, but once a good frost has softened and mellowed them up, they are reasonably palatable. They have helped more than one poor mountain family endure through the winter, as a tasty and sweet addition to an otherwise terribly monotonous diet of 'taters and cornbread. A good possum, fat from eating persimmons, may have looked pretty good, too.

Persimmons can be made into pies, cakes, and jam. They take some work to prepare, though, because of the tough skin and a number of big seeds in each one. And it is those seeds that set me off on this story. It turns out that there are a bunch of people, not including me, who already knew the secret of how to predict the weather from persimmons. And it goes like this:

If one splits a persimmon seed in half lengthwise, you come upon a small white pattern in the center of the seed, actually formed by the seed's embryo of the next tree. And in the shape of the white pattern lies the key. If the white pattern is shaped like a spoon, you're going to be shoveling snow. If it's shaped like a knife, you're going to have a bitter cold winter, with winds that cut you like a knife. But if it's shaped like a fork, the winter will be mild, and I suppose we all sit around and eat.

One inquisitive person has studied this phenomenon and found that, in his area of Arkansas, the persimmon seeds yielded spoons in about 60% of cases, a knife in around one-third, and a fork in only about 7% of seeds. So, if you really need a prediction of a mild winter, you may have to fall back on the always-reliable height of the hornet's nests above the ground, or the number of foggy mornings in September, or the relative amounts of brown and black on the woolly bear caterpillars.

And, if the winter turns out a lot harsher than expected, don't risk your life shoveling snow; hole up and eat biscuits and persimmon jam. It works for the possums.

AFTER THE STORM

This story was published two and a half years after Hurricane Katrina. Our church disaster relief group ultimately made 17 week-long work trips to the coast, with many more adventures and many more stories. I have left this article as it was originally written as of January 2nd, 2007.

Pearlington is a small, unincorporated town in southern Mississippi. Way south. Its southern end fades into salt marshes and bayous, and from them, on into the Gulf of Mexico. To its west is its namesake, the Pearl River, boundary line between Mississippi and Louisiana. New Orleans is another 50 miles to the west, a world away.

We first heard about Pearlington through a rather remarkable series of events. In November 2005, things were really bad in coastal Mississippi. Hurricane Katrina, which the locals now refer to as "the Storm," had been through 6 weeks earlier, on August 29th. New Orleans got most of the publicity, but Mississippi got the storm surge. Most of the homes along the Mississippi coast south of Interstate 10 had water up to their ceilings. A lot of them washed completely away.

A group of us from Fountain City Presbyterian Church went down to join the throngs of people from everywhere in the United States to do what we could to help out. We stayed at the First Presbyterian Church in Bay St. Louis, Mississippi. Their building had somehow been spared from the water, but most of their people had left. There were few usable homes, no grocery stores or restaurants, no gas stations—not much of anything that had to do with the needs of daily living. The church had only an elderly pastor and his wife and eight members.

Brother Benny is a freelance fundamentalist and independent Baptist preacher from North Carolina. His past, he told us, included drugs, alcohol, and prison. His home church had a special ministry going for victims of drugs and alcohol. They met in his church basement where they could smoke, worship, and feel comfortable. Attendance was huge. Brother Benny was a facilitator in all that, a big job. But he felt called to Mississippi, and arrived soon after the Storm, "to see what he could do." He set up a soup kitchen in the parking lot of an abandoned supermarket. He sought out donations, he found supplies, and before long, he was feeding hundreds of people a day. This made us think of the biblical story of the loaves and fishes.

At any rate, while the hungry waited in line, Brother Benny fed their souls with his Gospel message and came up with some 45 new believers. After some searching, he found them a church home at First Presbyterian Church, Bay St. Louis. When we got there, we worshipped in a church with a congregation made up of 8 old Presbyterians, 45 newly converted Baptists, and a bunch of transient emergency relief volunteers in T-shirts and shorts. We had Communion that Sunday. It worked just fine.

Our group needed work. We were there, eager and ready, but the bureaucracy was grinding very slowly on assigning work details. Brother Benny, who seemed to know everything about everybody, came to the rescue. He suggested a family he knew who could really use some help in getting back on their feet. They lived 15 miles away in a place called Pearlington. And that was the beginning of an amazing journey for us all.

Jimmy and Robin had bought a run-down house in the pine woods of Pearlington. It sat at the end of a bayou, and they could get in their outboard boat and wind all the way down to the Gulf. They had worked really hard, getting it all fixed up. They finished just before the Storm.

We followed Brother Benny out to Pearlington from Bay St. Louis, past miles of mountains of household goods piled along the roadsides, past overturned cars and boats in trees. At one spot in Jimmy's neighborhood, the road went between the two halves of a house. We drove through, looking into someone's ruined living room.

Jimmy was in Bay St. Louis for the Storm. As director for food services for the local county hospital, he was a member of the ride-out crew, the ones who rode out Katrina there in the hospital. He later told us about being on the second floor that morning and watching all of Bay St. Louis disappear under the water, just the tips of the big live oaks sticking up to show where the town was drowning.

Six weeks later, Jimmy's wife Robin and the children were scattered but safe. Jimmy was just hoping the hospital would reopen and he would have his job, and all his people would have theirs. He hoped his house, now only four walls and a bunch of bare two-by-fours, could somehow be saved. Like everybody else south of Interstate 10, he didn't know where to begin.

So, *we* began. Our crew of amateur carpenters and drywall hangers and finishers worked at Jimmy's house for four and a half days. We got most of the drywall done. The last day Jimmy drove up from work at lunchtime with fried catfish, gumbo, French fries, and bread pudding. We sat at a picnic table outside his FEMA-provided trailer in the hot Mississippi November sun and feasted. What a great "thank you"! And he has fed us very well, many times since.

Yes, we've been back, some of us as many as six times. And every time, it's the same. We meet discouraged and bewildered people at the first of the week. At the end, we leave not some "poor unfortunate people we were glad to help", but encouraged, warm, friendly folks that we will care about and be in touch with from now on. They become friends; they are almost family.

And then there are the stories. Every person in coastal Mississippi has their own story of the Storm. We could fill a book. Most of them bring a lump to the throat. There was the 80-year-old couple in Biloxi who had gathered in their house with all their family for their 50th wedding anniversary celebration. The water roared in their front door, and 11 people and a dog spent several very scary hours, watching from the attic crawl space as the water lapped at their ceiling.

There was the retired nurse who found herself in charge of an emergency shelter in an elementary school for 3 days after the Storm. There were no lights, no water, no air conditioning (it was 100 degrees after the Storm—August, remember?). She had 350 people in her shelter, from newborn infants to demented elderly. Didn't lose a one.

And, one of the more touching sights we saw: An elderly man, with only a concrete slab where his home had been, out patiently, maybe aimlessly, hoeing away in his dead garden.

We called Jimmy and Robin on December 31st last year, when we were down in Gulfport on our second trip. There was a lot of joyful noise in the background. They were back in their house, and it was full of family. And they were very excited; they had gotten their front door put up in time for

Christmas! And most remarkable of all, now that they were back on their feet, they had already started helping neighbors. They and others had cleared the debris and muck from 20 nearby homes!

I think that's what draws us back to Pearlington. The folks there aren't whining and waiting for the federal government to fix their problem. They have set up a distribution center for food and goods in the elementary school gym. The classroom building of the school is gone, but the library is now a place for volunteers to stay, and there are showers and a laundry in trailers, and a dining room in a tent. Several citizens are responsible for coordinating relief efforts; they know who in the little town needs what, and they direct the right kind of help their way. New houses are going up; damaged ones are getting repaired. A gas station just reopened in Pearlington, and they were putting up an ATM where the bank had been on the main street when we were there last. But years of work remain to be done.

Jimmy and Robin came up to East Tennessee this past October. They wanted to get away for a few days and to see one of their favorite places, Cades Cove. And we all wanted to see them. They spoke at our church one Sunday morning. They talked about how life goes on, how even if you're trying to rebuild your home from bare two-by-fours there are still kids to get to school, neighbors to help, and birthday parties to be celebrated. They gave everyone some insight into the courage, energy, and dogged determination of the people of Pearlington, Mississippi. It's wonderful to see them coming back from such misery and doing OK.

We'll be going back to Pearlington in January. There's a lot more drywall to hang. Happy New Year, Jimmy and Robin!

EBIRD—AMAZING!

eBird (ebird.org) is indeed amazing. Maybe not so much for those of you in the computer generation, who learned to count at a year old by playing kiddie computer games and who are able to fluently communicate your lives minute by minute on social media.

However, in my world it's a fact that I can still remember my grand-mother's crank-dial, four-party-line telephone from when I was small, and I still tell errant callers on my home phone that they have "dialed" the wrong number. So maybe you can understand why I am in awe of a system that can collect 10 million bird sightings from around the world, over a 4-day period, and have them all neatly stored away, to be accessed and used in every way imaginable. That amazing process would be eBird. Here's some background about how it came to be.

Cornell University, located in Ithaca, New York, in the scenic environs of the Finger Lakes District in upper New York State, has been the epicenter of academic bird study for a very long time. A hometown example of what they've been doing all those years comes from right here in Knoxville. UT professor and Knoxville Bird Club member, the late Dr. James Tanner, was working on his doctoral thesis at Cornell University over the years of 1937 to 1939, studying the ivory-billed woodpeckers in the swamps of Louisiana. That published thesis has become a classic, a detailed study of those now-extinct birds. Jim and his wife Nancy last saw an ivory-billed woodpecker in December 1941. Nancy, also a member of our bird club, lived to be 96 and was apparently the last person on earth to have seen a living ivory-billed woodpecker. We in the bird club were privileged to hear the Tanners tell their stories about working with those gone-forever birds.

These days, the big birding events at Ithaca happen at the Cornell Laboratory of Ornithology, set high on a wooded hill above the town. Spouse and I included it on the itinerary of one of our spring Northeast birding trips and had a really fine visit there. The lab consists of a big main building nestled in the woods, with huge two-story windows looking out over a beautiful tree-lined lake. The lake has an active great blue heron nest, there are birdfeeders everywhere, and birding scopes are set up for watching all the activity.

Off the main lobby, you can access the famous Macaulay Library of bird songs and calls, the largest collection of bird songs in the world. A person can sit in there and listen to most any bird in the world, one by one, to his or her heart's content. And behind the scenes, there are lots of labs and cubicles filled with bright young computer-savvy ornithology-type people doing amazing things with birds, computers, and data.

The Cornell folks call all of us amateurs "citizen scientists," and they happily gather our millions of observations and bird lists into a giant database of information that they can organize, use, and study in ways that no single group of researchers or academic institutions could ever achieve.

That is where eBird began. We first heard of it years ago from Chris Wood, one of the young people at the Cornell lab, who helped dream it up and who was the eBird Project Leader. He has been our guide on several of the birding trips we have enjoyed around the country, and he has patiently tried to help me understand the group's vision of a worldwide depository of bird information, fed by tens of thousands of birders everywhere reporting the species they were seeing throughout each year. Launched in 2002, the vision has come to pass, with remarkable success!

So, what sort of information do they get from all us citizen scientists? They learn where the many species of birds are, in real time, where they spend the winter, where they are to be found while nesting and rearing young, and when and where they are when on the move during migration.

Now with all the data they have collected, the lab has produced animated maps for individual species of migrating birds with subtitle dates, similar to TV weather maps, showing the tsunami-like waves of birds ebbing and flowing to and from North and South America season by season. Those maps give a visual face to the hard-to-imagine concepts of millions of birds passing to and fro over our heads year after year.

The folks at eBird have come up with a lot of other fun and interesting things. Probably the biggest is the system whereby individuals can sign up for membership, and then can at any time send in a list of birds they've seen, on a walk around the yard, a trip to the beach, or wherever. Your sightings go into the huge database, but they are also stored specifically for you, so you can check on your own list of birds and sighting records any time you wish.

Yet another feature, called eBird-alert, lets you subscribe free to receive daily emails from any state you wish, reporting the locations of especially interesting or rare birds, complete with detailed Google maps of their locations, so you can hop in the car and go find them. It even tells you the locations of the nearest good places to eat! And then there's Merlin, a free app for your mobile device that helps you identify the 400 most common birds in the United States, especially helpful for beginning and intermediate birders.

For many years now, we have counted the birds at our feeders at intervals from November to March and sent those counts in—initially on long paper forms at the end of each season, but now via a spiffy data-reporting site that even I can navigate—to Operation Feederwatch, another data-gathering program from Cornell; it is great fun during an otherwise rather sparse bird-watching period of time. And we just finished the Great Backyard Bird Count in February. People from all over the world counted birds anywhere they wanted, over the 4-day timespan, and sent their results in to eBird. Incredibly, they have so far received 157,272 checklists, listing a total of 5,545 species of birds, over half of all known species on Earth, for a total number of individual birds topping 18 million. Not bad for a bunch of amateurs! Err, I mean, citizen scientists.

It appears to me that this computer thing may actually prove to have some useful applications after all, especially if it helps us know more about the birds. You might want to check out the eBird site (http://ebird.org), maybe even sign up for something, and try it out!

ENJOYING A RARE BIRD

One of the real joys of birding is to find and get great looks at the occasional rare, unusual, or hard-to-find bird, and wintertime is often a good time to discover a rare bird or two. In the winter, one of the more dependable families of birds that we can count on being around is the woodpeckers. And of the eight species of woodpeckers that can be found here in the Southeast in winter, one of those fits the above description to a "T."

Motoring out on a roundabout route from Powell to north Alabama for the holidays, Spouse and I did a bird-watching loop through the state of Mississippi the week before Christmas. One of our prime scheduled stops was a day at the 48,000-acre Noxubee National Wildlife Refuge, located about 20 miles south of Starkville. It has ponds and lakes full of wintering waterfowl, mowed agricultural fields with open-country birds, and lots of woods, including old-growth pine forest. It was just what our Bird of the Trip, the endangered red-cockaded woodpecker, ordered.

Red-cockaded woodpeckers are found nowhere in the world other than the southeastern United States. They are widely scattered from Virginia and North Carolina south into Florida, and west into Texas and Arkansas. Sadly, you needn't look for one in Tennessee. They once lived in a few counties in our state, but the last known sighting was of a lonely male that was nesting down in Polk County, in the far southeast corner of Tennessee. Discovered in 1991, he was gone by 1994, and as far as anybody knows, there are no others.

There aren't that many red-cockaded woodpeckers anywhere. From a low of perhaps 4,000 birds when they were placed on the endangered species list in 1970, and with a lot of expert help and attention, they have come back to a total population of about 12,000 today. Through the years, Spouse and I have been fortunate enough to see them at various special areas in North Carolina, South Carolina, and Florida. But we got our best and closest observation of one there in the Noxubee Refuge.

Red-cockaded woodpeckers are busy little guys, intermediate in size between downy and hairy woodpeckers. Instead of the white backs and black faces of those two, the red-cockadeds have black backs with white barring, and big white patches on their faces. The red cockades that give these birds their name are little red marks on the side of their heads, so small that they are seldom visible.

As mentioned, red-cockaded woodpeckers are scarce, and this is because they are very picky about where they live. They make their nest holes only in large, mature pine trees that are at least 60–120 years of age. The problem here is that, of the 60 to 90 million acres of old growth longleaf pine savannah that once covered the Southeast, only about 3 million acres remain. The rest has been cut for timber and cleared for agriculture and housing, or broken up into little patches or small groves of the big trees. So, it turns out, there is less than 1% left of the habitat these birds require.

The nest holes are a curious thing in themselves. The birds select a big old tree that has what is called red heart rot, a fungal disease that softens the heartwood. They take an amazing 1 to 3 years—sometimes more—to excavate any given nest hole. And then they peck the tree all around the hole to make the tree ooze sap, coating the whole trunk in the area of the hole with a whitewash of sticky pine rosin. This apparently protects the nest from their most dreaded predator, those skillful tree climbers the rat snakes.

And the birds require more than just a little patch of the big trees; each of their family groups, with a batch of nest trees called a "cluster," takes around 200 acres of old-growth pine forest to meet their nesting and foraging needs.

And speaking of family groups, in addition to being choosy about their real estate, they also have some peculiar social habits, at least for birds. The family unit consists of a male and female pair, that own the nest and produce the usual three or four eggs, but in addition, there are up to four helper birds, usually young, single male birds from the previous year's batch. They really do help, staying with the family and joining in on incubating the eggs and then feeding the new hatchlings. This makes an active, chattering family group of several birds if you are lucky enough to find them.

Visitors to a place like the Noxubee Refuge will find active red-cockaded nest trees marked with a ring of paint; once you see those, the rosin-coated trunks and nest holes become obvious. There at Noxubee, a few days before Christmas, we walked through an area like that, a parklike place with big, stately pines and almost no undergrowth. Numerous nest trees were marked with rings of white paint. Our ears perked up when we came upon a mixed flock of foraging birds, including red- and white-breasted nuthatches, singing pine warblers, and even a spiffy red-headed woodpecker.

Then we heard it: the chittering call of a red-cockaded woodpecker! And there it was—hooray!—some 12 feet up in one of the big pines, ripping off half-dollar-sized flakes of bark as it searched industriously for hidden insect snacks in the nooks and crannies. We stood and watched the rare bird, and oohed and aahed, for 10 minutes or so. Our day was happily made!

Only two woodpeckers have been on the endangered species list: the ivory-billed and the redcockaded. It was too late for the ivory-billed; its last stronghold, in the old-growth swampland of Louisiana, was converted into hundreds of acres of rice fields. The last sighting was in 1941. With the red-cockaded, perhaps the warning has been sounded in time. There are lots of smart and caring people working to help them survive. Maybe someday we, or our grandchildren, will be able to experience the joy of watching one of those busy little birds making the chips fly once again here in Tennessee.

AN INTRIGUING EVERGREEN, UMMM, CONIFER

For the past several years, Spouse and I have headed up the road to Vermont for Thanksgiving. We have family up there, including a grandson, and we take great pleasure in having a delicious New England Thanksgiving dinner with loved ones and watching the snow gather outside the windows.

Another interesting highlight of these journeys is as follows. Naturalists, who know about such things, like to say that going up through the various life zones in the Smoky Mountains, from the lowest valleys to the highest peaks, is the equivalent of going from here to the natural communities and habitats 1,000 miles to the north. And it so happens, that is the distance from here to our daughter's house. We've found that the things we see up there tend to bear out the naturalists' rule of thumb.

They have spruces, mountain ash, Clinton's lilies, and trilliums, the same or very similar to those in the Smokies, except that they are pretty much at sea level up there. So, we like to look around and see what's up as we progress up the thousand miles of highways and byways to our destination.

This year as we cruised along the interstate east of Binghamton, in upstate New York, we noticed clusters of golden-yellow trees, standing here and there on the hillsides, among the nearly bare oaks and hickories. We were reminded of the aspens that are so spectacular in the fall out west, golden groves against barren rocky bluffs or contrasting with the dark ponderosa pines. Were these Eastern yellow trees poplars, or maybe birch trees, we wondered?

Finally, when we got settled down in Vermont, we had an opportunity to examine a grove of the golden mystery trees up closer. And we discovered that the gold wasn't from a tree full of brightly colored late autumn leaves; it was from trees covered with golden-yellow, autumn-colored *needles*!

This is not the usual goings-on in nature. Everybody knows that trees with needles are evergreens, and being covered with yellow needles usually means they are either dead or well on their way to becoming so. Pines, spruces, firs, and the like, all needle-bearing trees, are called conifers as a group, because they all bear cones. And they are also generally called softwoods, because their wood is softer and lighter than the hardwoods such as the oaks, hickories, and maples. The hardwoods are mostly deciduous trees; they lose their leaves in the winter. The conifers are evergreens.

But there are exceptions. For example, consider the magnolias. While the other four species of magnolias in the Smokies all lose their leaves in the fall, like proper deciduous trees, the Southern magnolias, with their big, dark green waxy leaves, stay green all year. This accounts for their popularity as landscaping trees for yards and parks. And the stately live oaks of the Gulf Coast area stay green all year, sometimes for hundreds of years.

It turns out that there are exceptions the other way, too. There are two native North American conifers—needle-bearing trees—that lose their needles every fall. One is the bald cypress, that great tree of the swamps, that stands in the still, black water on a huge, buttressed base surrounded by "knees," draped in Spanish moss, giving shade to 'gators, cottonmouths, and just maybe, somewhere, an ivory-billed woodpecker.

The other species of deciduous conifer in North America is, sure enough, our Vermont fall-yellow-grove tree. It is the American larch, *Larix laricina*, also known as tamarack.

These are unquestionably northern trees. Although they have been shown to have grown as far south as Louisiana during the last Ice Age, some 18,000 years ago, their presentday range is far north, all across Canada from Labrador to the Yukon, and down into New England as far as the northern borders of Pennsylvania. Who knows how many millions of them there are!

Conifers can tolerate harsher growing conditions than broad-leaved trees because their needles act to conserve water better than leaves, and they can remain active and carry on photosynthesis even in the winter, on mild days. The evergreen ones replace only about 20% of their needles each year, and so save the resources it would take to make all new leaves every spring. That is why the trackless miles of boreal forest, the Great North Woods stretching across Canada, Scandinavia, and Siberia, are home mainly to conifers.

The larches, though, go one step further to increase their chances of survival in their cold, harsh climate. They not only have needles, but they drop them in the winter, when things are really bad where they live and the temperatures hover near or below zero for weeks at a time.

Paleobotanists have an interesting theory about how the larches developed their needledropping habit. They say that they evolved from conifers that used to live high in the Arctic, where the sun completely disappears during the winter. With nothing for needles to do all that dark time, it was more efficient to just drop them.

Even among needle-bearing trees, the larch groves have a unique appearance. Larches are tall, straight trees with horizontal branches. They have fine little needles about three-quarters of an inch long, growing from short, spur-like shoots along the branches, giving them a sparse, airy look. Indeed, larches are believed to shade the ground beneath them less than any other conifer. This allows a dense thicket of undergrowth to thrive beneath the trees, far different from the parklike appearance of a spruce or hemlock forest.

And the larch's needles, though short and fine, do not decay for 3 or more years after they fall, longer than even oak leaves, so they build up into a deep, spongy carpet on the forest floor. Larch forests are home to a large number of species of birds and animals that feed on their cones and inner bark and that nest in their branches or in the dense undergrowth beneath.

Larch wood is among the hardest and densest of the softwood trees, and it resists rot and decay very well. It is used for poles, posts, and railroad ties. There are two other interesting uses for the larch tree. The trunk and roots form an angle that makes that part of the tree just the right shape for knees, a part of the framework for small boats. And the Algonquin Indians used the long, strong, thinner roots of the larch tree to sew together the birch bark for their famous canoes.

So, there you have it. . . . Mother Nature does it again! Just when we thought we had evergreens figured out, here come ones that aren't, well, "evergreen." Think about those cold, bare, deadlooking larch trees this winter. I'd rather be in East Tennessee.

WOOD DUCKS AND WARBLERS

January's Noah's Ark–type floods had not yet come to the Beaver Creek bottomlands when, on the fifth of the month, we put up wood duck boxes in the wetlands along my stretch of the creek. It was a nice mild January morning when I joined a bright young lady who had crafted together some excellent nest boxes as part of a Girl Scout Silver Award project, on a family expedition to find just the right places for the boxes and to put them up.

Lest you think that we were over-eager, out there all bundled up and putting out nest boxes in the dead of winter, let me remind you that April will come in only 2 months! The owls are feeding nestlings, the tree swallows' average arrival date is around the first of February, and the purple martins will be close behind. It was time to be cleaning out those bluebird houses and, as we were doing, putting up more housing.

There are 85 species of North American birds that prefer or require cavities in which to hatch and raise their young. Before there were any people around, there were plenty of natural cavities, in large old trees with rotten places and holes where dead limbs had broken off. And the woodpeckers, as we have discussed previously, are prime real estate developers, most of them excavating a new cavity each year for nesting, and often, a second one in the fall, for winter roosting. Then later on, these real estate opportunities are available to all those other cavity nesters.

Now, with a lot of our woods giving way to subdivisions and malls, and overachieving tidy types cutting all the dead trees and snags in yards and parks, nesting cavities have become scarce. That whole situation was greatly

compounded with the arrival of the alien, aggressive European starlings and house sparrows. They take whichever nesting holes they want from the smaller birds, tossing out the hatchlings and often killing the parents.

On the positive side, a considerable number of our native birds have been given a significant boost in their numbers by us humans providing manmade nest boxes. The most noticeable success has been with our Eastern bluebirds, now brought back from perilously low numbers to a respectable population. And the largest and most enduring housing development for the cavity-nesting birds has been all those folks who through the years have tended to their beloved purple martins.

But many other birds will take to a manmade home: owls, kestrels, wrens (when they're not nesting in an old hat in your garage), chickadees, titmice, and tree swallows. Which brings us back to the wood ducks, our most gaudy, flamboyantly dressed North American duck, and why the swamp people were down in the creek bottom in January.

There are actually two species of brightly colored birds in our area that like to live in nest boxes in lowland, watery places. The wood duck and the prothonotary warbler both nest in water-oriented habitats; both like their homes leaning out over the water, if not actually standing in it. Otherwise, the two birds are about as different as any two birds can be.

Wood ducks are waterbirds, they eat stuff that lives in the water, and their babies can care for themselves and find food almost from the moment they hatch. The warblers, on the other hand, are regular, bug-eating landbirds that just happen to like waterfront property, and produce the ugly, helpless little babies we're accustomed to see in birds' nests.

Wood ducks are widespread now across the eastern United States, but by the early 1900s they had been hunted nearly to extinction. Just in time, hunting laws were passed, and many wildlife agencies as well as lots of private citizens began setting out wood duck nest boxes, such as the ones we were putting up along Beaver Creek. Fortunately, the wood ducks have rebounded. They are our most beautiful duck; check out that male in his breeding plumage in your bird book!

Their family life is amazing, too. The females lay 10–15 eggs in a nest. Then sometimes, other female wood ducks will lay their eggs in there, too, in a practice called, appropriately, dumping. The first mama duck can end up with two or three dozen eggs! When the baby ducks all hatch, they climb out of their nest hole or box, and jump, to either bounce or splash, depending on the nest location. If the family nest is not already at the water, Mama Duck leads them off, across the golf course or busy highway, to the nearest water. The fuzzy baby ducks can swim and find their own food immediately. I have often seen a batch of fluffy wood duck chicks, all in a row, swimming along Beaver Creek behind the mama duck, a really nice scene.

And good news for us people—wood ducks exhibit what the ornithologists call strong nest site tenacity; they usually return to the same place to nest year after year. So, we're hoping our Beaver Creek nest boxes will have tenants this year, and the next and the next. We'll keep you posted.

That other water-oriented, cavity-nesting bird, the prothonotary warbler, also named the golden swamp warbler, is truly golden. They are named after certain Vatican officials who are dressed in splendid golden-yellow robes. The male warbler's head, throat, and breast light up a gloomy swamp like a ray of sunshine. I saw my first one from a canoe. The bird was making a nest in an old hollow stump by the dark, still waters of the Okefenokee Swamp—one of those instant and brief sights you never forget.

Prothonotary warblers live over most of the eastern United States, mainly south of the Ohio River. In our area they often nest in woodpecker-excavated cavities in the soft wood of dead willow snags, typically standing near or in the water. I've heard of their nesting near the Island Home airport and around the lake shore at Kingston, Tennessee. But my favorite place to hear their song in the spring, and usually see them, is Cove Lake State Park. The hollow willow snags standing in the water there make perfect habitat for the golden swamp warblers. I try to go up and stand on the observation platform there at least once every spring, just to get my yearly prothonotary warbler fix.

Prothonotary warblers will use manmade boxes, too. They like boxes about the size of a bluebird box, only with a smaller entrance hole, about 1¼ inches in diameter; this lets warblers in and hopefully keeps some of their competitors, as well as predators, out. They lay an unusually large number of eggs for a warbler, about 8 to 10. But once hatched, their babies follow a more standard program and stay in the nest until they can fly. And being out over the water, they have to get it right the first time!

Maybe that's why they lay so many eggs. You know, birds can really be interesting!

SUGGESTED READING

General

Louv, Richard. *Last Child in the Woods: Saving Our Children from Nature-Deficit Disorder.* Chapel Hill, NC: Algonquin Books, 2008.

Pielou, E. C. *After the Ice Age: A Return of Life to Glaciated North America.* The University of Chicago Press, 1991.

Stokes, Donald W. *A Guide to Nature in Winter.* New York: Little, Brown and Company, 1976.

Stutchberry, Bridget. *Silence of the Songbirds.* New York: Walker and Company, 2007.

Tallamy, Douglas W. *Bringing Nature Home: How Native Plants Sustain Wildlife in Our Gardens.* Portland, OR: Timber Press, 2007.

Williams, Ernest H., Jr. *The Nature Handbook: A Guide to Observing the Great Outdoors.* Oxford, England: Oxford University Press, 2005.

Wilson, Edward O. *In Search of Nature.* Washington, DC: Island Press, 1996.

Appalachian Mountains

Brown, Margaret Lynn. *The Wild East: A Biography of the Great Smoky Mountains.* Gainesville: The University Press of Florida, 2000.

Davis, Donald Edward. *Where the Mountains Are: An Environmental History of the Southern Appalachians.* Athens: The University of Georgia Press, 2000.

DeLaughter, Jerry. *Mountain Roads and Quiet Places: A Complete Guide to the Roads of Great Smoky Mountains National Park.* Gatlinburg, Tennessee: Great Smoky Mountains Natural History Association, 1986.

Nolt, John. *A Land Imperiled: The Declining Health of the Southern Appalachian Bioregion.* Knoxville: The University of Tennessee Press, 2005.

Spira, Timothy P. *Wildflower and Plant Communities of the Southern Appalachian Mountains and Piedmont.* Chapel Hill: The University of North Carolina Press, 2011.

Weidensaul, Scott. *Mountains of the Heart: A Natural History of the Appalachians.* Golden, Colorado: Fulcrum Publishing, 1994.

Birds

Dunn, Jon L., and Jonathan Alderfer. *Field Guide to the Birds of North America*, 7th ed. Des Moines, IA: National Geographic Society, 2017.

Peterson, Roger Tory. *Birds of Eastern and Central North America*, 6th ed. Boston: Houghton Mifflin, 2010.

Sibley, David Allen. *Field Guide to the Birds of Eastern North America*, 2nd ed. New York: Alfred A. Knopf, 2016.

Simpson, Marcus B., Jr. *Birds of the Blue Ridge Mountains.* Chapel Hill: The University of North Carolina Press, 1992.

Gardening

Hunter, Margie. *Gardening with the Native Plants of Tennessee*. Knoxville: The University of Tennessee Press, 2002.

The Xerces Society. *Gardening for Butterflies*. Portland, OR: Timber Press, 2016.

Insects

Brock, Jim P., and Kenn Kaufman. *Kaufmann's Field Guide to the Butterflies of North America*. Boston: Houghton Mifflin, 2003.

Hoyt, Erich and Ted Schultz, eds. *Insect Lives: Stories of Mystery and Romance from a Hidden World*. Cambridge, Massachusetts: Harvard University Press, 1999.

Nikula, Blair and Jackie Sones with Donald and Lillian Stokes. *Beginner's Guide to Dragonflies*. Boston: Little, Brown and Company, 2002.

Paulson, Dennis. *Dragonflies and Damselflies of the East*. Princeton, NJ: Princeton University Press, 2011.

Stokes, Donald W. *A Guide to Observing Insect Lives*. Boston: Little, Brown and Company, 1983.

Venable, Rita. *Butterflies of Tennessee*. Franklin, TN: Maywood Publishing, 2014.

Wagner, David L. *Caterpillars of Eastern North America*. Princeton, NJ: Princeton University Press, 2005.

Trees

Duncan, William H., and Marion B. Duncan. *Trees of the Southeastern United States*. Athens: The University of Georgia Press, 1988.

Kershner, Bruce et al. *Field Guide to the Trees of North America*. Merrifield, VA: National Wildlife Federation, 2008.

Sibley, David Allen. *The Sibley Guide to Trees*. New York: Alfred A. Knopf, 2009.

Plants and Wildflowers

Carman, Jack B. *Wildflowers of Tennessee*. Highland Rim Press, 2001.

Cobb, Boughton, Elizabeth Farnsworth, and Cheryl Lowe. *Peterson Field Guide to Ferns and Their Related Families*. Boston: Houghton Mifflin Company, 1995.

Horn, Dennis, and Tavia Cathcart. *Wildflowers of Tennessee, the Ohio Valley, and the Southern Appalachians: The Official Field Guide of the Tennessee Native Plant Society*. Auburn, WA: Lone Pine Publishing, 2005.

Hutson, Robert W., William F. Hutson and Aaron J. Sharp. *Great Smoky Mountain Wildflowers, 5th ed.* Northbrook, Illinois: Windy Pines Publishing, LLC, 1995.

Newcomb, Lawrence. *Newcomb's Wildflower Guide*. Boston: Little, Brown and Company, 1989.

Smith, Richard M. *Wildflowers of the Southern Mountains*. Knoxville: The University of Tennessee Press, 1998.

Stokes, Donald, and Lillian Stokes. *A Guide to Enjoying Wildflowers*. Boston: Little, Brown and Company, 1985.

The Great Smoky Mountains Association has produced a series of small, pocket-sized books over a period of several years filled with information on a number of fascinating natural history subjects:

Birds of the Smokies
Day Hikes of the Smokies
Ferns of the Smokies
Mammals of the Smokies
Reptiles and Amphibians of the Smokies
Trees of the Smokies
Waterfalls of the Smokies
Wildflowers of the Smokies

BIBLIOGRAPHY

Adams, Paul J. *Mt. LeConte*. Knoxville, The University of Tennessee Press, 2016.

Adler, Bill Jr. *Outwitting Squirrels*. Chicago: Chicago Review Press, 1996.

Alsop, Fred. *Birds of North America*. New York: DK Publishing, Inc., 2002.

Atkins, James A., Wingo, Curtis W., and Sodeman, William A. "Probable Cause of Necrotic Spider Bites in the Midwest," *Science,* Vol. 126, No. 3263 (12 July 1957), 53.

Audubon, John James. *Ornithological Biography, or an Account of the Habits of the Birds of the United States of America; Accompanied by Descriptions of the Objects Represented in the Work Entitled The Birds of America, and Interspersed with Delineations of American Scenery and Manners*. Philadelphia: E. L. Cary and A. Hart, 1832 (Vol 1); Boston; Hilliard, Gray, 1835 (Vol. 2); Edinburg: Adam & Charles Black, 1835–49 (Vols. 3–5).

Bales, Stephen Lyn. *Ghost Birds*. Knoxville: The University of Tennessee Press, 2010.

Bierly, Michael Lee. *Bird Finding in Tennessee*. Nashville, Tennessee: Privately Published, 1980.

Bourne, Joel K. "Loving Our Coasts to Death," *National Geographic,* Vol. 210, No.1 (July 2006), 60–87.

Brown, Larry N. *A Guide to the Mammals of the Southeastern United States*. Knoxville: The University of Tennessee Press, 1997.

Byerly, Don W. *The Last Billion Years: A Geologic History of Tennessee*. Knoxville: The University of Tennessee Press, 2013.

Campbell, C. Carlos. *Birth of a National Park*. Knoxville: The University of Tennessee Press, 1960.

Carson, Rachel. *Silent Spring*. Boston: Houghton Mifflin Company, 1962.

Conner, Jack. "Cache and Carry," *Living Bird,* Vol. 22, No.1 (winter 2003), 42–45.

Craighead, Charlie. *"Who Ate the Backyard?" Living with Wildlife on Private Lands*. Moose, Wyoming: Grand Teton Natural History Association, 1997.

Cubie, Doreen. "Water Wars Move East," *National Wildlife,* Vol. 47, No.6 (October/November 2009), 16, 18.

Dana, Mrs. William Starr. *How to Know the Wildflowers*. New York: Charles Scribner's Sons, 1893. Reprinted, Boston: Houghton Mifflin Company, 1989.

Davis, Ren and Helen. *Our Mark on This Land*. Granville, Ohio: The McDonald and Woodward Publishing Company, 2011.

Delcourt, Hazel R. *Forests in Peril: Tracking Deciduous Trees from Ice-Age Refuges into the Greenhouse World*. Blacksburg, VA: The McDonald and Woodward Publishing Company, 2002.

Doughty, Robin. *The Mockingbird*. Austin: The University of Texas Press, 1988.

Dunkle, Sydney W. *Dragonflies through Binoculars*. New York: Oxford University Press, 2000.

Dunn, Durwood. *Cades Cove: The Life and Death of a Southern Appalachian Community, 1818–1937*. Knoxville: The University of Tennessee Press, 1988.

Gaines, David. *Mono Lake Guidebook*. Lee Vining, CA: Kutsavi Books, 1989.

Halfpenny, James C., and Douglas Ozanne. *Winter: An Ecological Handbook*. Boulder, Colorado: Johnson Publishing Company, 1989.

Hauser, Susan Carol. *Outwitting Poison Ivy*. Guilford, Connecticut: The Lyons Press, 2001.

Hayler, Nicole, ed. *Sound Wormy: Memoir of Andrew Gennett, Lumberman.* Athens: The University of Georgia Press, 2002.

Heinrich, Berndt. *Winter World: The Ingenuity of Animal Survival.* New York: HarperCollins Publishers, Inc., 2003.

Jolley, Harley E. *The Blue Ridge Parkway.* Knoxville: The University of Tennessee Press, 1969.

Lembke, Janet. *Despicable Species: On Cowbirds, Kudzu, Hornworms and Other Scourges.* New York: The Lyons Press, 1999.

Lockwood, Jeffrey A. *Locust. The Devastating Rise and Mysterious Disappearance of the Insect that Shaped the American Frontier.* New York: Basic Books, 2004.

Logan, William Bryant. *Oak: The Frame of Civilization.* New York: W. W. Norton & Company, 2005.

Mason, Adrienne. *The World of the Spider.* San Francisco: Sierra Club Books, 1999.

Miller, James H. *Nonnative Invasive Plants of Southern Forests: A Field Guide for Identification and Control.* Asheville, NC: U.S. Department of Agriculture Forest Service, Southern Research Station General Technical Report SRS-62, 2003.

Moore, Andrew. *Pawpaw: In Search of America's Forgotten Fruit.* White River Junction, VT: Chelsea Green Publishing, 2015.

Moore, Harry. *A Roadside Guide to the Geology of the Great Smoky Mountains National Park.* Knoxville: The University of Tennessee Press, 1988.

Phillips, H. Wayne. *Plants of the Lewis and Clark Expedition.* Missoula, Montana: Mountain Press Publishing Company, 2003.

Rombauer, Irma S., Marion Rombauer Becker and Ethan Becker. *The Joy of Cooking.* New York: Scribner, 1997.

Spencer, Marci. *Clingman's Dome: Highest Mountain in the Great Smokies.* Charleston, SC: Natural History Press, 2013.

Steers, Edward Jr. *His Name Is Still Mudd: The Case Against Dr. Samuel Alexander Mudd.* Gettysburg, PA: Thomas Publications, 1997.

Stokes, Don and Lillian, and Justin L. Brown. *Stokes Purple Martin Book: The Complete Guide to Attracting and Housing Purple Martins.* Boston: Little, Brown and Company, 1997.

Terres, John K. *The Audubon Society Encyclopedia of North American Birds.* New York: Wings Books, 1991.

Thomas, Robert B. *The Old Farmer's Almanac.* Dublin, NH: Yankee Publishing Inc., 2018.

Tolme, Paul. "The Bountiful Boreal," *National Wildlife,* Vol. 42, No. 6 (October/November 2004), 22–28, 30–31.

Urquhart, Fred A. "Found at Last: the Monarch's Winter Home," *National Geographic,* Vol. 150, No.2 (August 1976), 161–73.

Wexler, Mark. "Coping with Chronic Clamor," *National Wildlife,* Vol.55, No.2 (February/ March 2017), 40–43.

Winchester, Simon. *The Map that Changed the World: William Smith and the Birth of Modern Geology.* New York: HarperCollins Publishers, 2001.

Wise, Kenneth and Ron Petersen. *A Natural History of Mt. LeConte.* Knoxville: The University of Tennessee Press, 1998.

Wright, Lizzie. "Native Tennessee Ants: Not So Black and Red," *The Tennessee Conservationist,* Vol. LXXXII, No.2 (March/April 2016), 32–35.

Wynne, Peter. *Apples.* New York: Hawthorn Books, Inc., 1975.

INDEX